Non-discursive Rhetoric

Non-discursive Rhetoric

Image and Affect in
Multimodal Composition

JODDY MURRAY

Cover image: Drew Jason Mounce, "Recognition." Acrylic on canvas.
Courtesy of the artist.

Published by
State University of New York Press, Albany

Printed in the United States of America

For information, contact State University of New York Press, Albany, NY
www.sunypress.edu

Production by Eileen Meehan
Marketing by Anne M. Valentine

Library of Congress Cataloging-in-Publication Data

Murray, Joddy, 1968–
    Non-discursive rhetoric : image and affect in multimodal composition /
Joddy Murray.
        p. cm.
    Includes bibliographical references and index.
    ISBN 978-0-7914-7675-8 (hardcover : alk. paper)
    ISBN 978-0-7914-7676-5 (pbk. : alk. paper)
    1. Rhetoric.   2. Communication.   I. Title.

PN175.M87 2009
808—dc22   2008024987

10 9 8 7 6 5 4 3 2 1

Contents

Figures

Acknowledgments

I want to thank all those mentors and colleagues who have helped me in one way or another in the past—their intellectual support and rigor, their close readings, and their willingness to engage in some of these ideas helped me in innumerable ways. It is impossible to tell at what point the influence and example of one mentor or colleague starts, and at what point it stops; it is therefore more fitting that I just thank them all and dedicate this book to them.

I also want to thank Texas Christian University for their support and encouragement, and, especially, my colleagues in the English Department. Writers compose in communities, even if they are typing alone. TCU has been a terrific supporter of my work.

Drew Jason Mounce's artwork is an inspiration—go to his website and see his work (www.lefthandart.com) because I really appreciate his allowing me to use "Recognition" on the cover of this book.

Finally, but most importantly, I wish to express my gratitude to my wife, Cisalee Morris, who has always been my best reader, confidant, and muse. Without her love and support, this book would not have been possible.

Introduction

The rhetorical theory espoused in this book is one that attempts to replenish our symbol-making practices with all of our symbol-making textual forms. This theory of non-discursive rhetoric is meant to provide a more integrated view of composing better suited to the contemporary composition classroom. Such a classroom often ask students to compose various hybridized, multimodal texts, and in doing so, students must learn how the imagination is required for logical, reasoned, claim-based argument; how the emotions are not only omnipresent but integral to image and textual production; and how choosing colors for the background of a web page, or choosing the rhythm of a particular kind of drum, or choosing a particular camera angle in snapping a photograph can all work rhetorically in compositions. But how do writing teachers teach these things when most rhetorical training focuses on discursive, print-oriented rhetoric? This book theorizes a new composing model, one that views symbolization and the rhetorics it produces as having two distinct types: discursive and non-discursive. Though each type of symbolization is needed, useful, and important, the latter type is the most neglected in many discussions about symbolization and language.

As I talk to other scholars about the term "language," however, it has become clear that suggesting an expanded definition of the term has its difficulties. The word and its variants resonate in a Bakhtinian way throughout many discourses, many theorists, many philosophies, and, as such, there seems to be significant resistance among many language theorists to expanding the common use of the term so that it can include all modes of symbolization. The reason I wish to broaden the term language is similar to my reason for suggesting that rhetoric has both discursive and non-discursive symbol systems. Not only should the term language include the specific syntaxes and lexicons of German or Chinese or American Sign Language (i.e., any word-based system, etc.), I would like to also suggest that the term "language" include the symbol systems of music, film, sculpture, dance, et cetera. I could speculate as to the reasons for this resistance, but for now it may be enough to emphasize terms like "symbolization" and

"textual production" rather than exclusively language—though not synonymous, they serve similar purposes here. I point to this resistance in order to
broaden this term (which has already been done in many other fields, such
as computer science, poetry, and even dance) as only one more indication
of the extent to which discursive language is privileged in academia today.
Part of this text, then, includes a discussion of what language is or is not,
what symbolization is or is not, and what symbol-making tools are actually
in use for textual production.

Non-discursive rhetoric, as theorized here, is an important development to rhetors and teachers alike because it provides us a way to talk about
rhetoric as it is experienced in many multiple and layered textual modes and
media. We are currently experiencing a Gutenberg-like explosion of textual
production, one that radically changes the way texts are produced, consumed,
and distributed. I avoid using the terms "revolution" or "paradigm shift"
because, from a rhetorical point of view, the same tools once available to
only a few are becoming more available to an increasing number of people.
Textual production itself is being distributed and, consequently, the texts
and those who author them are changing and being changed. Rhetoric has
always suffered from distribution problems—from the distance one voice
may carry in a forum, to the limited production of books and textiles and
the limited literacies able to consume these books, to a gradual, though
not complete, distribution of rhetorical agency to those who were fortunate
enough to learn reading and writing. Historically, rhetoric has been dogged
as much by its lack of distribution as by its lack of mass education, and,
on a global perspective, this is as true now regarding digital literacy as it
was in ancient Greece regarding print literacy.[1] Rhetors have always valued
image and emotions, for example, but they both have lacked sufficient consideration within rhetorical theory. Language, often defined traditionally as
"articulated sound" or written orality, necessarily limits what can be counted
as rhetorical text because of the way it is constructed to function: "abstractly
sequential, classificatory, explanatory examination of phenomena or of stated
truths" (Ong 8). But rhetoric must be able to escape the confines of any
single medium, and as long as the term "language" is only associated with
discursive text, it cannot take advantage of all that image and emotions bring
to rhetorical texts and their production, much less handle the challenges of
hybrid texts that incorporate many modes at once.

This book attempts to emphasize non-discursive text, image, and
emotion (or affectivity). Discursive text and the sequentiality of spoken and
written language are important, but, as Langer has shown us, it is only part
of what we can do with our symbol-making skills. The prevalence of digital
tools, as well as the importance of emotions to inventing and composing,
both make it necessary to reiterate how language is much more than words;
language includes non-discursive forms of meaning-making, forms that take

advantage of image, emotion, and nonsequentiality. In other words, non-discursive symbolization makes it possible to emphasize, analyze, and teach non-discursive rhetoric.

Image, it turns out, is vital to both discursive and non-discursive symbol-making practices. All symbolization, including traditional notions of language, is based in image because our brains function through image. No matter how abstract and disassociated they may become from pictures or illustrations, no matter how mechanical and practical their articles and linguistic placeholders, no matter how fallible and distanced they are from direct communication, symbol and image are virtually synonymous. Though this may not be an entirely new claim, the conflation of symbolization and image in rhetoric and composition may be increasingly important at this current intersection in time: new media studies, visual rhetoric, and visual literacy have all become important new areas of research in our field as scholars begin to get a glimpse of the importance of image to the symbols we make. Communication studies, and most of the history of rhetoric before it, has long accepted the fact that communication takes place through nonverbal means; the suggestion that rhetoric applies to more than just words is not a new one. What I suggest, however, is (1) that although non-discursive symbol systems are somewhat known and theorized, they are largely eclipsed by a strong bias toward alphacentric, or word-based, discursive symbol systems, especially in rhetoric and composition; and (2) that image is central to all symbol systems no matter what its medium or mode.

In addition, there exists a need to acknowledge just how image is theoretically important to our composing practices and pedagogies, as well as a full conception of symbolization itself. This book—drawing from philosophy,[2] rhetorical theory, neuroscience, and composition studies—posits a theoretical view of image that is elemental to thought, to emotion, and ultimately to composing. In doing so, it provides a conception of symbolization that is not limited to discursive meaning-making but one that values non-discursive symbolization, especially as it applies to rhetorical practice. Such interdisciplinary work carries with it the danger that individual disciplines will not find the work done by others as convincing. However, it also carries the promise that such interdisciplinarity is characteristic of images and image studies in general. By ultimately theorizing a new composing model that incorporates both discursive and non-discursive textual production, I provide a pedagogical aid for contemporary writers.

Connections to Langer

In 1942, Susanne Langer first defined the terms "discursive" and "non-discursive" in *Philosophy in a New Key: A Study in the Symbolism of Reason*,

Rite, and Art. The discursive, the form of symbolization most common to composition classrooms and associated with verbal and written or printed text, includes the kind of language-making in which we "string out" our ideas; it relies on language to be ordered, sequential, and adherent to the "laws of reasoning" often assumed to be synonymous with the "laws of discursive thought" (82). Discursive texts often take the form of the expository essay, the oral presentation, research and argument papers, and the common modes such as narrative and description. The discursive is bound by semantic forms and, consequently, limits itself by those forms because it assumes that the "word" is the only means to articulate thought, and that anything that cannot be directly conveyed by discursive means—i.e., anything unsayable or ineffable—is mere feeling, or too "fuzzy" for serious study. The discursive, therefore, is commonly referred to as "verbal" or "written" communication because, like this paragraph, it aims to convey one idea after another.[3]

Conversely, the non-discursive is free of such ordering. In fact, its most apparent difference from discursive symbolization is that it often happens at once, is primarily reliant on image (taken here to mean both sensory and mental images), and that it most often becomes employed to symbolize what cannot be said or written directly by the word. Here is what Langer says about the non-discursive:

> Visual forms—lines, colors, proportions, etc.—are just as capable of articulation, i.e., of complex combination, as words. But the laws that govern this sort of articulation are altogether different from the laws of syntax that govern language. The most radical difference is that visual forms are not discursive. They do not present their constituents successively, but simultaneously, so the relations determining a visual structure are grasped in one act of vision. Their complexity, consequently, is not limited, as the complexity of discourse is limited, by what the mind can retain from the beginning of an apperceptive act to the end of it [. . . .] An idea that contains too many minute yet closely related parts, too many relations within relations, cannot be "projected" into discursive forms; it is too subtle for speech [. . . .] But the symbolism furnished by our purely sensory appreciation of forms is a non-discursive symbolism, peculiarly well suited to the expression of ideas that defy linguistic "projection." (93)

Langer frames the difference between "visual forms" and "words" (her way of simplifying the difference between "non-discursive" text and "discursive" text) as differing primarily through "laws" that "govern" them. What Langer clarifies later is that images are not just "visual forms" but any form taken by the senses, and these forms are necessarily more complex, in part because they are "simultaneously" received. A non-discursive text is also complex because it "contains too many minute yet closely related parts." Non-discursive symbolization, therefore, includes those "things which do not fit the grammatical scheme of expression" (88). It is symbolized language, but it is a form not limited to the chain-of-reasoning we require in discursive text. Its strength, in part, is that it can accommodate meaning unsuited to sequencing—unutterable, affective, ephemeral—and that there are connections through images that may lead to further articulation. The value of non-discursive text, therefore, is that it thrives and derives its meaning-making from the complexity and ambiguity of its medium, whereas discursive language works best when it reifies and reduces complexity and ambiguity as it goes along.

Langer must have known that to theorize language one must also theorize the activity and purpose of the human mind. One reason I call for the broadening of the term "language" is precisely due to the discursive bias that exists in what is normally considered language. Langer says a symbol is anything that can "articulate" thought: "Such *expression* [of an idea] is the function of symbols: articulation and presentation of *concepts*" (*Feeling* 26). This kind of articulation can be both discursive or non-discursive, and both carry with them their own brand of logic. She spends a great deal of time, for example, in both *Feeling and Form* and in *Philosophy in a New Key* to situate her theory of symbolization with some consideration of what reason and rationality are mentally:

> Rationality is the essence of mind, and symbolic transformation its elementary process. It is a fundamental error, therefore, to recognize it only in the phenomenon of systematic, explicit reasoning [. . . .] Rationality, however, is embodied in every mental act, not only when the mind is "at the fullest stretch and compass." It permeates the peripheral activities of the human nervous system, just as truly as the cortical functions. (99)

Before the days of CAT, MRI, PET, or even reliable x-ray scans, Langer was asking and answering questions about the way our minds function, especially in terms of language.[4] Remarkably, the connections Langer intuited between the science of the mind and the philosophy of the mind remain today; remarkably still, many of these connections are being validated today by scientific methods she could only imagine.

Connections to Neuroscience

In addition to expanding and enriching the way language is viewed by the field, this book embraces an interdisciplinary view of image and emotions by bringing into composition the work done by neuroscience regarding new research on the way our brains function. As with Langer, these new theories now being investigated by neuroscientists are largely consistent with many of the other theories of language, image, and consciousness offered by theorists as varied as Vygotsky, Bakhtin, Cassirer, Berthoff, and others. The combination of these theorists and the recent work done in neuroscience indicates an emerging view of image that complicates and extends assumptions about the role of image in composing, and provides a great deal of rich theoretical potential for rhetoric and composition.

So how can philosophers and rhetoricians, who study image, emotion, and invention, connect with neuroscience and contribute to our understanding of writing in composition? Although there is more detail about this in chapter 3, it is enough to point out four claims relevant to image, emotions, and consciousness. First, neuroscientists and cognitive psychologists have begun to fully recognize the role image plays in the construction of knowledge: image is not only a basic unit of thought in the brain—the progenitor of language and a component of reason—but image also *shapes* the brain, constructs pathways and nodes which make up such potentialities as personality, health, and acumen. In other words, there are structural and functional elements in the brain that point to the centrality of image to thought—displacing alphacentric language.

Second, consciousness itself is becoming a valid object of study in science, even though consciousness has been eschewed by science in the past because it was thought of as too subjective or unpredictable to yield generalizable results.[5] Perhaps most relevant to this book is the research done by Antonio Damasio: his claim about consciousness as being made up of images is crucial. Damasio also claims that the making of symbols extends consciousness away from the core consciousness of our evolutionary ancestors to the more advanced, self-aware consciousness located in higher brain functions (such as the cortex and neocortex, as well as areas connected to the frontal lobes) (*Descartes'* 89–90). The difference between the brain and the mind, if there is one, might very well be the difference between perceiving images and being aware of and manipulating those same images.

Third, because image and consciousness are integrated, science is also invested in looking at the role of emotions in all brain functionality; consciousness and our ability to make images are set within an emotional, or affective, context. Damasio, in *"The Feeling of What Happens": Body and*

Emotion in the Making of Consciousness claims that the relationship between image and consciousness comes from our ability to *feel* that we have created images (26). Damasio's point has resonance for those of us studying image in the context of writing. He essentially asserts that it is precisely because we associate feelings with images that we eventually are able to achieve a state of higher consciousness. What this says in terms of this book is simply this: images are not only integral to non-discursive symbolization, they also help form our very sense of who we are.

Finally, the fourth valuable contribution from neuroscience for compositionists is that the connection between image and thought is not representational but cognitive. Damasio makes it clear that mental images are not mirror copies of the real image; we are only able to conjure approximations of images. Damasio finds that nothing less than thought itself is reliant on image: "The factual knowledge required for reasoning and decision making comes to the mind in the form of images" (96). There is therefore a connection between image and any or all of our cognitive abilities. That alone says much about the importance of image to who we are, how we symbolize, and, ultimately, how we think.

In sum, symbolization is dependent on image to do its work of meaning-making. Whether the symbol is a discursive one or a non-discursive one, images not only become stored as approximations in our brains by the experiences we have, but they drive our brains' functioning. Our relationship to image is not just a perceptual relationship; our brains require images in order to operate. Consequently, if we are to integrate this knowledge into our theories of composing and rhetoric, scholars must theorize the relationship of image and the affective domain in a much more complex and integrated way than we have done in the past.

This work from neuroscience, combined with including Langer's conception of non-discursive text, indicates a substantive change in the way rhetoric and composition treats image and composing. As soon as we ask students to consider image as rhetorical, as soon as we create hypertexts, for example, that attempt to displace the linearity of discourse, as soon as there is special attention played to invention and the role of prewriting in the writing process, we are also talking about the role of non-discursive texts in our pedagogy. As such, writers gain a view of composing that posits image as a lexicon of thought and emotion as a carrier of reason. We now have an opportunity to integrate the non-discursive as a framework in our teaching practice applicable to the use of electronic and multimodal texts. As we integrate non-discursive texts into our composition practice, we begin to practice a corresponding writing theory that accommodates the challenges and opportunities of multimodal rhetoric.

Connections to Multimodal Texts

As new media and digital production of symbols promulgates through our culture, writers are refortified in textual modes that were never really lost; due to the ease and historical prevalence of discursive production, these rhetorical practices are now somewhat strange and daunting to us.[6] The ability to produce text non-discursively is currently necessary—but largely unconsidered—while digital tools make it easier and easier for rhetors to produce multimedia texts: hardware and software with improved interfaces and accessibility are not ubiquitous, but strive to be. As composers, we can no longer ignore these multimodal texts in our classrooms, and this book joins several others in claiming the importance of bringing our classrooms into the twenty-first century by assigning the kinds of texts students will undoubtedly encounter outside of academia. The hegemony of discursive text and orality has worked hard to remove from itself any vestige of its author: we often teach how discursive texts are "logical" and organized, perspicacious and adherent to strict formatting and disciplinary expectations. This is important work and it must continue. The challenge presented here is not one of substitution, rather one of addition: we must continue to teach students to become adept at writing discursive text with its sequential structures, disciplinary expectations, and, ultimately, nonaffective tone; we must also teach students to become adept at "writing" non-discursive texts with its layers, images, and, without a doubt, pervasive affectivity. This particular time in history is not so much requiring that we apply fundamentally new questions to our pedagogy. Rather, it requires that we revalue and reauthorize what has always been important to our symbol-making process: image and affectivity. We can no longer rest on the assumptions that the body and the mind are separate, that affectivity and "logic" are opposites, or that rhetoric and design are fundamentally separate disciplines.

Similarly, inventing, composing, and designing need no longer sound like completely separate, stand-alone processes. One of the consequences of acknowledging the efficacy and rhetorical power of non-discursive text is the knowledge that not only are these elements iterative, they are consubstantial: they exist at once in body, and though their production could be broken down into these elements, they are happening simultaneously even while the text is being read. A theory of non-discursive rhetoric makes possible the advancement, analysis, and pedagogies of all rhetorics employed in multimedia, not just those based in the printed word, and not just those labeled "visual." We can include under the umbrella of non-discursive rhetoric all of the sensual ways information reception can be rhetorical: visual, haptic, aural, olfactory, and gustatory. By dividing symbol-making into discursive and non-discursive text, it is possible to consider the meaning potentialities of each form, one potentially good at leading the audience through a constructed sequence of meaning placed in time, and the other potentially providing an experience irrespective of time or sequence, built upon layers of unuttered and at times unutterable, meaning and affectivity.[7]

This book attempts to revisit the connections between symbolization and image in order to imagine a theory of non-discursive rhetoric: a theory that both acknowledges and values image and the affective domain as critical to the way writers invent and compose text—especially multimodal texts created with digital tools—as a way to achieve consensus, form communities, make connections, build knowledge and/or persuade. Chapters 1 and 2 revisit Susanne Langer's theories about language as a way to first make some claims about symbolization that are important to this theory, and then review some of the ways visual rhetoric and visual literacy are discussed in rhetoric and composition. Chapter 3 focuses on the way cognitive science and advances in neuroscience have begun to understand the connections between thought and language, specifically those advances relevant to image, and how important the affective is to the way our brains function. Finally, chapters 4 and 5 conceptualize ways in which we must help students invent and compose, advocating in the end a new composing model designed to accommodate the flux between discursive and non-discursive texts.

CHAPTER 1

Non-discursive Symbolization

*W*hat is non-discursive rhetoric? The following chapters attempt to answer this by proposing that the stuff of rhetoric—the symbols used—includes more than the ordered, grammatical, and codified linearity of discursive text. In fact, rhetoric throughout history has often taken advantage of our ability as a species to symbolize through non-discursive text, a text that is more than the linear, largely nonaffective, and enthymemic set of resources found in discursive text; more than the one-to-one correspondence between sender to message to receiver; and more than any supposition that symbolization is primarily a set of (arbitrary) linguistic sign systems useful in communicating thought transparently from sender to receiver. Rhetors have always known about the power of a particular orator's tone of voice, the use of gesture at key points in a speech, appeals to patriotism and the emotions, the use of vivid imagery and storytelling, and even the value of grooming and general appearance: manipulation of any one of these elements has a direct affect on the audience. Over time, however, as rhetoric became increasingly bound to the printed word, it also became bound to discursive symbol-making. As rhetoric became more and more reliant on written discourse, the non-discursive aspects of rhetoric became more and more ancillary, even rejected altogether as logical positivism and rational discourse prevailed during the modern age—vestiges of which still dominate today.[1]

As a result, the view that language is primarily a vehicle for the communication of ideas continues to dictate the way textual production is theorized today. One such discursive symbolization systems is the Shannon-Weaver view of communication—a paradigmatic example of how texts are discussed: symbols "communicate" by sending "information" through a medium between sender and receiver.[2] Obviously, this use of symbols is acceptable and necessary—as compositionists, it literally exemplifies what we most often are asked to do. However, even the Shannon-Weaver theory of communication eventually acknowledges the complexity that emerges from human symbol systems left unaccounted for in discursive symbolization. And as Langer states, "If the mind were simply a recorder and transmitter, typified by the simile of the telephone-exchange, we should act very differently than we do" (*New Key* 36). Non-discursive symbolization is simply a term that accounts for the many other ways humans use symbols to create meaning—methods wholly outside the realm of traditional, word-based, discursive text. With this distinction in symbolization, then, comes a distinction in rhetoric; non-discursive rhetoric is the study of how these symbol systems persuade, evoke consensus, become epistemological, and organize or employ intended results in human behavior. In short, non-discursive rhetoric is to non-discursive symbolization what discursive rhetoric is to discursive symbolization.[3]

The terms discursive and non-discursive provide another way to talk about symbolization, or language. Susanne Langer's main claim in *Philosophy in a New Key* is that humans are capable, even practiced, at much more than communicating discursive information in sequence. By including all symbol systems as a legitimate part of our repertoire of language (some of which—specifically ritual, art, and dreams—may only be internalized by the individual), the tools available to any composer become complete, no longer limited to convey merely the "facts of consciousness" (36). On the other hand, it is too often the case that the communicative role of symbols becomes the entire concept of symbolization; that in our efforts to create and clarify our discursive texts, we often overlook the pivotal role of non-discursive composition. In contrast, the view of meaning-making proposed here necessitates and values all that our symbols—though especially image—can do: affectivity, circularity, ambiguity, incongruity, and even ineffability.

The main consequence of Langer's insistence on including *both* discursive and non-discursive texts in her theory of symbolization is that it broadens the landscape for rhetoric. By considering non-discursive texts, all possibilities of symbolization become tools for the rhetor: the symbols of math, music, textiles, food, poetry, commerce, violence, inaction, and even silence. The world is text because we read the world as symbols, and, in turn, create symbols to be read.[4] Jacques Derrida acknowledges this in *Of Grammatology*, and his notion of the sign continually rewriting itself is consistent with the way symbolization is viewed here: what we know about the human ability to symbolize is that we must, and that we do it often, and that such symbolization itself recreates itself as it goes along.[5] We create and produce symbols whether or not we are educated or uneducated, within a community or alone, naïve or wise, destitute or wealthy, sleeping or awake. Symbol-making consists of more than its discursive function, more than Roman Jacobson's six "constitutive factors of any speech event" (as one example), more than the traditional sender-messenger-receiver paradigm.[6] Rather than consider symbolization to be primarily communication in the absence of noise, I prefer to think of symbolization as encompassing all of our powers to create and manipulate meaning and emotions through a wide variety of symbols beyond the discursive word.

As I illustrate more fully later, a view of symbolization that accounts for both discursive as well as non-discursive texts can provide a more integrated view of composing better suited to the contemporary composition classroom: one that encourages the powers of the imagination not just for what is often labeled "creative" writing, but for logical, reasoned, claim-based argument as well; one that acknowledges the value of emotions not just in so called "expressivist" or "personal" writing, but also in the kind of social awareness and normal, rational decision-making we encounter every day; one that views text not just as printed paragraphs on a 8.5 x 11 inch sheet of paper, but as any kind of symbolization: digital or analog, 2-D or 3-D, haptic, olfactory, or gustatory. The key element, the piece that has been missing in our composing models—in the way we view symbolization, and in the way we discuss the rhetorical implications of any text—is the value of the non-discursive.

Langerian Symbolization

It is crucial to begin with symbolization systems to show the impact image has to our textual production because traditional conceptions of language may be too narrow to allow for non-discursive elements—elements that I argue are often as important as discursive elements of text. The terms "symbolization," or, sometimes, "language," are not intended to refer to grammar systems, or a particular brand of linguistically codified rules and procedures that communicate or produce meaning and emotion.[7] Symbolization, as I mean it here, is the very nature of a human symbol-use in all forms—both discursive and non-discursive. By symbolization I mean the act of cognizance at the very beginning of our lives that is hard wired, innate, inevitable, and most characteristic of our species—a definition very similar to Suzanne Langer's: "The symbol-making function is one of man's primary activities, like eating, looking, or moving about. It is the fundamental process of his mind, and goes on all the time" (New Key 41). Symbolization, therefore, goes on all the time and is part of who we are.

As many other theorists have noted, symbolization is learned socially, within a culture, and with immediate emotional consequences and shadings. But symbolization or our use of language is rarely if ever talked about this way when it is mentioned in theoretical or pedagogical texts: language has traditionally been biased toward discursive meaning-making and little else (just as this text is). Although it is true that this line between discursive and non-discursive text is often blurry (that both have elements of each other to some degree), there is little question that what we do in traditional, monomodal writing classrooms is often to help students move toward the discursive without addressing the non-discursive. As Langer explains, insistence on focusing on only the discursive aspect of text leads to a reified conception of symbolization, leaving out an element which can be our most powerful tool:

> So long as we regard only scientific and "material" (semi-scientific) thought as really cognitive of the world, this peculiar picture of mental life must stand. And so long as we admit only discursive symbolism as a bearer of ideas, "thought" in this restricted sense must be regarded as our only intellectual activity. It begins and ends with language; without the elements, at least, of scientific grammar, conception must be impossible. A theory which implies such peculiar consequences is itself a suspicious character. But the error which it harbors is not in its reasoning. It is in the very premise from which the doctrine proceeds, namely that all articulate symbolism is discursive [. . . .] I do believe that in this physical, space-time world of our experience there are things which do not fit the grammatical scheme of expression. But they are not necessarily blind, inconceivable, mystical affairs; they are simply matters which require to be conceived through some symbolistic schema other than discursive language. (88–89)

Langer is not only making the case that not "all articulate symbolism is discursive," but she also calls into question any theory of language which fails to account for those types of expression that "do not fit the grammatical scheme of expression." Not only is Langer providing an alternative to the discursive bias in other symbolization theories, but she is also highlighting what she sees as the main failure of what she calls "discursive mentalism": humans exist in a "physical, space-time world of our experience," and to forget this is to forget all if not most of what it means to be human. In short, language theory must account for all of human experience, both the discursive and the non-discursive.

Symbolization, conceived in this way, becomes our sixth sense, our ultimate legacy, and it is completely natural and indicative of being human—as far as it is possible to know, we have created symbols since the dawn of our recorded history:

> The earliest people made art—whether they called it that or not—as evidenced by the cave paintings found in various parts of the world. Archaeologists tell us that in the Ice Age, about 35,000 years ago,

Cro-Magnon peoples in Europe "suddenly" began making objects that we would describe as art [. . .] They painted the walls of their caves, carved figurines, decorated their tools and everyday implements with fine designs, and even made musical instruments. (5)

Accordingly, symbol-making, whether considered "art" or not, exists across and among many different types of relationships: between voices within an individual, between groups, cultures, and beyond the constraints of time and, increasingly, place. Non-discursive symbolization, then, includes attempts to symbolize that are not necessarily statements made in printed text on paper, or vocalized words intended to communicate a main idea.[8] Such symbolization includes art, but it also includes photographs, graphs, music, textiles, ceramics, doodles, et cetera.

There might also be an erroneous temptation to look at language as being the sum of its symbols. Langer says in *Philosophy in a New Key* that "[o]ur confidence in language is due to the fact that it [. . .] shares the structure of the physical world, and therefore can express that structure" (88). On the contrary, language is not the sum of its symbols; language is not even limited by its symbols. James Kinneavy's book, *A Theory of Discourse*, provides one example of a reduced view of language. The aim of discourse, as Kinneavy proposes, can be broken-down and classified because it is made manifest, made objective, through words on paper (and this is usually what is meant by language in this case—words on paper). The shadings of symbolization, the difficulty of reading a painting, the feelings involved, the contributions to meaning by silence and ambiguity: all these things are too easily overlooked because symbolization is often written, discernable, expository, and interpreted as having a direct translation into discursive meaning.[9] Langer teaches us to open up what we view as language in order to understand all aspects of symbolization as a whole: we need to look also at non-discursive text.

In addressing language theory that includes the non-discursive, I hope to show how our view of language necessarily shapes views of rhetoric, philosophy, and communication. Cassirer, Vygotsky, Vološinov, Bakhtin, Langer, and others complicate what we mean when we talk about language in order to make their own theories relatable, even understandable. In order to examine what a theorist says, it is just as crucial to understand the theorists conception of language beneath the exhortation, whether that view is stated explicitly or implied (J. Murray 19). In fact, rhetoric and composition scholars are always necessarily theorists in language, even if such a theory remains subsumed by whatever emphasis or specialization is currently occupying the discussion (a point that I. A. Richards originally voiced years ago).[10] By starting at the level of symbols, by expanding the possibilities of symbolization to include non-discursive text, we may begin to understand image as crucial to all symbol-making and, consequently, the value of the imagination and, ultimately, the role of emotions in composing.

This chapter will review some of the ways language and symbolization have often been discussed in composition studies. The purpose is to lay to rest some of the criticisms that dismiss work such as this as "expressivist" or atomistic. Upon close analysis, those in composition studies who have made it a point to marginalize the importance of the non-discursive in our symbolizing lives are now having to rethink what it means to compose in the twenty-first century. By reviewing a few important language theorists in the field, I hope to show how broadening our conception of symbolization and language offers rich theoretical possibilities that connect our meaning making to image making. In some cases, such as with Cassirer, Vygotsky, Vološinov, Bakhtin, Langer, and to some extent Berthoff, a few of these theorists make direct claims about symbolization that are then supported in their original texts. In other cases, such as with Britton, Moffett, and Coles, their perspective on symbolization theory is more implicit and made opaque only through the way they advocate writing instruction and curricular design. Specifically, I intend to establish four main claims in this chapter:

1. Symbolization includes all forms of meaning-making through symbols, both discursive and non-discursive—accordingly, language must rely not only on discursive thought but also intuitive thought;

2. Language is used and practiced within a social, historical, and cultural fabric; it is therefore layered, stratified, by time and place—never wholly atomistic, individualized, or entirely introspective;

3. The ambiguities in language, the places where language fails to communicate or fails to convey a message, are crucial to both the process of learning about language, invention, and interpretation itself—in fact, it is within these cracks, these places where language works against itself to convey meaning, that we find possibility enough to invent new texts and discover new knowledge.

4. Language, image, and consciousness are intimately connected, so much so that theorists attempting to make claims about language often also account for image and consciousness.

In taking each of these claims in turn, I hope to build a theory of symbolization that is broader and more indicative of most language theories—one that is compatible with non-discursive texts.

At the end of this section, I review some of these theorists again to demonstrate that many of them anticipated some of the more salient points made about image, consciousness, and the imagination, especially within the context of language theory. Though most of these theorists were writing in the first half of the twentieth century, they anticipated many findings in neuroscience and psychology which are just now becoming available to a wider audience. Our field has yet to deal seriously with questions involving consciousness and the relationship between image and imagination to self and identity, though some of these theorists, such as Vygotsky and Bakhtin have, and their ideas are worth noting as a way of introducing the importance of non-discursive symbolization.

As I highlight lesser known aspects of the following theorists' work, or provide alternate interpretations of their writings, I also hope to reinvigorate the applicability of these theorists to modern composition studies. Some of these theorists may be considered dated or otherwise less relevant to contemporary scholarship than others: in short, some may think that these theorists have already run their due course in the field, such as those at the forefront of the social-epistemic view of rhetoric. On the contrary, I restore an expanded and, subsequently, slightly different view of some of these theorists' work as it becomes relevant to the present project: theorists, for example, such as Cassirer, Langer, and Berthoff who, as phenomenologists, may have been written off too early by critical theorists as ignoring the social, historical, and cultural consequences and elements of language; theorists such as Vygotsky, Vološinov, and Bakhtin are not readily known for their theories on image, imagination, and consciousness, yet all three touched on these topics; and, finally, theorists such as Britton, Moffett, and Coles shed some light on the value of ambiguity and abstraction in language, though they did not necessarily propose an explicit theory of language in their original texts. Therefore, to those who might ask "Why are you looking at these theorists again?" I would answer, "Because they have more to teach us."

Language as both Discursive and Non-discursive

Ernst Cassirer, Susanne Langer, and Ann Berthoff each posited language in such a way as to highlight the significance of the non-discursive, but more importantly, all three advocated a language theory which could account for the imagination.[11] Though Berthoff is the only one who might be considered a compositionist, Cassirer and Langer both constructed philosophies that heavily influenced her work. The most valuable contribution I take from them, however, is the way language comes to encompass both discursive and non-discursive text. It was Cassirer, then Langer, who proposed how it is our symbol systems work to include all of human articulation, not just speech or the written word (Ann Berthoff carries this work on in composition, and I discuss her contribution later in this chapter). Each of these language theories also make contributions to how symbolization connects to image and the mind.

Ernst Cassirer considered himself a neo-Kantian, meaning that his theories were in response to and aligned with Kant, and his language theory was an extension of Kantian philosophy:[12]

> The problem of language, however, is not treated in the work of Kant. He gives us a philosophy of knowledge, a philosophy of morality and art, but he does not give us a philosophy of language. But if we follow the general principles established by his critical philosophy we can fill this gap. According to these principles, we must study the world of language, not as if it were a substantial thing which possesses a reality of its own, an original or derivative reality, but as an instrument of human thought by which we are led to the construction of an objective world. If language means such a process of objectification, it is based on spontaneity, not on mere receptivity [. . . .] Language cannot be regarded as a copy of things but as a condition of our concepts of things. If we can show that it is one of the most valuable aids to, nay a necessary presupposition of, the formation of these concepts, we have done enough. We have proved that language, far from being a substantial thing, a reality of higher or lower order, is a prerequisite of our representation of empirical objects, of our concept of what we call the "external world." (*Symbol* 148)

Cassirer seems to point early to language as a means to understanding our world: that it objectifies our world for us, makes it tangible and a "condition of our concepts of things." In a significant way, Cassirer seems to posit that "in the beginning" there was language. Everything else soon followed: "Language grants us our first entrance into the objective. It is, as it were, the key word that unlocks the door of understanding to the world of concepts" (153). Cassirer's starting point is to show the primary way language functions—how it comes to objectify and thus, essentially, provide our experiences in the world.

Cassirer also attempts to distinguish between the mythic branch and the language branch by how the two engender thought differently as a way to introduce the difference between discursive and non-discursive text:

While certain contents of perception become verbal-mythical centers of force, centers of significance, there are others which remain, one might say, beneath the threshold of meaning [. . . .] Logical contemplation always has to be carefully directed toward the extension of concepts; classical syllogistic logic is ultimately nothing but a system of rules for combining, subsuming and superimposing concepts. But the conceptions embodied in language and myth must be taken not in extension, but in intension; not quantitatively, but qualitatively. Quantity is reduced to a purely casual property, a relatively immaterial and unimportant aspect [. . . .] In mythico-linguistic thought, however, exactly the opposite tendency prevails. Here we find in operation a law which might actually be called the law of the leveling and extinction of specific differences. Every part of a whole is the whole itself; every specimen is equivalent to the entire species. (*Language* 88)

I interpret "beneath the threshold of meaning" as Cassirer's way of talking about the non-discursive. It is not that the non-discursive is meaningless. Rather, the non-discursive, or "mythico-linguistic thought," does not have to be reliant on syllogistic or logical thought to express concepts. In fact, such non-discursive thought, as it exists in language, helps to create the whole of language: without it, there is only the discursive. Cassirer thus postulates a gap between "subjective impulses and excitations" (i.e., sensory information processed as thought) and "definite objective forms and figures" (i.e., symbolization). This gap, or "inner tension," is precisely where language and its failure to truly objectify occurs—that there is a difference between what is finally symbolized and the subjective impulses and excitations that originally led to ideation. This gap, then, is often continuously and repetitively navigated through discourse with varying degrees of success. But Cassirer stresses that this "indissoluble correlation" between myth and language is both "independent" and coincident: they combine at the substrate where mythico-linguistic thought exists. Any suggestion, then, that language or thought (or myth) could proceed one or the other is not tenable for Cassirer: "[N]o matter how widely the contents of myth and language may differ, yet the same form of mental conception is operative in both" (*Language* 84). This "mental conception" may be our innate ability to symbolize, or our imagination, or perhaps even the biological workings of mind in the presence of language. Whatever his intent, Cassirer was loathe to think of language as only discursive in nature, and through the mythico-linguistic, he postulates the existence of the non-discursive in language.

Another important contribution by Cassirer is that he critiques positivism by asserting that myth is not a "mental *defect*" but the primordial soup from which all language (both discursive and what he calls "the creative imagination") springs: "The Self feels steeped, as it were, in a mythico-religious atmosphere, which ever enfolds it, and in which it now lives and moves; it takes only a spark, a touch, to create the god or daemon out of this charged atmosphere" (*Language* 72). It is not enough to say that language springs from momentary gods known as the Word, and so Cassirer wishes to trace all theoretical knowledge to its base in myth:

> For all, the concepts of theoretical knowledge constitute merely an upper stratum of logic which is founded upon a lower stratum, that of the logic of language. Before the intellectual work of conceiving and understanding of phenomena can set in, the work of *naming* must have proceeded it [. . . .] All theoretical cognition takes its departure from a world already performed by language; the scientist, the historian, even the philosopher, lives with his objects only as language presents them to him. (28)

This kind of discursive thinking is marked by a totalizing nature, one that moves inductively from small observations to large concepts. "Mythical thinking," on the other hand, does not move in this way; it "does not dispose freely over the data of intuition" (32). Mythical thinking "comes to rest in the immediate experience" and consumes our senses with wonder:

> [I]t is as if the whole world were simply annihilated [. . . .] instead of expansion that would lead through greater spheres of being, we have here an impulse toward concentration; instead of extensive distribution, intensive compression. This focusing of all forces on a single point is the prerequisite for all mythical thinking and mythical formulation. (32–33)

From myth to "noticing," to naming, to ideation and conception, to discursive language (which includes the will-to-integrate), Cassirer takes his argument to community and the sociocultural fabric of our lives.

> Indeed, it is the Word, it is language, that really reveals to man that world which is closer to him than any world of natural objects and touches his weal and woe more directly than physical nature. For it is language that makes his existence in a *community* possible; and only in society, in relation to a "Thee," can his subjectivity assert itself as a "Me." (61)

Cassirer, therefore, also underscores the social nature of language, and he emphasizes how without language, community (and identity) would not be possible.

Perhaps most relevant to my purposes here, Cassirer also theorizes on the origins of language itself. He identifies a kind of "mental operation" which functions in the substance of myth and language. He calls this operation "metaphorical thinking" and it is fueled by a kind of inner tension mentioned already: "the nature and meaning of metaphor is what we must start with if we want to find on the one hand, the unity of the verbal and the mythical worlds and, on the other, their difference" (84). From this, Cassirer postulates a kind of symbolic formulation:

> Language and myth stand in an original and indissoluble correlation with one another, from which they both emerge but gradually as independent elements. They are two diverse shoots from the same parent stem, the same impulse of symbolic formulation, springing from the same basic mental activity, a concentration and heightening of simple sensory experience. In the vocables of speech and in primitive mythic figurations, the same inner process finds its consummation: they are both resolutions of an inner tension, the representation of subjective impulses and excitations in definite objective forms and figures. (88)

This "inner tension" marks the named from the unnamed, self from other, utterable from unutterable, and discursive from non-discursive. Tension is the motivating force behind language, behind ideation, behind all mental conceptions.

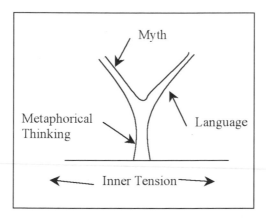

Fig. 1.1 Cassirer's Conception of Language

What Cassirer does is clear a space for Langer to talk about symbolization in a new way. By taking Cassirer's notion that language and thought are both "resolutions" to an inner tension, Langer reminds us that language is larger than mere discursive thought—that non-discursive thought *also* provides us a way to symbolize language. Rather than demarcating language into only symbol and object, Langer resists any notion that language exists solely as an objectifying tool for discursive thought:

> At best, human thought is but a tiny, grammar-bound island, in the midst of a sea of feeling expressed by 'Oh-oh' and sheer babble [. . . .] Most of us live the better part of our lives on this mud-flat; but in artistic moods we take to the deep, where we flounder about with symptomatic cries that sound like propositions about life and death, good and evil, substance, beauty, and other non-existent topics. (*New Key* 88)

Langer considers thought and language as Cassirer does—broader than discursive text, older than written history, and coincident with feeling and the way humans experience their existence. Langer seems to say here that our "mental life" includes much more by way of symbolization than discursive text alone would allow. She also stresses that we limit ourselves when we limit what we consider "language"—that language includes so much more in our "space-time world of our experience" than what is possible discursively (89). As I noted earlier, Langer's emphasis on the non-discursive broadens what is normally talked about when we talk about discourse, and it provides an essential insight into what she calls the "paragon of symbolic form": language itself (*Feeling* 28).

Some may be more familiar with Langer's term "presentational symbolism" rather than non-discursive symbolism. She uses both terms, and they have come to mean similar things, but in looking at *Philosophy in a New Key*, non-discursive symbolism is explained before presentational symbolism is mentioned, and it seems to be a broader category than presentational symbolism (93, 97). Arthur C. Danto, in "Mind as Feeling; Form as Presence; Langer as Philosopher," directly states that "presentational form" is "the most familiar sort of non-discursive symbol" (644–45). The terminology "presentational symbolism" may have been assimilated by some fields as a more meaningful opposite of discursive symbolism because Langer emphasizes its similarities to a presentation: "Their very functioning as symbols depends on the fact that they are involved in simultaneous, integral presentation" (97). In fact, Langer uses several terms to describe the non-discursive, each getting at different aspects of non-discursive text depending on her intended audience: the "art symbol" in *Feeling and Form* (3–41); the "expressive form" in *Problems of Art* (126); and "presentational symbols" in *Mind: An Essay on Human Feeling* (Vol. I, 156; Vol. II, 66). This apparent inconsistency is an effort by Langer to characterize more specifically for disciplinary scholars what she means with the term "non-discursive"; she is consistent in her opposition to discursive symbolization as the only recognized type of text. In addition, she relies on the term non-discursive to talk more about the general nature of that symbolization, as she does in the appendix of *Problems with Art*: "And although I am convinced that some abstractions cannot be made by the non-discursive forms we call 'works of art,' yet the basic abstractive processes are all exemplified in language at various stages of its ever-productive career" (168). What is the most salient here, despite Langer's seemingly inconsistent use of the term, is that our knowledge of feeling is "not alogical but prelogical: known without the mediating symbolism of discursive reason" (J. Johnson 64).

In addition to allowing a place in her language theory for the non-discursive, Langer also stresses "intuitive reasoning" as essential to our symbolizing practices: "Intuition is the basic process of all understanding, just as operative in discursive thought as in clear sense perception and immediate judgment" (19). Here Langer reveals her phenomenologist worldview, but she also demonstrates one paramount ramification of such an expanded view of language: that is, what we value in symbols indicates what we value in thought processes. A long history of valuing discursive language may imply a long history of valuing discursive reasoning. So, to define language theory as being both discursive and non-discursive is to make the case for intuitive reasoning *as an additional and critical component* of our conscious ability to understand.[13]

Another distinction Langer makes regarding language is the difference between signs and symbols. Whereas signs are proxy for their objects, symbols come to carry the meaning of objects:

> In talking *about* things we have conceptions of them, not the things themselves; and *it is the conceptions, not the things, that symbols directly "mean."* [. . . .] Of course, a word may be used as a sign, but that is not its primary role. Its signific character has to be indicated by some special modification—by a tone of voice, a gesture (such as pointing or staring), or the location of a placard bearing the word. In itself it is a symbol, associated with a conception, not directly with a public object or event. The fundamental difference between signs and symbols is this difference of association, and consequently of their *use* by the third party to the meaning function, the subject; signs *announce* their objects to him, whereas symbols *lead him to conceive* their objects. (*New Key* 61)

Clearly, Langer is emphasizing the role of the non-discursive even in the understanding and interpretation of the discursive. It may seem at times that I have been drawing the line between these two as a way to create a dichotomy, or a dualist philosophy, but that is not the case. Langer emphasizes how the non-discursive is necessarily part of the discursive, and vice versa. But because we so often privilege the discursive over the non-discursive, the latter is eclipsed in favor of the former. Because the distinction between sign and symbol is one, largely, of human interaction (the sign is just there; the symbol is our perception/interpretation of that sign), signs carry less weight in language than symbols do. In fact, the *New Key* Langer refers to in the title of her book is symbolization itself. The symbol, in fact, has a relationship to our perceptual "sense data" that must evoke awareness in order to be processed at all:

> Symbolization is pre-rationative, but not pre-rational. It is the starting point of all intellection in the human sense, and is more general than thinking, fancying, or taking action [. . . .] The current of experience that passes through it undergoes a change of character, not through the agency of the sense by which the perception entered, but by virtue of a primary use which is made of it immediately; it is sucked into the stream of symbols which constitutes a human mind. (42)

Langer considers perception a possible building block of conception, but not the exclusive building block.[14] Language, as a consequence, is not made up of signs at all; language becomes the result of these "vehicles for the conception of objects" taking shape as symbolic conceptions in the human mind (60–61). Language, in short, is made up of symbols, not signs.

Another consequence of thinking about language as both discursive and non-discursive is that writing—the composition of symbols—is no longer simply the articulation of words. In fact, words and sentences are only but one type of symbolization among a cosmology of many we as humans inhabit all the time. Langer stresses how these other kinds of articulation aid our formulation of concepts and conceptions: "Visual forms—lines, colors, proportions, etc.—are just as capable of *articulation*, i.e., of complex combination, as words" (93). Langer's symbolization theory, then, paves the way and even provides a theoretical frame for some of the recent trends in composition studies for composing with visual forms: for thinking of the visual not as merely representation or mimicry, but as crucial steps in our ability to form concepts—in other words, a fundamental part of language. Langer's theory, then, provides a way for language to include images (whether visual, auditory, haptic, olfactory, etc.) as an articulate form of symbolization.

Yet Langer does warn theorists from broadening the term "language" in relation to the arts (*Feeling* 225), but she does so because "language" for Langer is synonymous with speech: with oral communication (it is, in the end, translatable). In fact, true "language" for Langer is the same as "discourse": "Perhaps it were well to consider, here, the salient characteristics of true language, or discourse" (*New Key* 94). My interpretation of Langer contends that she regards the word "language" and symbols as synonymous *to the extent* that those symbols are discursive. Language, broadened to include non-discursive text (which is my argument, not Langer's), becomes capable of all symbolization—a distinction that works against the discursive bias that has held sway in language theory. Nevertheless, Langer's theory of non-discursive and discursive symbolization does offer an opportunity to refigure image as central to both.

Finally, another major contribution by Suzanne Langer is her theorization about virtuality—she is possibly one of the earliest philosophers willing to talk about nongeographic space. In *Feeling and Form*, Langer characterizes the virtual in this way:

> The harmoniously organized space in a picture is not experiential space, known by sight and touch, by free motion and restraint, far and near sounds, voices lost or re-echoed. It is an entirely visual affair; for touch and hearing and muscular action it does not exist. For them there is a flat canvas, relatively small, or a cool blank wall, where for the eye there is deep space full of shapes. This purely visual space is an illusion, for our sensory experiences do not agree on it in their report [. . . .] Like the space 'behind' the surface of a mirror, it is what the physicists call 'virtual space'—an intangible space." (72)

Langer expands on this "virtual space" by outlining the modes of virtual space ("illusory scene," "illusory organism," and "illusory [. . .] place"), virtual powers (symbols of "vital force" as in dance), and virtual memory ("narrative [. . .] the semblance of memory")—each are manifestations of the symbolic world as perceived by observers in the actual world (95, 175, 265). Langer's virtuality, then, places symbolization into our lives just to show us how much it is a part of what we do as humans: how much symbols offer us "a life of feeling" (372).

Language as both Individual and Social

The influence of Russian theorists is palpable in composition studies, so much so that their combined authority has helped to define how our discipline views issues as diverse as the nature of self and identity, the social nature of language, and the importance of cultural histories on writing instruction. What is not often mentioned, however, is how theorists such as Vološinov, Bakhtin, and Vygotsky also advocated an expanded view of language somewhat before its time, as well as the importance of the individual within the social. Generally considered as linguists and psychologists, these theorists reacted against the communication model of language, as well as the Saussurian notion that language is made up of the signified and the signifier (and that meaning is created by simply having "inherited" an understanding of both). Much has been written about these theorists and their work. I only wish to briefly summarize some of the main points here regarding the relationships between image and these theorists' own particular view of language.

One such language theorist is V. N. Vološinov.[15] In *Marxism and the Philosophy of Language*, Vološinov spends a great deal of time in defending his view of language:

> In somewhat simplified form, the idea of language as a system of conventional, arbitrary signs of a fundamentally rational nature was propounded by representatives of the Age of the Enlightenment in the 18th century [. . . .] Abstract objectivism finds its most striking expression at the present time in the so-called Geneva school of Ferdinand de Saussure [. . . .] It can be claimed that the majority of Russian thinkers in linguistics are under the determinative influence of Saussure.[16] (58)

In particular, Vološinov positions himself in opposition to Saussure by theorizing language as revealing ideological and social relationships. Unlike Saussure, Vološinov does not see language within an individual as any less social than that language used in the greater social fabric of speech acts:

> In point of fact, the speech act or, more accurately, its product—the utterance, cannot under any circumstances be considered an individual phenomenon in the precise meaning of the word and cannot be explained in terms of the individual psychological or psychophysiological conditions of the speaker. *The utterance is a social phenomenon.* (82)

He then contends that the relationship between the utterance and the individual are within a dynamic that is constantly changing and layered by history and social contexts. Language "exists not in and of itself but only in conjunction with the individual structure of a concrete utterance" (123). Again, the dominant emphasis by Vološinov is to challenge any static notion of language: that language is simply passed down from generation to generation. Instead, language "reflects, not subjective, psychological vacillations, but stable social interrelationships among speakers" (118). This fluidity, which is a direct challenge to Saussure's semiotics, stresses the give-or-take of language by emphasizing the human role in the way it is learned, used, and forgotten. Though commonly cited as a proponent of the social importance of language, it would be a misreading to say that Vološinov did not see the value of the individual because it is precisely at the intersection between the two that the forces of language interact: both are present, and both contribute to the dynamic nature of language.

Another Russian theorist, Lev Vygotsky, focuses his work on the study of language as reflected in the development of children—a methodology in sharp contrast to Vološinov's more philosophical methodology. He often stresses what is missing in discursive language, openly criticizing any effort to separate metaphor or emotion from the relationship between thought and language:

> When we approach the problem of the interrelation between thought and language and other aspects of mind, the first question that arises is that of intellect and affect. Their separation as subjects of study is a major weakness of traditional psychology, since it makes the thought process appear as an autonomous flow of 'thoughts thinking themselves,' segregated from the fullness of life, from the personal needs and interests, the inclinations and impulses, of the thinker [. . . .] Unit analysis points the way to the solution of these vitally important problems. It demonstrates the existence of a dynamic system of meaning in which the affective and the intellectual unite. It shows that every idea contains a transmuted affective attitude toward the bit of reality to which it refers. (Vygotsky 10)

Language for Vygotsky must be dynamic, and it must come from an individual within a social context. He outright refutes any notion that thought can be "segregated from the fullness of life," and by associating intellect and affect, Vygotsky is allowing language to be a "dynamic system of meaning," helping to reintegrate the otherwise too easily separated realms of affect and intellect. These two realms may be so easily separable precisely because language, through its symbolization, materializes into a *thing* (symbols on a medium that are usually—or ultimately—static) that can then be perceived by the senses. Language itself seems isolated from the "thinker," or the "personal needs and interests, the inclinations and impulses" of the person behind the symbolization. In uniting intellect and affect, Vygotsky allows definitions of language to broaden significantly.

For Vygotsky, and like Vološinov, the relationship between thought and word is dynamic and depends on the presence of a symbol. But Vygotsky does not necessarily limit his discussion to what we translate as speech or printed text on a piece of paper: "Language does not have to depend on sound [. . .] The medium is beside the point; what matters is the *functional use of signs*, any signs that could play a role corresponding to that of speech in humans" (75–76). Vygotsky expands the popular notion of the time that language is just words or speech, or that it consists only of sign and referent:

> Schematically, we may imagine thought and speech as two inter-secting circles [see Figure 1.2]. In their overlapping parts, thought and speech coincide to produce what is called verbal thought [. . . .] **There is a vast area of thought that has no direct relation to speech** [. . . .] Nor are there any psychological reasons to derive all forms of speech activity from thought [. . . .] Finally, there is 'lyrical' speech, prompted by emotion" (88, bold my emphasis).

Again, Vygotsky is more interested in stressing the separateness of thought and speech than in defining a new area of cognition. In order to wrangle thought away from linguists who saw thought and speech the defining elements of language, Vygotsky is actually helping to define language in such a way that is broader than simply the use of speech.

But Vygotsky goes only so far in defining the separation of thought and language, and it is possible to conflate the idea of verbal thought with speaking to oneself silently. James T. Zebroski, in analyzing Vygotsky, makes the distinction between inner speech and inner speaking clearer:

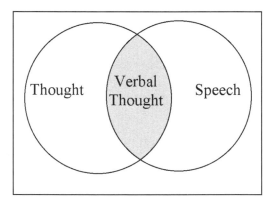

Fig. 1.2 Vygotsky's Thought-Speech Relationship

Inner speaking is subvocalized speaking, one of the psychological functions most distant from deeper levels of thinking, yet still too often confused for Vygotsky's inner speech. Inner speech in the strict sense is the intermediate and transactional form of thinking-speaking that has its own speeded up movement, its own peculiar syntax, semantics, and pragmatics [. . .] It is beyond the threshold of consciousness but plays an important role in helping to *prepare* for specific kinds of utterances. (*Thinking* 199–200)

The inner speech area shown in Figure 1.2, is preconscious, fueled by "motive" or will, and that it contains a "subvocalized" form of language ready to "prepare" for an utterance, whether vocalized or not. Because this brand of speech is clearly internal to the speaker, Vygotsky is stressing the importance of the individual in our use of language. It would be too simplistic to say that language for Vygotsky is primarily or entirely a social construction.[17]

Similar to Vygotsky, M. M. Bakhtin also aims to broaden notions of language. He is arguably the most popular language theorist in composition studies, and his works are cited within many different, even competing, areas in the field. Bakhtin's work on language, like Vygotsky and Vološinov, is long and complex, and I will only try to highlight his most relevant contributions to language theory, especially regarding its reliance on both the social and the individual forces in language.

Though his object of study is often narrative and the novel, Bakhtin has a lot to say about the dialogic nature of language:

Language—like the living concrete environment in which the consciousness of the verbal artist lives—is never unitary. It is unitary only as an abstract grammatical system of normative forms, taken in isolation from the concrete, ideological conceptualizations that fill it, and in isolation from the uninterrupted process of historical becoming that is a characteristic of all living language. Actual social life and historical becoming create within an abstractly unitary national language a multitude of concrete worlds, a multitude of bounded verbal-ideological and social belief systems; within these various systems (identical in the abstract) are elements of language filled with various semantic and axiological content and each with its own different sound. (288)

The sound element and the semantic element form a heteroglot in language layered with possibility. The position that language is never unitary—and that the consciousness of the "verbal artist" is also, necessarily, never unitary—is not inconsistent with modern views of consciousness as both integrated and differentiated.[18] Both Bakhtin and Vygotsky work to expand thought and language to include more than simple communication, or the sender-message-receiver model of language. Bakhtin often characterizes language as a "world" in which thought and speech intersect:

> [L]anguage is a heteroglot from top to bottom: it represents the co-existence of socio-ideological contradictions between the present and the past, between differing epochs of the past, between different socio-ideological groups in the present, between tendencies, schools, circles and so forth, all given a bodily form. (291)

Bakhtin posits layers, much like Vygotsky does, with inner speech as a layer between thought and speech, and these layers are made up of epochs and worlds unto themselves. The consequence of such layering is a view of language that is both social and individual: the world is an ecosystem where individuals interact with their environment. Though Bakhtin's emphasis is on the social, he acknowledges the "bodily form" which ultimately provides the nexus for these layers. The social, in order to make any sense whatsoever, must also be embodied.

Especially relevant is the way Bakhtin incorporates space and time into his theory of language. Both Vygotsky and Vološinov posit how language is dynamic, changing, and social, but Bakhtin takes this further by making language rife with layers of different places and times—an element he labels the "chronotope": "We will give the name *chronotope* (literally, 'time space') to the intrinsic connectedness of temporal and spatial relationships that are artistically expressed in literature" (84). He then relates the chronotope to language by situating discourse within a context: "Also chronotopic is the **internal form of a word**, that is, the mediating marker with whose help the root meanings of spatial categories are carried over into temporal relation-ships (in the broadest sense)" (251, bold my emphasis). This "internal form of a word" is a mediating form entrenched in spatial as well as temporal relationships. What is pertinent here is the fact that Bakhtin's language theory is also laced with its own history and location(s): it is social, it is dynamic, and it is linked to its own time and place just as individuals are within a social context.[19] As a consequence, Bakhtin's language theory is in opposition to a simple sender-message-receiver model because every element of that exchange carries along with it different times and different places: associations that make up the full "internal form of a word." In short, language is inherently connected, not just to other words, but to the past layers, voices, and eras contained within each utterance.

Bakhtin's interests in the utterance, though he would call it the "word," emphasizes the give and take of language. By looking at the way language has ties to its own history, its own etymological evolution, Bakhtin stresses the dialogic nature of language. Each word has connections not only to its own historical meanings, but also to all the other meanings it implies or is culturally associated with because it is part of an ever-changing social network. As a consequence, the dialogic principle states that language is never unitary: it is a "multitude of concrete worlds, a multitude of bounded verbal-ideological and social belief systems" (288). Because language is made up of a nonunitary set of worlds, it is a "heteroglot" of languages, beliefs, and socio-ideological "contradictions," which extend through time and through place. These levels, or strata, form from social strata that exist in culture: language is "stratified" because "each word tastes of the context and contexts in which it has lived its socially charged life" and that each of these words are "populated by intentions" and, therefore, "for the individual consciousness, lies on the borderline between oneself and other" (293). Bakhtin looks at dialogism not necessarily as a conversation between two people, but as a conversation between layers within a single word. Each word is a hyperlink, if you will, to its own layers, its own strata made up of other cultures, historical meanings, and contradictions. But while the word is living in a conversation, all its forces are radicalized into centralizing forces and decentralizing forces: Bakhtin calls this the centrifugal and centripetal tensions in language. The very ambiguity and complex stratification within the heteroglossia of the word decentralizes it, remains centrifugal; the act of the utterance, however also forms new layers in the strata, adding new voices to the heteroglossia, and thus works as a centrifugal force, or a centralizing force. Intertextuality, therefore, simply reinforces how no single utterance is unitary; all utterance builds upon the strata of previous utterances, and, thus, is intertextual. James Zebroski summarizes Bakhtin's theory of language this way:

> Bakhtin sees language—itself too dead and reified a term—as a landscape of interacting forces, a field of energies that penetrate and withdraw, that converge and break up, that obliterate and wash away the kind of neat categories and boundaries that the communication model is based on. Language is a battlefield of clashing and merging armies. It is a multivoiced plurality. Language is dialogue in a literal kind of way. It is dialogic because even the most complete monologic utterance can never be understood in and of itself, always being part of a wider context [. . .] Language is, for Bakhtin, simultaneously being built up and torn down. (*Thinking* 186)

This view of language emphasizes the constructive/deconstructive (or centripetal/centrifugal, to use Bakhtin's terms) forces in language, a move which acknowledges the innate heuristic nature of language itself: like bone, language, within its various strata and ideologies, can build or reduce in order to grow—a conflict that strengthens as it changes. This is different from Derrida's deconstruction in that the signified is already signified, and this continual signification works to rewrite and fragment language rather than enrich and layer it. According to Derrida language becomes diluted and rewritten; in Bakhtin language becomes multilayered and textured with other worlds.

There can be no doubt about the social nature of language. Whether discursive or non-discursive, language thrives within a social context that influences and is directly influenced by the way others use it. What these Russian theorists have emphasized, then, is not that language is only social, or even that language is *primarily* social. On the contrary, Bakhtin, Vygotsky, and Vološinov all emphasize the social as it is embodied in the individual: that the two are related by forces both ideological and communal. It is as much a reduction to view language as sign and signifier within the individual's brain as it is to view language as a purely social phenomena. These theorists acknowledge how the social and the individual are integral to language: Vološinov emphasizes language as operating "in conjunction" with an individual's concrete social experience; Vygotsky emphasizes language as made up of both intellect and affect; and Bakhtin emphasizes language as being given "bodily form" even as it constructs and tears down worlds of meaning. It is often the case that these theorists are cited as upholding the social influences of language above the individual. In actuality, both the social and the individual work together to create text, and, significantly, such work can and often does fail.

Language Failure and Ambiguity as Important to Writing

Ann Berthoff shifts the focus of language theory from production to reception as she highlights what happens as we attempt to interpret the symbols of others. Though Langer also stresses interpretation as a part of concept formation, Berthoff theorizes what happens when language fails or, at least, is ambiguous. Like Bakhtin, Berthoff expands on the notion that language is both self-destructive as much as it is generative:

> In the perspective of a triadic semiotic, gaps function as part of the semiotic structure itself [. . .] The triangle with the dotted base line is an emblem of a triadic semiotics. By differentiating referent and reference and showing their interdependence, the curious triangle reminds us that the heuristic power of the symbol depends dialectally on separation and conjunction [. . .] But triadicity has no explanatory

> power unless interpretation is seen as a logical, not a psychological matter [. . .] The point is, rather, that it is by being a barrier that it is a bridge: language *as such*—the formal system, the arbitrary structure, unconscious and historically determined—language is itself the great heuristic. (*Barricades* 49)

Thus, language is at once able to bridge meaning as much as it can become a barrier to meaning. It is made up of a dialectic dependent on "separation and conjunction," and as the interpreter interacts with this tension, "meaning could be brought into the picture" depending on the interpreters access to the logic of triadicity. Just as Cassirer would link language and myth making (though "noticing" in the mythic consciousness), Berthoff repeats the relationship internally, making language itself the thought that is interpreted through what she calls "triadicity." The "thirdness" of the interpretant makes every symbolization an act of active connection for the receiver. Because language creates ambiguity as it goes along, users of language *create* "bridges" to overcome the ambiguity.

But overcoming ambiguity does not mean that we necessarily interpret a meaning once and forever. A natural extension of Berthoff's heuristic would be that we may hold several possible interpretations of any one unit of meaning at the same time, connecting and disconnecting between alternatives at will or convenience. Berthoff reinforces how language and thought have inertia: they do not begin and end with a symbolization of ideas within a social context. Rather, symbolization may lead to language, which may lead to thought or symbolization, which may again lead to language. In this way, Berthoff is reinforcing the interconnectedness of symbolization: language is recursive, active, and changing.

Though others have offered theories of triadicity before, each has as its interpretant a different agent (represented as apexes in Fig. 1.3). Berthoff,

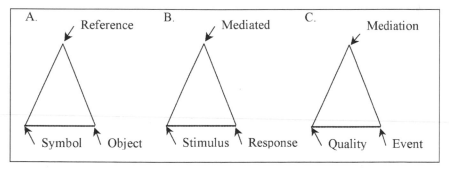

Fig. 1.3 Three Triadicity Models

in *Mysterious Barricades*, takes her notion of the interpretant most directly from C. S. Peirce and his concept of mediation (or what Berthoff calls "thirdness"). The reason this model more closely represents her theory of language is that "mediation" is the connectedness in language:

> What is least understood is Peirce's idea of representation: given the radical skepticism of much contemporary criticism, perhaps representation should also be hailed as a revolutionary doctrine. But then so should semiosis: Peirce's emphasis on the process whereby one sign requires another for its interpretation leads to his very powerful idea of Synechism—the continuity of all things, including ideas including man. (65)

The apexes of these triangles differ due to the degree each respective theorist emphasizes the power of interpretation in language: Ogden and Richards barely acknowledge this link (A), Vygotsky more so (B), and Peirce most of all (C). The interpretive thirdness of language both creates and obscures language: ambiguities between symbol/object, stimulus/response, and quality/event drive the heuristic power of language while, at the same time, limits its ability to convey unaltered meaning.

Berthoff, as a compositionist, is especially interested in linking these theories about language with composing. She stresses the generative nature of language itself as one way to make meaning in the world:

> Observing, thinking, writing: these are all forming activities [. . .] How you construe *is* how you construct; how you understand is how you compose. To "construe" is to interpret or make meaning [. . .] "Construct is defined as a verb meaning to build [. . .] Construing and constructing are both acts of forming. Thus, writing is a matter of learning how to use the forms of language to discover the forms of thought, and vice versa. (*Forming* 21)

Simply put, composing is a type of forming, or writing, from the world about the world. Berthoff emphasizes how language is actively formed from the way we observe our experiences and construct meaning out of them. But meaning in language is not a result of a pure, one-to-one relationship between symbol and object, stimulus and response, or quality and event. Berthoff is careful to stress how language must be interpreted, ambivalences must be navigated, and meanings do not arrive as ontological givens: "Since 'perfect accuracy of thought is unattainable,' we must be on guard against claiming too much for our interpretations. We must cultivate fallibilism because it is practical, because it makes a difference in our logic" (61). By emphasizing how the interpretation of language is fallible or varied, Berthoff's language theory expands beyond simple communication theory. Rather than avoid and bemoan the fallibility of language with its ambivalences and failures, we should learn to embrace it—to acknowledge its complexity as its most generative feature.

Although Berthoff theorizes the reception of language, she has a lot to say about the production of language as well. Despite the fact that they are often criticized for their phenomenological views, Cassirer, Langer, and Berthoff all acknowledge and stress the role of the social in language—that language is social as much as it is individual. Berthoff in particular stresses how the social and communal nature of language lead philosophers to a more integrated theory: "Showing how the linguistic process and the process of perception are interdependent, how they unfold in social contexts, can guide us towards an authentic phenomenology of knowledge" (*Barricades* 27). That is to say, a social context is the stage on which these linguistic and perceptive processes interact, compound, and even barricade each other's meaning. When Berthoff stresses individual selves, it must be read in conjunction with the other claims she makes about social context. It's not just individual or just social; Berthoff grounds her language theory within the perspective that both the social and the individual interact, and that this interaction takes place both in the act of text production and text reception.

Other composition scholars have addressed language theory in their work, but to a lesser extent than those already mentioned in this chapter. They are largely the practitioners, the writing teachers, who directly enact language theory in their classrooms, but not necessarily on paper. Consequently, it is through their writing about pedagogy and about the way language ought to be taught that their theory of language becomes at least implicitly obvious, if not directly explicit. In the analysis to come, I do not claim that these authors are talking about language theory *per se*, but I do claim that they may indicate a particular stance about language (in terms of its use and its formation, for example) in the way they advocate writing and writing instruction. Taken together, these theorists play an crucial role in the way language has been understood in composition studies, and though they are not as consistently aligned with the theorists already mentioned, they are often cited as dominant influences in the way symbolization is talked about and theorized in the field. I mention Moffett, Britton, and Coles because they too address the function of ambiguity and failure in language.

In *Teaching the Universe of Discourse*, James Moffett posits a theory of education based on Piaget's principle of egocentrism, Vygotsky's theories of language, and Langer's theories of symbol-making. In general, Moffett concludes that students (who, for Moffett, are children) learn by abstracting experience into symbols—that language comes directly and naturally from the everyday give-or-take of symbol-making and verbalization. As language becomes more abstract, children are able to decenter themselves and move from telling, to generalizing, to predicting (something he calls chronologic, analogic, tautologic, respectively). Students best learn about language use not through textbooks, but through using language at every point along these abstractive levels. Moffett is also interested in removing the "ghost" of grammar from language instruction, replacing it with "structure" (or rhetoric) so students not be "duped" by information in the future.

> Yes, language is about itself, but [. . .] higher abstractions are about lower abstractions, never about themselves. That is, some English words refer to the outer world, other words (like relative pronouns) refer to these first words, and all syntax is about tacit rules for putting together the concrete words (like relative pronouns) [. . .] and all syntax is about tacit rules for putting together the concrete words. Some notion of a hierarchy of abstraction, defined as greater and greater processing of phenomena by the human mind, is indispensable. Thus, the more abstract language is, the more it is meta-language, culminating in mathematics as the ultimate language about language. So we imagine a symbolic hierarchy going from the codification of our world that most nearly reflects the structure of that world to codification that more and more resembles the structure of the mind. Basically this is what abstraction is all about. To enable the student to learn about this process, we must first separate in the curriculum, and hence in the student's mind, symbolic systems from empirical subjects, and then help him discover both the dependence and independence of one and the other. (9)

Moffett's analysis of abstraction, then, partially mirrors the way Langer talks about the forming of concepts, but his intent seems to be to "separate" symbols from signs in order for students to see the difference. Like Bakhtin, he refers to words as having "worlds," a sure sign that words, as symbols, carry more than just an intended meaning. He is not concerned with whether or not a child knows how to abstract, but whether a child knows the difference between levels of abstraction. In fact, mathematics "is the ultimate language about language" because it is the ultimate example of discursive symbolization: language representing itself as transparently as possible without error or ambiguity. These levels of abstraction are important to Moffett because he wishes to show how language is sometimes made more abstract as it is made more discursive. He then constructs a curriculum that progresses from lowest level narration ("chronologic"), to generalization ("analogic"), to claims about the future ("tautologic"), all in progressive, regulated, deliberate steps (34).

> The essential purpose of such a curriculum would be to have the student abstract at all ranges of the symbolic spectrum and progressively to integrate his abstractions into thought structures that assimilate both autistic and public modes of cognition. The discourses that are successively more abstract makes it possible for the learner to understand better what is entailed at each stage of the hierarchy, to relate one stage to another, and thus to become aware of how he and others create information and ideas. (25)

Moffett is simultaneously acknowledging the importance of the social and individual influences on language as the child learns to use "all ranges of the symbolic spectrum." Learning about these levels of abstraction is, if nothing else, acknowledging the importance of abstraction to symbol-making, and at the same time supporting the position that students must learn to cope with ambiguity as he or she becomes more familiar with these different levels: "To be a master, and not the dupe, of symbols, the symbol-maker must understand the nature and value of his abstractions. This takes consciousness and an integrated view of the hierarchical, inner processing" (25). Not only are students becoming more rhetorically competent in such a curriculum, but they are also having to deal with these abstractions and ambiguities emotionally: "The relations among feeling, thought, and values are such that this course seems not only possible but in the end necessary" (25–26). In the end, Moffett's curriculum indicates a theory of language that must value the importance of ambiguity and language failure if students are to progress from one level of abstraction to another.

In addition, by writing about abstraction, Moffett does provide an interesting way of conceptualizing the relationship between thought and language. For him, the difference between the two is dependent on different levels of abstraction:

> The qualifying of thought and elaborating of sentence structures develop together. Outside the classroom this development through vocal exchange occurs all the time, but in the classroom it can be furthered deliberately by creating kinds of dialogue in which questioning, collaborating, qualifying, and calling for qualification, are habitual give-and-take operations. (82)

What Moffett is advocating is an implicit view of language that values the learning that happens when discursive language fails. As these students question each other, as they listen and learn to qualify their responses, they are also learning how language is *not* a transparent conveyance of thought: language often fails to work, and it is the experience of both having it fail for you and for someone else that is so instructional here. That is to say, Moffett's levels of abstraction acknowledge the ambiguity of language because of the various "levels" that are ongoing at the same time in both the listener and the questioner. Further, it may be that the tolerance for this ambiguity actually indicates the development level of the reader (or receiver). The development of a tolerance for the ambiguous is what enables us to interpret, at the different levels of abstraction, what Moffett delineates in his curriculum. Moffett is relevant to the present study because his levels of abstraction may indicate levels of ambiguity that both children and adults alike must navigate in order to participate in discursive and non-discursive symbol-making.

Unlike Moffett, James Britton implies a language theory that is not based on abstraction, but on the concretization of experience. Britton claims experience drives our representations of the world. By borrowing from both Cassirer and Vygotsky, Britton rejects "reason" as the essential human characteristic with regard to language. Though he talks mostly about discursive language, he accounts for the possibility of the non-discursive this way:

> But language, as we shall see, is only one way of symbolizing what is in the universe, and we cannot explain the particular workings of language unless we see their relations with other ways of symbolizing and with the nature of the symbolizing process itself." (13)

The "other ways of symbolizing" may be a reference to the non-discursive (he refers on the same page to Cassirer's characterization of language as being one of "the most characteristic features of human life"), but the most significant point here is that Britton understands language as relational, not just between meaning and meaning, but between one symbolic group and another (as evidenced in part by his reliance on Cassirer). The main benefit, according to Britton, of learning about "other ways of symbolizing" (or non-discursive symbolization) comes from the exposure of relationships between "symbolizing" systems. This, in turn, leaves an opening for methods other than discursive logic. By learning more about intuitive logic, to use Langer's term, we may learn more about discursive logic and the very "workings of language" in general. It is through relationships that we are able to understand the whole, and relationships are usually ambiguous.

Another implied aspect of Britton's language theory, one that is closely tied to his emphasis on the relationships between various symbolic systems, is the way our language and perception can actually change what is symbolized or perceived.[20] Britton hits upon one more way language is inherently ambiguous and prone to failure: language shapes what we see, and language relays the way our feelings and our logic are linked.

> We must take into account the fact that we shape the objects of our perception in the act of perceiving them; thus, we regularize, simplify, give a more satisfying shape to what we look at in the very act of looking at it; and this ordering is reflected in the way we speak and write about our experiences. We must take into account also the fact that an organization of our *feelings*, by some means or another, must always accompany the process of arriving at a logical conclusion by the means we have been considering. (214)

Britton emphasizes these two pivotal points, but also stresses that we ultimately may not be able to explain them using traditional, logical means. As such, the very fact that non-discursive language "embraces both cognitive and affective aspects of experience" may make it impossible to translate it fully by discursive means—a good reason that this book addresses the affective domain in chapter 3.

To say that we shape what we see is not a particularly new or radical idea in Britton's time. But Britton writes in the context of other language theories (Cassirer, Langer, Vygotsky, etc.) and, therefore, may implicitly call into question our act of looking at language in the first place. I propose that as language theorists strive to understand language, they are shaping it. In fact, as I write these words to better understand Britton's contribution to language theory in composition, I am shaping them, constraining them in a new context, stripping them of context, and, perhaps, even distorting their original intent. To do so, at any level, is inevitable, but it is also normal practice, something we are used to in our reception practices. As we read more and get used to adjusting to the point of view of the one who symbolizes through language, we must acknowledge that even in the most discursive of texts, we don't just read discursively. This is what Berthoff emphasizes with interpretation and "thirdness": even in the most discursive, most logical, most mathematical of texts, we *read* with a combination of cognitive and affective capacities in order to mediate between how the author is shaping, or in some cases, changing the object being viewed.[21] Just as we may not wholly discredit whether the animals depicted in the cave paintings in Lascaux, France, actually existed, or existed in the manner portrayed, we may not wholly discredit a given set of symbols just because it does not hold true to our notions of discursive logic. Britton, perhaps without intention, highlights how we may be shaping what we see through our representations in language—that the object of language actually changes through the way we represent it within language. Conversely, he also implies that we shape what we interpret as well—that even our interpretations change through our representations of them in language. We shape both what and how we symbolize as we produce and receive text.

Britton connects the ambiguity of language to the way we feel as we interpret or compose. Our feelings are connected to our logic, and so discursive thought is constantly shaped and shadowed by our feelings. In fact, according to Britton, thought can no longer be conceived as pure rational thought: it includes "almost every intuitive process, semantic and formal (logical), and passes from insight to insight not only by recognised processes, but as often as not by short cuts and personal, incommunicable means" (215). Acknowledging these "incommunicable means"—or the non-discursive—is precisely what has been missing, though sometimes hoped for, in talking to students about writing. The incommunicable and the unutterable are relevant aspects of any theory of writing or textual production, just as silence and absence are relevant to discourse theory. As Britton reminds us, the relationships help us understand the items being related. It is precisely where discursive language fails that non-discursive symbolization excels, and it is here that the non-discursive must be emphasized and employed within a language theory able to account for not only discursive logic but also intuitive logic.

William E. Coles, Jr., provides a logical extension to the way Britton talks about language, and in doing so he narrates what happens when you attempt to helps students experience the ineffable—the unsayable, the unutterable—through writing. In his book *The Plural I—and After*, Coles shares reflections and assignments from an undergraduate humanities course he taught. Along the way he makes some reflective observations about language. In fact, rather than make language simpler for students to understand (i.e., in a set or rules, or checklists, or methods of composing), the overall pedagogical impulse is to complicate, obscure, and challenge what students thought they knew about both writing and reading texts. He works against what Britton said is inevitable about language: that it tends to "regularize" and "simplify" as it goes. Coles, above everything else, seem to successfully work against that notion in order to provide students with some glimpse of the mystery in language. "Dictionaries define words," he says, "they cannot define word users who seek in their use of words to be someones as well" (50). Like Britton, Coles implicitly values how language can fail, and he does this by providing experiences of language failure for students within his writing assignments.

Language failure means more here than simply the inability to communicate a particular meaning. Coles explains that the success of writing comes from the efforts a writer makes through failure. In fact, Coles took pains to point out the problem with "proficient" writing, the kind that is always clear and formulaic. Whether termed "Engfish" by Ken Macrorie, or "Englishclassese" by Coles, these student writers were so good at following a formula that their writing seemed disengaging and rote. Growth, then, is measured not by the continued use of discursive logic, but by other, more intangible elements of style and voice:

> His [the student] difficulty as a writer was that he was generally too damned Proficient for his own good. He had never had anyone demand of him that he write a sentence that was *about* anything, and he responded to the demand initially as though he had been asked to drop his pants. (265)

The student improved when Coles could finally hear a voice, a self, in the writing. Or, perhaps, what Coles was really looking for is what Langer and Britton both emphasize: evidence of intuitive thought underneath all that programmed discursive thought. Coles required students in his class to look at language not just as a set of discursive symbols with a logical framework (i.e., introduction, body, conclusion), but a view of language that required students to acknowledge themselves in their writing: their uncontested assumptions and their reasons for using language in the first place. It is a distinct possibility that Coles helped students understand the ineffable in language; he helped them learn about language by pushing them towards failing in it. Through cryptic and brash instruction, Coles kept asking students to press language to its limits, to move outside any codified or systemized conveyance of meaning. In short, Coles asked students to break their own ability to use language. Though the students may have thought they were failing to "get" what Coles wanted from them, Coles was trying to have them fail at their own use of language. As a consequence, Coles' narrative indicates that he values the lessons learned when language fails.

Failure, however, is perhaps the wrong word. Instead, let's consider the inaccuracies of language as synonymous with the fecundity of language. Just as there are instances when a writer struggles and struggles to express a particular (objectified) meaning and fails, there are opportunities for epistemology. Jacob Bronowski, in *The Origins of Knowledge and Imagination*, explains this phenomenon this way:

> Ambiguity, multivalence, the fact that language simply cannot be regarded as a clear and final exposition of what it says, is central both to science and, of course, to literature. Why to science? [. . . .] [W]henever you try to press the symbolism to do more than it can do, you fail [. . . .] What distinguishes science is that it is a

systematic attempt to establish closed systems one after another. But all fundamental scientific discovery opens the system again. The symbolism of the language is found to be richer than had been supposed. New connections are discovered. The symbolism has to be broadened. Symbolism, language, scientific formulae here are all synonymous. (108–09)

In the end, even science must "open the system" through the imagination, otherwise new knowledge would be impossible as old knowledge gets infinitely redescribed. Language, though its failures, accesses the imagination: "The act of imagination is the opening of the system so that it shows connections" (109). It is the set of new connections spawned by a symbolism pressed too far that makes reformulations possible.

Valuing ambiguity, of course, might seem controversial for those who view language as only a means to communicate or send messages. After all, if the goal is communication, why would you ever want to purposely create miscommunication? The consequence of valuing and learning from the way language fails is not only to improve the message (should that be the goal) but also to decenter discursive *meaning* as the primary motivation or purpose of language. Berthoff iterates this centrality of meaning in the following way: "the analysis appropriate to the relationship of language and thought must begin not with one or the other but (as Vygotsky has it) with 'the unit of meaning,' with what language and thought create in their peculiar independence" (*Barricades* 160). For Berthoff, the "unit of meaning" (and, therefore, the idea that meaning is the unit of language) is the center of scholarship regarding thought and language. But what I wish to emphasize here is that this unit of meaning, this basic element of the thought-language-interpretation triad in rhetoric, is comprised of *image*. As Cassirer notes in his work, the impetus toward language comes, ultimately, from the focus of our attention: noticing begins the act of symbolizing. Langer takes this even further by saying "No human impression is only a signal from the outer world; it always is *also* an image in which possible impressions are formulated, that is, a symbol for the conception of *such* experience" (*Feeling* 376). By displacing discursive meaning as the center of all language and replacing it with image, it becomes possible to value non-discursive meaning as equally essential to the way we compose meaning in language. It is now possible to talk about language without making the error Langer warns us against regarding the non-discursive: that because it lacks the formal, chain-of-reasoning logic of discursive text it must also necessarily lack articulation (89).[22] If image is regarded as language, we are then free to talk about *either* discursive or non-discursive meaning in language theory.

Language is Closely Tied to Image and Consciousness

Many of the language theorists already mentioned wrote about the relationship between language and consciousness as a way to substantiate their claims. In fact, many, like Langer and Vygotsky, posited that it is impossible if not downright irresponsible to make any claims about language without accounting for the way consciousness and language interact. This section deepens the connection between image to language as it explores the way theorists have talked about consciousness in relation to textual production.

One such theorist, V. N. Vološinov, defines something he calls "pictorial reflective speech" in *Marxism and the Philosophy of Language*:

> the reporting context strives to break down the self-contained compactness of the reported speech, to resolve it, to obliterate its boundaries [. . .] Its tendency is to obliterate the precise, external contours of reported speech; at the same time, the reported speech is individualized to a much greater degree—the tangibility of the various facets of an utterance may be subtly differentiated. (120–21)

Here Vološinov creates a space for individual intonation, including such elements as "humor, irony, love or hate, enthusiasm or scorn" (121). In a way, pictorial reflective speech is also made up of non-discursive text, even if only in the intonations present in the speech itself. Vološinov is pointing here to an extra-communicative facet of language, one that remains fluid, historical, and social. His particular view of language—especially the notion that actual, concrete context is "inseverable" from any utterance—refutes the notion that language is simply a reflection of thought intended by a transmission source because there is so much more than just the words involved. Add the "pictorial reflective speech" of intonation, and the reason he called it "pictorial" may become clearer: the concrete, ideological context reveals itself through the imagistic qualities of non-discursive language. The "intonation" that accompanies speech is, in effect, a non-discursive image made up of everything other than the actual discursive language being conveyed.

The image, for Vygotsky, belongs to the more "primitive," or older aspects of consciousness—a distinction that is not meant to be negative. Image forms the basis for language for Vygotsky, but his aim is to talk about concept formation through language, and to do so means to relegate image as one central element among many:

> Concept formation is the result of such a complex activity, in which all basic intellectual functions take part. This process cannot,

therefore, be reduced either to association, attention (G. E. Miller), imagery and judgment (K. Buhler), or determining tendencies (N. Ach). All these moments are indispensable, but they are insufficient without the use of a sign, or word. Words and other signs are those means that direct our mental operations, control their course, and channel them toward the solution of the problem confronting us" (*Thinking* 106–07).

So what is the role of images within inner speech for Vygotsky? To answer this, we must first look at how Vygotsky theorizes consciousness.

In "Consciousness as a Problem of Psychology of Behavior" (1925), Vygotsky argues for the study of consciousness in psychology, an area previously left to philosophy due to its highly subjective nature. One of his primary points was that consciousness was social—that it was built from interaction with the environment: "The mechanism of social behavior and the mechanism of consciousness are the same [. . . .] We are aware of ourselves for we are aware of others, and in the same way as we know others; and this is as it is because in relation to ourselves we are in the same [position] as others are to us" (19). Consciousness is as social, then, as language is. This is one of the more considerable ideas Vygotsky brings to his field, one that stands as controversial to this day. Consciousness within an individual exists, but not without the exchange of images (perceived by all the senses) which occurs within social relationships: a set of relationships embedded within the identity of the individual as well as within the detonations, connotations, and intonations of the word. An overriding theme for Vygotsky is to blur, if not deconstruct the barrier between what is traditionally considered purely social and purely individual. They are both dynamically woven within layers of relationships which cannot be teased apart by merely asserting that an author is alone or among many—it is always already built into the symbols themselves.

Images, for Vygotsky, are therefore indispensable and primitive: they form the basis of the "word" in consciousness, but the form of thinking they inhabit at this level may be itself incommunicable, as in autism: "Autistic thinking is not social but individual. It serves wishes that have nothing in common with man's social reality. It is a nonverbal form of thinking, a form of thinking based on images and symbols. These images and symbols penetrate the structure of fantasy and are not communicable" (*Collected* 344). I interpret this to mean that images themselves are indispensable, so much so that in the extreme, images may dominate to the point of rendering the verbal mute. What Vygotsky calls autistic thinking (a term he uses to label asocial thinking) is a form of extreme, imagistic thinking. His connection to "fantasy" here is also a connection to the imagination, perhaps giving some acknowledgement as to the centrality of how images operate within consciousness.

In *The Dialogic Imagination*, Bakhtin stresses how language is "always a servant" but "never a goal," begging the question *who or what is the master?* (193). Perhaps the answer can be found in his view of consciousness: "Consciousness finds itself inevitably facing the necessity of *having* to *choose a language*. With each literary-verbal performance, consciousness must actively orient itself amidst heteroglossia, it must move in and occupy a position for itself within it, it chooses, in other words, a 'language' (*Dialogic* 295). In other words, consciousness decides how to move through and among the heteroglossia of symbol-systems we can access. It would seem, then, that consciousness is comprised of languages. In addition, while discussing the chronotope, Bakhtin states that "Language, as a treasure-house of images, is fundamentally chronotopic" indicating that images comprise the various forms of language we have stored within consciousness (251). This may be represented by a triangle (see Fig. 1.4) with images at the bottom, languages in the middle, and consciousness at the apex.[23] According to Bakhtin, as we gather images through the senses, languages form, stretch, change, and fall away. These various languages, then, make up the consciousness, but not necessarily in a way that defines it wholly. Nothing in Bakhtin implies that the entirety of consciousness is language, but he does certainly indicate a close relationship between the three.

Unlike Bakhtin, Cassirer postulates how images enter consciousness in the first place. For Cassirer, before there can be image there must be "noticing": "For only what is related somehow to the focus point of willing and doing, only what proves to be essential to the whole scheme of life and activity, is selected from the uniform flux of sense impressions, and is 'noticed' in the midst of them—that is to say, receives a special linguistic accent, a name" (38). To notice is to perceive with attention, a kind of

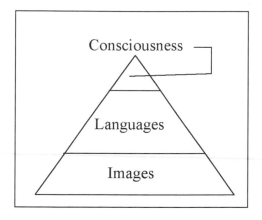

Fig. 1.4 Bakhtinian Language Triangle

general receptivity to images. Cassirer elevates the image as a basic requirement to any kind of "higher order" thinking: "before man thinks in terms
of logical concepts, he holds his experiences by means of clear, separate,
mythical images" (37). In order for the aforementioned "inner tension" to
manifest itself—a kind of fertile ground for language and myth—and create
the conditions required for "metaphorical thinking," we must be receptive to
the myriad images around us. Cassirer also states that "Our common words
are not mere semantic signs but they are charged with images," an obvious
rebuke of abstract objectivism and Saussurian linguistics, something both
Vološinov and Vygotsky also condemn in their work (*Essay* 153). Cassirer
begins at the beginning, so to speak, by insisting that images must not only
be present, but we must be willing to notice them, consume them.

    In *An Essay on Man*, Cassirer links the consciousness to our unity of
experiential understanding of our objective reality:

> Experience, [Kant] says, is no doubt the first product of our
> understanding. But it is not a simple fact; it is a compound of two
> opposite factors, of matter and form. The material factor is given
> in our sense perceptions; the formal factor is represented by our
> scientific concepts. These concepts [. . .] give to the phenomena
> their synthetic unity. What we call unity of an object cannot be
> anything but the formal unity of our consciousness in the synthesis
> of the manifold in our representations. Then and then only can we
> say that we know an object if we have produced synthetic unity in
> the manifold of intuition. (208)

Consciousness, therefore, comes from the "pure understanding" of our
experiences, and experiences are made up of the unity between our "sense
perceptions" and what we already know (or, as Cassirer labels it, our "scientific
concepts"). These sense perceptions are vital, yet they exist epistemologi-
cally not in the phenomenal world but in the noumenal world. We must
acknowledge the world of images as being just as important (if not more
so) than the cognitive, phenomenal experience we already know. Images
provide the link to the social. The two together, according to Cassirer,
form our consciousness and, presumably, our ability to create symbols and
languages.

    At this point I would like to restate that though Cassirer and Langer
are important to this theory of non-discursive rhetoric, they themselves
probably would not consider their theories and perspectives on language
and consciousness as part of any kind of rhetorical theory. I am continuously
amazed how relevant these theorists are to rhetoric, yet they are excluded
from most histories of rhetoric or anthologies of rhetorical theory. Again,
I want to emphasize that by highlighting their theories in this book, I am

also making room for an argument that they be included in our discussions about rhetoric, especially since they speak so readily to issues of symbolization, multimodality, image, and consciousness.

Langer, too, has a lot to say about image and consciousness. Like many other language theorists, Langer begins with perception and the senses. She constructs her notions about image and consciousness out of the idea that at some level, we must choose "certain prominent forms," and in doing so, we perceive objects, or "things" in the world: "An object is not a datum, but a form construed by the sensitive and intelligent organ, a form which is at once an experienced individual thing and a symbol for the concept of it, for *this sort of thing*" (89). This is clearly a definition of image, since image does not refer to just the objects our eyes see. Images are a "form construed by the sensitive and intelligent organ"; they are constructed by our brain as a symbol of a thing. It can come from all or any combination of sensations we perceive, and it may be conscious or, according to Langer, unconscious:

> [T]his unconscious appreciation of forms is the primitive root of all abstraction, which in turn is the keynote of rationality [. . .] *Familiarity* is nothing but the quality of fitting very neatly into the form of a previous experience. I believe our ingrained habit of hypostatizing impressions, of seeing *things* and not sense-data, rests on the fact that we promptly and unconsciously abstract a form from each sensory experience, and use this form to *conceive* the experience as a whole, as a "thing." (89–90)

Image becomes more than sense-data. Images are symbols that help us see the familiar in the unknown, or, said differently, to link the unknown with the known.

Langer's conception of consciousness, therefore, seems to be divided into different types depending on the purpose of symbolization at issue: mythic consciousness (which she takes directly from Cassirer); artistic consciousness; and scientific consciousness. What is common between these three is a kind of purposeful, attentive conception—whether discursive or non-discursive. This is not to say that Langer envisions consciousness to be some kind of "thought engine" which then transfers meaning into symbols. Rather, consciousness is differentiated into its different purposes, like in Cassirer, where form and matter construct symbols toward some kind of goal (mythical, artistic, or scientific):

> [T]he so-called "inner life"—our whole subjective reality, woven of thought and emotion, imagination and sense perception—is entirely a vital phenomenon, most developed where the organic unity of the precarious, individual form is most complete and intricate, i.e.,

in human beings. What we call mind, soul, consciousness, or (in current vocabulary) experience, is an intensified vitality, a sort of distillate of all sensitive, teleological, organized functioning. The human brain, with all its ramifications, is wide open to the world outside, and undergoes profound, more or less permanent changes by impressions that the "older," less variable organs record only by transient responses, the bodily symptoms of emotion. (127)

Langer weaves the consciousness out of an "inner life" comprised of "thought and emotion, imagination, and sense perception" with the "world outside"; this inner world is the consciousness, a word she uses haltingly in order to account for so many other common synonyms. This conception of consciousness denies any interpretation that it could be static, unitary, or purely individual. In fact, as we shall see later, Langer suggests here exactly what recent studies in neuroscience have confirmed: that the brain is not just affected by its experiences, but that it is chemically and forever altered by them. Langer predicts that these "profound, more or less permanent changes" to the brain are changes also at the level of consciousness. Interestingly, Langer also puts a primary value of the social on the consciousness, taking away any possibility that it may be regarded as atomistic, or locked away within the skull of each and every individual. By connecting the "intensified vitality" of our experience to the world, Langer is also stressing the social aspect of consciousness, just as Vološinov and Bakhtin did.

Like Langer, the image is a fundamental concept to Berthoff and it is omnipresent in her language theory. From the beginning, Berthoff stresses the usefulness of close observation, of being in the world, and of our use of images in writing:

Visualizing images that can represent concepts is a skill of fundamental importance to anyone who has to explain, argue, persuade—all of us. Even scientists, some would claim, are dependent on imagery, once they forsake mathematical formulations. For any writer, exploring the relationships between images and concepts can be useful in getting the dialectic started and in forming a concept. The relationship of an *image* to what it represents or expresses is as complex as the relationship of a name and an idea, a word and a thing [. . .] You can think of an image as a visual name. (*Forming* 143)

To characterize the image as a "visual name" has many striking consequences, especially in context with Berthoff's theory. First, "naming" is one of the most basic (and one of the first) steps in concept formation. This is because language is a simultaneous act of both classification and identification: "Naming means identifying, which is inconceivable without classifying [. . .] naming both creates chaos and discovers the way out of chaos" (111). According to Berthoff, we form concepts by "generalizing from particular examples and by interpreting those examples," and this is done within various classified structures already formed (115). Because naming initiates concept formation, then so do images. And if this is so, if images *initiate* concepts, then the relationship of images to language is as generative, as heuristic, as naming them is. Images, taken this way, foster textual production.

In fact, the role images play comes into full light only when looking at Berthoff's composing model in *Forming, Thinking, Writing*. Although "everything happens at once," this model depends on naming, opposing, and defining. Because images are a kind of naming, then this could also be read as imaging, opposing, and defining, and because these activities are going on all the time, imaging and naming are not just modes of critical thinking. Each twist of the spiral is more and more dependent on image because defining and opposing are referential to what is named. The image—the named—is the symbolization that drives the other two processes.

The second consequence of Berthoff's characterization of image as a visual name is that it is *relational*. Image is too often viewed as a bunch of nouns—chair, hat, fork—and not necessarily as often as verbs or the connecting aspects of language. Berthoff uses the phrase "seeing relationships" often, and it is significant because these relationships are connections from one symbol to another, and the connections themselves are images. Like the connective tissue of a bone, they help us understand function, action, and affect. The visual name of relationships, then, act to connect images and concepts to its context, or dialectical environment:

> Seeing means "seeing relationships," whether we are talking about seeing as perception or seeing as understanding [. . . .] The way we make sense of the world is to see something *with respect to, in terms of, in relation to* something else. We cannot make sense of one thing by itself; it must be seen as being *like* another thing; or *next to, across from, coming after* another thing; or as a *repetition* of another thing. *Something* makes sense—is meaningful—only if it is taken with *something else* [. . . .] Relationships, whether perceptual (I see) or conceptual (I know), are compositions. (51)

These images do not stand alone. They are not any more atomistic as language itself is, and they are imperative in not just *what* they symbolize, but *how* and *why* they are symbolizing within an embedded context of relationships. Image, for Berthoff, is both noun and verb.

Consciousness, as an explicit concept, is not a primary concern for Berthoff. In fact, she really doesn't focus much of her theoretical attention on the word at all. But she does talk about the mind, specifically about the processes of generalizing and abstracting. The further away from the concrete writers are, the more likely that generalizing and abstracting can take place. In fact, the act of creating language is first-order testimony to the act of abstraction. Consciousness is the stage for these activities, along with forming, shaping, and imagining. Berthoff often theorizes the imagination, but usually at the expense of consciousness and will.

The basic tenets about language offered by Vološinov, Vygotsky, and Bakhtin are basically consistent with Cassirer, Langer, and Berthoff. All six of these theorists discuss the relationship between image and consciousness to language theory despite the fact that the theorists themselves are often cited in opposition with each other (i.e., as in critical theory against phenomenology). By looking at the way these theorists theorize language, I have come to four major conclusions regarding image and language: (1) Language includes all forms of symbol-making, not just the discursive; (2) Language is both social and individual, and it is used and practiced within a social, historical, and cultural fabric; (3) The ambiguities in language, the places where language fails, are vital to both the process of learning about language, and to textual production and interpretation itself; and (4) Language, image, and consciousness are intimately connected. There are several other theorists worthy of inclusion in this section, but I wanted only to highlight these few in order to emphasize the link between image and language theory.

The next section attempts to recount how image and visual rhetoric have influenced composition, and as such it explores the ways in which image has often been talked about in the field: both implicitly and explicitly. We must fully understand how image and language are related in order to begin to understand its centrality in language theory and, therefore, the way the non-discursive becomes integral to the affective domain and our composing practices.

Non-discursive Symbolization, the Ineffable, and Invention

One consequence of the centrality of image to language is that image must be of a fundamental consequence to both discursive and non-discursive text. Inasmuch as language may be limited by discursive forms, language has within it the ability to overcome its own limitation through the use of non-discursive forms. One potential consequence of such a view is that writing, no longer limited to the "chain of reasoning" or to discursive thought as a whole, has an entirely different realm to explore: images, emotions, and the non-discursive. Writing suddenly has the ability to literally "be in the world"—to experience, to live, to feel—when it is no longer limited by a discursive view of language. But in the same way that we come to view language as exclusively inhabiting the discursive realm, we also come to view image as having value only within the discursive realm. While in the hands of those with a discursive bias, image must often *re*present something to have value—the more images are limited to simply representation, the more discursive they themselves are, and, consequentially, the easier it is to translate them into printed text. But like language, compositionists must learn to value the non-discursive image, or at least the non-discursive *within* the image, if they are to understand the full potential of images in composing and inventing—even if the images are not functioning in a discursive way. Images that are ambiguous, that defy translation into words, are precisely the kind of images that are themselves the most generative, the most non-discursive.

Using images to unlock the barriers that discursive, linear, or rational symbols create is not new. Both Plato and Aristotle emphasize that the success of the rhetor may in large part be measured by the images he or she can evoke in the audience (Lalicker *Interdisciplinary* 3–14). Lucille Schultz, in *The Young Composers: Composition's Beginnings in Nineteenth-Century Schools*, traces the influence of object teaching in nineteenth-century schools to the paratactic "nature walks" of Johann Heinrich Pestalozzi (1746–1827) in which students wrote about common, everyday objects in the course of their study (57). Schultz traces the use of everyday images in Pestalozzi's pedagogy to the 1835 publication of a primer textbook published by John Frost entitled *Lessons on Common Things; Their Origin, Nature, and Uses*, a book containing over fifty illustrations used as the basis for writing assignments (68). Though Schultz addresses this only indirectly, the use of visual images (whether real or illustrated) proved useful precisely because it gave students something to write about from experience: it became an inventional scheme. The significance of this is only in that the marriage between writing pedagogy and the use of images has a long history. Discursive invention—that is, the formulaic, procedural-bound inventional schemes so often discussed in rhetoric—has always been the first choice by teachers and students because, like discursive image-making, it seems the most directly transferable into a sender-message-receiver format. It is only because of these "experimental" pedagogical methods were many students encouraged to imagine text from their own perception or experience—to form images in response to images as a way to have something to write about.[24]

However, other uses of images are common when it comes to writing, even if such uses are not written down or published in pedagogical accounts.

Writers have often relied on images not only to make discursive points, but to also generate text and create non-discursive moods, tones, and feeling (remember that images come in the form of auditory, haptic, and olfactory stimuli, as well as visual stimuli).[25] It may even go without saying that even in printed language, a writer's choice of describing a dog as "starving" versus describing the same dog as "hollow" has consequences that are not only discursive (one that may provide a kind of logical causation for what such a physical representation of starvation may do to a dog), but such a choice also has a non-discursive consequence (the emotional consequence of emptiness, the possibility of also seeing the ribs or hearing the echoed sound of petting such a dog, to hear it whine, or even pity). Every effort to symbolize is made up of countless choices such as this, and those choices indicate the extent to which writers create a world for their readers.

Both rhetors and poets have long known the centrality of image to writing, but few compositionists view what they are doing when they write as composing images. It might not be a huge cognitive leap to propose that writers, in general, do learn to compose texts that are non-discursive, but such a suggestion calls forth many difficulties. The most obvious one begs the question, Is non-discursive text valuable if it is devoid of discursive meaning? To this, the response is "yes" because its value does not depend on its inherent meaning as much as it depends on the ability of others to construct meaning for themselves (a point that many reception theorists contend already). Instead of insisting on the role of language as communication (of the transfer of information with as little error as possible), an alternative view consistent with the power of the non-discursive in language would necessitate a willingness by the author and by the audience to construct their own meaning (or not). Such a shift can be characterized as moving from exposition to disposition: from the desire to master to the desire to "be." Writing images, then, leaves open the question "What does it mean?" and substitutes the condition of being with language.

Why is it necessary to "be" with language? One answer may very well be that discursive language (after it is able to be invented, or generated, in the first place) often fails: fails to communicate, fails to express, fails to convey knowledge, fails to describe a problem, fails to employ a solution. In order to view the impact of image to language, then, we must acknowledge that without our ability to conceive of non-discursive images, we may never be able to symbolize the ineffable. In his book *Ineffability: The Failure of Words in Philosophy and Religion*, Ben-Ami Scharfstein defines ineffability as a more-or-less common phenomena. I quote him at length because he adds a certain kind of social and cultural logic behind ineffability and its complexity:

We are the animals that use words and that complain rather often
that they fail us [. . . .] It seems that we all share in the dream,
however latent, of perfect communication and communion, and we
are unhappy whenever our attention is drawn to the dream's failure
[. . . .] My view of ineffability takes into account all such complaints
because it is my strong conviction [. . .] that the various forms of
ineffability are relevant to one another [. . . .] The reason for this
[. . .] is the mutual inclusiveness and entanglement of worlds: each
of us alone and in company is an approximately unified world
in itself; and all these approximately unified worlds constitute a
single, encompassing, unimaginably various world of worlds; and
in all these worlds, as in the encompassing maybe limitless world
of all worlds, every distinguishable quality is related to every other
in somewhat the same way as our bodily activity is related to our
emotionality, to our social needs, to our logic, and to the rhythms
and intonations, both individually and generically human, in which
we speak and remain silent. We are all divided, subdivided, joined,
ruled, and self-ruled in complex, subtly related and unrelated ways;
and so it is no wonder that our problems with words are not simple
to categorize or easy to grasp. (xvii–xviii)

That is to say our very social nature makes the interaction of our individual
"worlds" both necessary and difficult: that writing discursively can often
become ineffable because the connections or relationships between these
worlds are too complex or for discursive logic. What non-discursive text allows
us, then, is to inhabit these worlds to simply interact: to be. Discursive text
can (and usually does) come later, but in acknowledging and even privileging the non-discursive, there is value in simply allowing the experience to
occur: allowing images to form and become combined or contrasted with
experience and personal identities. The ineffable is ineffable, then, because
it attempts to circumvent the experience of the non-discursive in order to
move directly to discursive symbolization. This may be why the term "hollow
dog" may be richer in some contexts than simply saying "starving dog": the
former provides different access to our image-making abilities and, as such,
connects to the image-making abilities of the non-discursive.

Scharfstein, therefore, is also pointing to an crucial aspect of language
that privileges the intuitive, the fallible, and the non-discursive. It is precisely this kind of "entanglement of worlds" which offers the greatest gift
in language, and it is the social networks and historical layering of meaning
within these worlds which keeps language alive, allows for the possibility of
epistemic growth, and allows rhetoric to reach its audience. In other words,

Scharfstein is pointing how that the ineffable is a border or boundary for the discursive. By authorizing the non-discursive, then, this kind of boundary may be negotiated as the full force of symbolization becomes available. As discursive language fails within a paradigm of exclusively discursive language, as the rhetor runs into what Berthoff calls the "mysterious barricade," then there is nowhere to turn until the writer or rhetor acknowledges and is able to theorize the non-discursive through access to images and the emotions those images carry.

If it is possible, then, to assume that non-discursive imaging leads to discursive text, and if image is indeed the central concept of cognition (including consciousness, ideation, and emotions), then non-discursive symbolization is simply an indefinable and inexhaustible set of symbols that allow for a different access to thought. Text generation is no longer necessarily conceived of a set of topics, or a shift of perspectives, or a bank of knowledge stored in memory (though it is not exclusive of these things either). Non-discursive writing creates, combines, associates, juxtaposes, compares, leaps, bridges, and synthesizes through the composition of images (brought to us by any one sense, or any combination of senses). The theory acknowledges image as the lexicon of thought, and it privileges the imagination as its core experience. It is social because language and consciousness are social, and it is in context with the individual's own constantly revised sense of self through the metaself. Non-discursive composition is not a procedure or a mechanistic list of parameters; it is part of the innumerable connections made by consciousness as it accesses images throughout the brain. Eric Charles White, in *Kaironomia: On the Will-to-Invent*, says something very similar regarding the ability of an inventor to use *kairos* to avoid repetitious procedures in inventing:

> The rhetorical practice of the sophist who allows *kairos* to figure in the invention of speech will issue, then, in an endlessly proliferating style deployed according to **no overarching principle or rational design**. The orator who invents on the basis of *kairos* must in fact always go beyond the bounds of the "rational" to the extent that this "will-to-spontaneity" succeeds in evading the burden of the past, the repertoire of collective norms that dissemble the ambiguous, ambivalent nature of reality. (21, bold my emphasis)

I would add to this that *kairos* means little without our ability to attend to image, and that this "will-to-spontaneity" exists only insofar as we are able to access our ability to create non-discursive text.

In sum, non-discursive composing is not in itself an heuristic: a procedural or mechanistic manual for generating text. Although it is possible to create many procedures or lists of actions based on this conception of language, I caution against such an effort. As instructors of writing, it is easy to forget how reified a concept of writing is when it is looked at as a skill or something requiring mastery. Writing, the composition of discursive and non-discursive symbolizations, is above else a "will-to-spontaneity" because consciousness is a exposure to worlds of text: images into memory, images into identity, images into emotions, images into language. Non-discursive text can point to exposition and explication, but it never *is* necessarily exposition and explication because the images used are multilayered, multimodal, and multimediated—they simply do not yet fit within a grammatical form of discursive expression. To reduce the nondiscursive to a step-by-step procedure would be to undo all that it tries to do for composers and all that consciousness relies upon: integration *and* differentiation.

Such a view of symbolization generates further questions and a further need for additional study. How do we import these ideas of image into current curricular designs? What other kinds of "knowledge making" occurs when non-discursive text moves us toward discursive text? How may we use our increased ability to produce, consume, and distribute images so that we may strengthen our ability to invent non-discursive text which may or may not become discursive text? And, finally, what does such a view of symbolization do to help students come to terms with issues of identity, ideology, and the future? Questions such as these may take this research on image and inventing into new and productive areas for rhetoric and composition, as it should.

What is needed is a model of composing that incorporates non-discursive textual production as a primary generative force in writing. Such a composing model would account for the way composers of text can move from non-discursive language filled with the "inner workings" of the mind/body, to discursive text. Such a model would also have to account for the influence of the writer's own will-to-symbolize, since it must be the case that symbolization requires the will in order for it to manifest. This book, in fact, exhibits my will-to-symbolize because within, before, and among all of the discursive language in this text are images within my own mind/body, and these images indicate a clear direction toward a composing model and a multimodal writing theory as one possible future direction for this work.

CHAPTER 2

Non-discursive Symbolization, Image, and New Media

This chapter pulls the three main concepts of this book together into one main idea: image, as non-discursive text, is the most important underlying compositional element in creating multimodal text precisely because of its ability to access something *other* than discursive meaning. In fact, it is through image that meaning (discursive or not) is assembled and made available through our senses: our world is experienced in multimodal ways, and as such, as humans, our texts must both acknowledge and grow out of this messy yet generative collection of multi-sensual images that surround our everyday experience.

There is a growing body of scholarship within composition that investigates the relationship between images and writing. Scholars differ in their approach as they investigate this relationship: some see it as a result of the increasing influence of computer technology in education and culture, others focus on the relationship between image and printed text as an opportunity to bring yet another kind of literacy into the classroom (and, eventually, a more diverse notion of the term itself, giving rise to the value of teaching multiple literacies). When the term "visual rhetoric" is used, studies often become immediately social, giving rise to cultural critique and inquiry. All of these approaches are useful in their own way, but what is rarely done in the field is to link image to emotion, emotion to language, and language to mentality in such a way as to theorize how images also function as non-discursive text for composers of discursive text. In other words, rhetoric and composition has taken up the non-discursive through visual rhetoric, yet it does so by primarily privileging the discursive elements of image and ignoring the non-discursive elements (not to mention the rhetorics derived from the other senses). This chapter reviews some of the work done regarding image and visual rhetoric in composition while, at the same time, attempting to articulate what is missing in the scholarship—specifically, the way images provide links to non-discursive language forms and emotions, links that are essential to rhetoric.

In general, image and the visual have often been treated as prompts, aids to explanation, or methods to gain an audience's attention. Thus, there seems to be a lack of theory as to why images operate the way they do for readers and writers, and in cases where some explanation is given there is sometimes an effort to relegate non-discursive elements such as emotion as insignificant, or as a source for error. The last chapter makes manifest the connections between images and the non-discursive in language, and this chapter suggests how this very connection seems to be what is missing in much of the existing scholarship in rhetoric.

In defining visual rhetoric, some scholars take the word "visual" very literally, and this is problematic. Marguerite Helmers and Charles Hill, editors for *Defining Visual Rhetorics*, highlight the difficulty of defining the term:

> Some scholars seemed to consider visual elements only in rela-tion to expressing quantitative relationships in charts and graphs. Others concentrated solely on the ubiquity of visual elements on the Internet, which might give the impression that visual elements are important only in online communication. Much of the more culturally oriented work was based in art history and art theory, sometimes using the terms *visual rhetoric* and *visual culture* to refer to artistic images exclusively. In still other cases, the use of the word *visual* included *visualizing*, the mental construction of inter-nal images, while other scholars seemed to use it to refer solely to conventional two-dimensional images. (ix)

The editors go on to explain that their book studies "the relationship of visual images to persuasion" (1). All of this is fine and good, and many of the essays are theoretically dense. But what is immediately clear is the fact that the term "visual" in visual rhetoric *can* refer to images in the mind, and once that happens, then we are no longer discussing only the visual anymore—our sense data become synesthetic in the mind, not discreet, and as such we can no longer readily separate what is truly what the eye sees from any number of other sensual inputs. Increasingly, "visual" refers to the electrical signals the eyes construct and send to the brain.

On the other hand, scholars who discuss these rhetorics in terms of "image" or non-discursive text are free from the confusion the term "visual" can cause. In cognitive studies as well as in literary studies, *image* as a term is similar in that it does not just refer to the act of seeing with the eyes—as in the definition of literary image.[1] Rather, the term *image* refers to what the mind forms and stores, not just what our eyes convey to the brain. Conse-quently, image is not beholden to any particular single sense but is instead a cognitive placeholder made up of a maelstrom of sensual experience. We construct images based on all of our available senses, not just the visual.[2] The other half of this term, rhetoric, I take to be closer to rhetorical theory. Specifically, to borrow from C. H. Knoblauch's definition, "rhetorical theory" is "a field of statements pertaining to language, knowledge, and discourse," and, because the word is in conjunction with the term "image" (as defined above), the two together come to mean a field of statements pertaining to image *as* language, knowledge, and both non-discursive and discursive text (126). Consequently, terms such as "visual literacy" and "digital literacy" and the like become a subset of such an expanded view of rhetoric because they comprise individual discourses within a larger framework of image rhetorics, or non-discursive rhetorics.[3]

The connection between language and image, as I explore it in this book, works as a bridge between studies done by neuroscience and language theorists. Scholarship in image studies may just help to revive this connection because image becomes more than simply illustration or ornamentation to discursive text: as suggested already, image operates as non-discursive text within language, and therefore requires special attention in the composing of both non-discursive and discursive texts. Such a view of image addresses the work already done in multiple-literacy pedagogy, computer and digital media pedagogy, and the historical use of images as prompts. In the end, these applications of visual rhetoric become useful to the degree that they remain discursive, and this view is simply too reductive. Image functions as the primary conveyor of thought and emotion in the brain, and it is this insight that has led both scientists and rhetoricians to begin theorizing mind and identity along with the visual.

Though image studies is discussed more and more in the field, image and its relationship to language remain undertheorized in most accounts of visual rhetoric: a point made more explicit in the following review of visual rhetoric scholarship. We must reestablish the impact of the non-discursive within image studies if we are to better understand how image-as-language works to generate text and communicate meaning discursively. Visual rhetoric remains a catch phrase until these connections to mind and language are made manifest.

Before arguing these claims, however, it is important to first stress how image has been applied in composition studies by dividing the scholarship into three categories: (1) advocates of visual literacy and pedagogy, or the visual as one among multiple literacies available to the composition classroom (consumption);[4] (2) scholars who cite image studies as essential to technical communications and visual design, often stressing the role of digital media in the consumption and production of such documents (production); and (3) scholarship which inquires into the visual realm through the lens of cultural studies (distribution).[5] This taxonomy of production, consumption, and distribution highlights the reliance of a discursive view of image—one that is therefore very closely tied to market forces and the exchange value of encoding and decoding. The taxonomy also makes it possible to emphasize elements of the non-discursive that do not fit within these three categories. Once the symbolization is free of this exchange of symbol for discursive meaning, we are able to talk about the non-discursive elements of that symbol as it exists free of discursive value. Scholarship in visual rhetoric, as a subdiscipline within rhetoric and composition, relies too heavily on the discursive analysis of consumption, production, and dissemination and not enough on the non-discursive elements that are just as crucial. In sum, this taxonomy clarifies how the centrality of emotions to the meaning of images is all but left out of our scholarship on the visual. Consequently, by the end of this book, I hope to highlight pertinent work done in classical rhetoric, language theory, and science—all of which suggests a more integrated notion of the relationship between image and emotions though non-discursive elements.

Visual Literacy and Pedagogy

Perhaps the earliest use of the image in composition comes from pedagogical practice—a necessary literacy for the modern student of writing. This may partly be due to the founding of an independent, nonprofit group in 1969 called the International Visual Literacy Association (IVLA). Foregrounding the need to incorporate visuals into the classroom, as well as the need to teach students how to negotiate the onslaught of visual images inundating our culture, the IVLA was one of the first to call official attention to the term visual literacy, expanding its meaning beyond the ability to read or write printed text:

> Visual literacy refers to a group of vision competencies a human being can develop by seeing at the same time he has and integrates other sensory experiences. The development of these competencies is fundamental to normal human learning. When developed, they enable a visually literate person to discriminate and interpret the visible actions, objects, and/or symbols, natural or manmade, that he encounters in his environment. Through the creative use of these competencies, he is able to communicate with others. Through the appreciative use of these competencies he is able to comprehend and enjoy the masterworks of visual communication. (IVLA Conference, 1969)

Much of the scholarship done in our field seems to reflect this call to action, positioning the visual primarily as a new literacy for students to learn. Reminiscent of the "literacy crisis" which crops up in our national dialogue every few years, this kind of crisis rhetoric maintains a very narrow conception of "visual" and "literacy," relegating these terms to pedagogy in the most pragmatic, most efficient way for practitioners to adopt these new methods in their classrooms (as evidenced especially by the reference to "masterworks" in the above quote).[6] Of little help was NCTE's own statement regarding visual literacy in 1996: "Resolved, that the National Council of Teachers of English through its publications, conferences, and affiliates support professional development and promote public awareness of the role that viewing and visually representing our world have as forms of literacy" ("NCTE Resolutions"). Though this is an initial step in acknowledging the visual as text germane to students, it falls short of valuing the image as another type of textual production that is primarily discursive: what it says, what it argues, how it manipulates, et cetera. It privileges the perspective that students must come to learn how to read this kind of text (and, implicitly, not be overly manipulated by it), but by only referring to images as yet another literacy students must learn such a statement fails to recognize what, exactly, the role images play in composing. Scholars in this category tend to view image and non-discursive text as visual aids, prompts, or methods to help students access their ideas about discursive texts—the implication being, of course, that it is the primary texts, the discursive texts, that are more "academic" and therefore useful to students.

In 1952, *College English* published "In Teaching Freshman English" by Cortell K. Holsapple and Warren Wood as part of a themed issue called "Experiments with Audio-Visual Aids." In it, the authors describe an experiment using what might now be called an overhead projector to teach "the fundamentals of composition" to freshman by projecting their "themes" for the class to critique (324).[7] But this kind of article is somewhat typical of the research being done at the time on kinesthetic learning. In fact, this article represents one of the more common misconceptions of visual rhetoric or visual literacy: that the aim of these terms is to simply provide a variety of multisensory (sometimes specifically visual) presentations of course material. In fact, there have been many similar follow-up publications advocating the use of this or that visual aid, this or that handout, this or that "visualizing exercise" in class. All of these claims for pedagogy have their purpose, but few operate at the level of theoretical discourse concerning the way image and learning interact.[8] Many other articles of this nature can be found in journals that emphasize specific pedagogical practices for primary and secondary educators, but it is not uncommon to see similar applications of this sort even in contemporary conference presentations, as well as offhand references in leading rhetoric and composition journals.

More recently, however, other calls for the visual as a type of literacy have fused their appeals with theories based in semiotics, social theory, social formation of language (namely Vygotsky), and technology. One such essay is Colleen Tremonte's "Film, Classical Rhetoric, and Visual Literacy" (1995). Beyond explaining her use of film to stimulate her students analytical and critical thinking skills, Tremonte makes the point that students need to become literate in how to "read" film images. She calls for teachers to help students become more literate in visual cues because, in using film in her composition classes, she notices that students "tend to overgeneralize or to confuse descriptive response with analysis," and, as compositionists, we "need to reconceptualize pedagogy and praxis so that students can recognize the play between literacies demanded by the visual rhetorics of electronic discourses such as popular film" (5). How, exactly, this need to teach close reading skills is different from *any* kind of text is not immediately clear, but Tremonte makes the case that her students were not as "equipped" to actively view film as they were active in reading printed texts. Though Tremonte's essay emphasizes the use of nontraditional texts in the classroom, it fails to develop a theory as to *why* analysis of such visual texts benefited her students, or even *how* such texts ought to be analyzed.

Rather than encouraging students to become better at reading visual text, other scholars encourage students to use the visual as a means to interpret printed text. Phyllis E. Whitin, in "Exploring Visual Response to Literature," suggests teachers "provide opportunities for students of all ages to make and share meaning through multiple sign systems" advocating one method she used to improve her seventh graders' ability to make meaning about literature by asking them to create and discuss visual representations about stories read in class (114).[9] By having students actively create visuals in class in response to a reading, Whitin documents an improvement in reading comprehension and social meaning-making (i.e., collaborative learning).[10] What this approach provides is another means by which students can use the non-discursive nature of images to access discursive reasoning, but, like others of this ilk, Whitin neither draws upon or offers any explanation as to why this phenomenon exists with her students. These images are also secondary to the literary texts, implying a primacy of all things printed and relegating the non-discursive as a helpful way to prompt students along. Though I applaud the use of images in the classroom, this sort of limited application of image is too reductionary. What is needed is an account for why students connect with images (as non-discursive text), and an explanation about how this connection helps them generate their own multimodal texts. Image used merely as illustration or ancillary material to printed text misses the point altogether because image becomes merely a visual accompaniment intended to increase comprehension, not a viable mode of symbolization itself.

Probably the most influential writer regarding the visual as a specific literacy, however, is Gunther Kress and the New London School. Though Kress has written many articles and edited other books about the subject, *Before Writing: Rethinking the Paths to Literacy* is particularly helpful in understanding why a theory of non-discursive rhetoric is needed.[11] In this seminal work, Kress studies the cognitive development of children and the central role of images in their meaning-making. Specifically, Kress is interested in allowing multiple literacies, especially nonlinguistic literacies, to have a central role in the education of children. He asserts that all signs and messages are multimodal and meaningful, and that the images created by children are not to be underestimated in their ability to signify (5–10). In a sense, Kress is highlighting the nascent meaning-making composed by children in *both* discursive and non-discursive forms. Though he does not use Langer's terminology and he does not generally broaden his argument to adults in this book, Kress does point to the way non-discursive images are crucial in the development of children's verbal skills. And because he is dealing with predominantly preliterate children, "visual literacy" becomes a convenient way to talk about this meaning-making as distinct from "print literacy." The distinction, however, is not generally intended to advocate "literacy" as such; rather he works to elevate these preliterate image compositions to the level of early print literacies as a way of authorizing the meaning-making done by these children.[12]

Though she doesn't cite Kress, Patricia Dunn's book, *Talking, Sketching, Moving: Multiple Literacies in the Teaching of Writing* (2001) is similar to Kress' work in that she emphasizes the need to stress nonlinguistic literacies, though Dunn expands the argument to also claim writing as a privileged way of knowing in adult composition classrooms. The book encourages compositionists to "investigate and use whatever intellectual pathways we can to help writers generate, organize, reconceptualize, and revise thoughts and texts" (1). But despite this willingness, Dunn makes the mistake of pigeonholing thinkers as having expertise in one mode over another, either by choice or design. In her discussion about "visual thinkers," she makes several claims that imply there are people who do not rely on images to form thought or construct ideas, and that our inattention to the needs of these kinds of thinkers eventually penalizes them (23). I see this tendency as one of the most ominous dangers of framing image studies through literacy: it assumes students operate under a deficiency model of learning with the teachers operating mainly as content providers. Not only is there an impulse to treat students as through they are deficient, but there is also a tendency to label and, by the act of naming that label, to characterize students as *incapable* or *un-predisposed* to one particular kind of literacy over another (i.e., print literacy over visual literacy). Consequently, to say that there are some students who are "visual thinkers" and others who are not is effectively *typing* those students, possibly fostering a notion that teachers need not spend energy in pursuit of the visual over, say, printed text because it is believed "harder" for these students than it is for others. This also results from maintaining a separation between texts in terms of media (i.e., print, image, dance) rather than whether that text can is primarily discursive or non-discursive.[13] The implication here is that, because a student does not often read or compose visual texts, they are somehow incapable or not predisposed to learn to read or compose with visual texts. In effect, such a judgment actually equates their abilities to compose with their potential to think visually when, in truth, images are integral to the way our brains function (something discussed more thoroughly in chapter 3). Though I doubt this was Dunn's intention, such labeling results in the privileging of one sense over another based on what is an insufficiently investigated trend of student performance.[14] Kress's work, as a minimum, would take issue with such a reductionist view of writers in favor of a more integrated, multimodal view of language use.

Specifically, a student or teacher who resists producing, consuming, or distributing an image because they themselves are not "visual" or they do not consider themselves "visually literate" are doing a disservice to their students or themselves. There is an essential difference between knowing certain "image grammars" and knowing, intuitively, how to read and produce images. The same is true with print: there is a difference between knowing a particular grammar and knowing how to compose text using that grammar. To think otherwise is to essentialize one grammar over another, or make symbolization wholly dependent on socially codified rules and procedures. The same is true for image text: though there may be some codified rules for certain audiences regarding the selection of color, the representation of space, line, weight, et cetera, the grammar itself does not preclude our ability to read, compose, or analyze image text. In fact, labeling or accepting the label of "not visual" is really labeling or accepting the label of "not visual for a particular audience" and that is all. Not only is there a biological reason why such labeling makes little sense, there is also a conceptual reason: various media do not limit the inherent skills of the composer's image-making abilities. Because image and the non-discursive are not being thought of as part of language as a whole, theorists may propagate this misconception and may actually do harm to students who simply have not practiced reading and writing visual forms for various audiences.

There is another reason why discussing image rhetorics as a literacy is problematic: it is often confused with critical literacy or social critique. I do not wish to critique the notion of critical literacy that encourages the independent analysis of ideologies toward being "critically careful," to use Keith Gilyard's words (269). Students can and should begin a journey towards the "attainment of insight and energy to be spent on achieving social justice" (269–71). On the contrary, this kind of critical literacy is just as, if not more, important to image texts as it is to printed texts. The point is that the concept of critical literacy must still be applied to all texts, not just visually-based or print-based texts. The term "literacy" is problematic precisely because in conflates the kind of hard critical analysis implicit in critical literacy with the act of producing, composing, or distributing image texts. Just as with print composition, image composition must be allowed to have an analysis applied to it, rather than assume students are already critical of it. Simply put, students must be critical of images just as they are critical of printed texts, and that work is best done as a critical literacy and not as a visual literacy: being critically literate ought to include being critically literate about all texts, including the visual.

As is perhaps evident by these few examples, the work done in visual rhetoric/visual literacy has gradually moved from the use of visual aids in the classroom to a more complex, multimodal use of visual language in the classroom—though little of this work theorizes why or how images function the way they do.[15] These articles have in common a pedagogical aim, as well as a passion for alternative sense-making media (film, television, video, drawing, dance, etc.). They each have their strengths and they each help to broaden the way pedagogies conceive of the writing course. Though I would question whether or not these authors are aware of the rhetorical nature of literacy claims—that all literacies are persuasive appeals by the dominant culture which tend to privilege one skill set, medium, or point of view as to what *ought* to be taught in the classroom—I would suggest that this scholarship has nevertheless been pivotal in the gradual acceptance of visual rhetoric as a viable subdiscipline of composition studies.[16] On the other hand, the efforts to bring technology and digital literacy into the classroom—the subject of the next category of what is often referred to as "visual rhetoric"—has had an even greater impact on the field as a whole.

Technical Communications and Digital Literacy

In an introduction to a recent edition of *Computers and Composition*, Carolyn Handa emphasizes the need to "think more critically" about how digital innovations "impact our writing classes in terms of rhetoric and literacy" (1). Handa, like other authors in this category, points to the infusion of computer technology as reason enough to question whether we are doing enough in composition to accommodate the *kinds* of products being produced today.[17] Others, through the influence of workplace and professional writing, have critiqued the usability of the traditional visual design of most documents created in the composition classroom.[18] In both cases, the chief aspect of this category in terms of visual rhetoric is its refusal to stay connected to the essay as the only, or primary, kind of textual production. In fact, technical communication scholars insist that to neglect teaching our students the fundamentals of visual design, or the role it plays in usability, is to do students a grave disservice as they step into the world of professional writing.[19] For this group of scholars, the age of the blocky, monochromatic, print-only essay is coming to its end. The image *of the document*, then, becomes a message in itself; it communicates something about the way that same document conveys information and the way readers *use* it. The visual literally becomes a service to the verbal by making it more efficient, more pleasing, even more directly relevant to a given audience (as is the case in texts with multiple intended audiences).

As an example, Elizabeth Tebeaux's essay "Writing in Academe: Writing at Work: Using Visual Rhetoric to Bridge the Gap" (1988) chronicles her experiences teaching writing in the workplace, stressing how useful attention to the visual is to writing documents: in design, organization, and in the very prose used to communicate ideas.[20] She highlights visual qualities of paramount concern for workplace writing and usability: (1) the use of headings and segmented text for ease of skimming and searching information; (2) the use levels with hierarchies, putting the most relevant information first; and (3) putting topics of hierarchies in the subject position of initial, supporting sentences (225). Obviously, these features are more than efforts to chunk information or make massive piles of data easier to use: they are also rhetorical in that they indicate visually something for their audiences as well as about the writers who composed them. The visual elements themselves serve as images that define relationships (including emotions) and carry information beyond the data itself. The non-discursive *look* of a document has everything to do with the way that document is used discursively. Features such as the alternating grey and white stripes in accounting or tables with many rows of numbers not only add a certain kind of visual usability, but because of this usability they also give the document a formal, businesslike appearance that evokes efficiency and productivity. The visual, as it is often regarded here in technical communications and digital literacy studies, becomes yet another way to quickly sift through and organize the relationships in text. As a tool to usability, image in this category becomes another tool for discursive text while its non-discursive associations and messages remain largely uninvestigated.

Another example of the image being used as an organizational (or usability) can be seen in "Seeing Student Texts" (2000) by Michael Hassett and Rachel W. Lott. This article prioritizes the needs of the readers over the traditionally held concepts of an unfolding essay, and they do that through the look of the document: its layout, its type, its use of headings, et cetera. Readers must be able to find information they need while, at the same time, filtering out (even if temporarily) the information they do not need. Specifically, Hassett and Lott outline Charles Kostelnick's four levels of visual design as essential guidelines in making a document have more of a rhetorical impact: (1) the intratextual image refers to the typeface; (2) the inter-textual image highlights the relationship among different elements, such as headings and subtitles; (3) the extra-textual items include photos, graphs, charts, lines, etc.; and (4) the super-textual, which includes those items which make a cohesive whole navigable through features such as tables of contents, indices, and appendices. The super-textual also cover "the overall shape and size of the document" (42–43).[21] Clearly, the prefixes before each of these categories are attempts to get at the elements of text that are non-discursive, the implication being that "text" is by definition always discursive or such prefixes would not otherwise be necessary. The authors in this article have in common a distaste for the traditional essay format, and they effectively show how writing problems that manifest in workplace come directly from a heritage of traditional essay instruction in college composition courses. Clearly, this kind of attention concerning the visual design of documents indicates how images (here taken to mean the image of the design itself) allow for a kind of asynchronous meaning that is much faster and almost instantaneously understood by readers. The more these non-discursive elements are neglected the more readers must rely on discursive reception methods (that is word by word, line by line) to organize and filter they information they desire. The non-discursive elements found in these documents allow both a conceptual and organizational picture to be formed regarding the relationships of ideas in the text as well keys to understanding the actual data itself.

But not all technical communication and digital literacy scholarship focuses on just the product in considering the visual; some focus on the interface involved in the process. The idea is to build an interface (usually a computer interface) that provides the user with a richly visual means of textual production. Unlike Hassett and Lott, Clay Spinuzzi's " 'Light Green Doesn't Mean Hydrology!': Toward a Visual-Rhetorical Framework for Interface Design" (2001) focuses not on students and their writing practices but users and their computer interfaces. Spinuzzi argues for computer interfaces which reject the static, indexical visual model of a metaphor (desktop, window, file cabinet, etc.) in order to embrace a "genre ecology," defined as "an interrelated, relatively stable group of genres that comediate their users' work in a shifting variety of ways" (42). By stressing a group of genres rather than a single metaphor, Spinuzzi claims that the visual interface can then change, or grow, with the user. This brings an element of *kairos* to visual design, allowing it to change over time as required by the demands of the rhetorical situation, which, in this case, is the dialogue between user and the visual components of the interface.[22] Once again, the impact of composing the visual for the user is highlighted, yet Spinuzzi does not account for his assumption that this is a good thing. His system for accommodating for the user visually is useful, but there is no mention as to why this reliance on the non-discursive impacts our reading practices to such a degree.

Another apparent theme in the way technical communication or digital literacy theories refer to the visual is the insistence that the visual and the verbal must be in dialogue. In "Part 1: Thinking Out of the Pro-Verbal Box," Sean D. Williams claims that our composition classrooms too often focus on "a single mode of representation—the verbal" and not enough on the visual and its combination with the verbal in documents of "modern society." Williams highlights the "exclusive logic" of a classroom focused entirely on verbal literacies, effectively ignoring the visual:

> A new form of composition pedagogy must, therefore, equip students with the skills necessary to read, write, and critique the 'old-forms' of literacy—specifically verbal literacy—and to read, write, and critique the 'new forms' of visual representation that exist in digital media like the World Wide Web. (29–30)

Though the call to action here is similar to those of the "visual literacy" category already mentioned, the stress is placed on the way documents become rhetorical in their visual design (rather than exclusively in the printed text), and that because students have access to a large number of the easily manipulated visual elements (fonts, charts, tables, drawings, pictures, etc.), students need to be able to critique these visual elements.[23] Williams seems open to the legitimacy of the non-discursive, and this work seems to be consistent with a broadened notion of text consumption and production. It is this emphasis on the rhetorical that most separates this scholarship from the previous category of "visual literacy," because it maintains the persuasive qualities of all text—both discursive and non-discursive.

Other than just looking at visual rhetoric as textual production—such as in document design, writing interface, and being critical of the manipulation in tables and charts—some of the scholarship in technical communication and digital literacy endeavor to show how a few historical texts also attempt to persuade through the visual. One such article, "Ramus, Visual Rhetoric, and the Emergence of Page Design in Medical Writing of the English

Renaissance," by Elizabeth Tebeaux, marks the evolution of medical documents as one of the earliest examples of visual design influencing clarity—a feature highly encouraged by Ramus's rhetoric because it made "the truth more accessible" through the use of partition (414). She shows, for example, how authors of medical texts used tablature to increase the amount of white space in a document and construct visual categories (and, thus, opposites) of complex ideas. Tebeaux likens this technique with the way Ramus decided to "clarify" the Aristotle's divisions of dialectic in 1584.

Like Tebeaux's piece, another article takes a look at the way images are used as a function of document layout in order to create a more sophisticated rhetorical argument: "On the Reefs: The Verbal and Visual Rhetoric of Darwin's Other Big Theory" by Rodney Farnsworth and Avon Crismore. The article analyzes the visual elements of one of Charles Darwin's early books, *The Structure And Distribution of Coral Reefs*. The authors contend that Darwin's prolific use of drawings, diagrams, and maps are placed exactly in such a way to maximize their persuasive affect, where "the tension between his audience preconceptions and the new theory being presented threatens to reach a dangerous level" (11). In the end, the essay performs a sophisticated visual analysis of the rhetorical placement of visual elements, even highlighting Darwin's use of metadiscourse which explains how these visuals are to be read by his audience.[24] Farnsworth and Crismore demonstrate, then, how the resulting document was persuasive both verbally and visually.

Both the Tebeaux essay and the Farnsworth and Crismore essay manage to not only highlight the impact of visual rhetoric in the way arguments are delivered as a product, but they also help to resist the idea that visual rhetoric has become increasingly common throughout history—a fallacy common to technologists and designers who more often than not see technological change as a progress narrative. Cynthia Self's book, *Technology and Literacy in the Twenty-First Century* addresses this same issue in this way:

> [O]ur cultural tendency to sketch complex technology issues and the technology-literacy link along the lines of a reductive binary—technology as a boon or technology as a bane—encourages a widespread lack of attention to the complexities and nuances of the issues with which we are now faced [. . . .] And yet it is just this kind of careful paying attention that our culture needs so desperately if we hope to make change, to effect a productive influence on the technology-literacy link and the projects surrounding technological literacy in our lives. (39)

This is to say that technology, especially its relationship to textual production, cannot be idealized as either the ultimate answer or the ultimate problem. Technology and literacy, or textual production, are connected throughout known history: they take turns influencing, shaping, changing, or even eradicating one another in no predictable, or necessarily ideological, manner. Visual rhetoric, if it must be linked to technology, must be seen as always present, always important, and just one of the many modes of non-discursive texts (the others include aural, haptic, gustatory, and olfactory, and they each could be listed as having their own rhetoric).[25]

However, as composition classes become more and more infused with digital technologies, as faculty become more aware of the kind of writing students will do in the workplace, and as students become more and more comfortable with the relatively inexpensive options in visual design available to them through software programs, there will be a continued emphasis on the visual as a means of improving technical communication and the use of digital literacy.[26] Some authors have called for a review of the entire discipline of English studies, noting how the analysis of image is usually regarded as less analytical than the analysis of printed text in most English department curricula.[27] Image in technical communication, therefore, is often encouraged to the degree that the image is discursive: images are the most encouraged as a way to illustrate or chart meaning. As a result, the use of images in this category often ignores the non-discursive strengths of symbolization—the colors, typefaces, lines, shades, boxes, etc., are used do impart emotional meaning, even if that emotional text is trying to adhere to the conservative principles of a conservative culture (i.e., no pink paper), or even if that emotional text emphasizes a lopsided bar graph that empha-sizes the companies profits this year over last.

On the other hand, one great contribution from technical com-munication and digital literacy is that it elevates the discourse about the visual into the purview of rhetoric, making the image an equally suasive element in both contemporary and historical writing. Because these studies in digital literacy, interface design, and usability highlight certain cultural aspects of non-discursive rhetoric, they also suggest the next category of research done within visual rhetoric: those impacted by cultural studies and the distribution of texts.

Cultural Studies and the Image

One of the most common, though flawed, justifications for bringing the visual into the composition classroom is that our culture is somehow more visual than it used to be: that films, television, computers, and even print are more and more reliant on bold, striking images to gain the attention of an audience who is nearly constantly bombarded with an increasing amount of visual stimulation.[28] One of the consequences of the first two categories of visual rhetoric, then, is the insistence that we become better an analyzing, discriminating, and criticizing the effects these images have on our behavior, both personal and societal—in fact, one could say that the first category emphasizes the reception of such texts while the second emphasizes the production of such texts. John Trimbur, in "Composition and the Circulation of Writing," recognizes this trend as well by calling attention to the ideologies inherent in the distribution of cultural texts, and he does so by "representing circulation as a historically contingent process of interdependent moments" that fit "quite readily into [. . .] the cultural studies agenda of developing a non-reductionist, non-linear model to understand cultural production and communication in all their complexity" (206).[29] Research in this third category, therefore, can be considered to have as its intellectual parent the fairly recent field of cultural studies, a field which places as its subject the dynamic, multifaceted face of culture. In doing so, cultural studies as a field has always been willing to take up artifacts of cultural production that include nontraditional texts. The research done in cultural studies focuses not only on the inherent rhetorical aspects within nontraditional texts, but also the distribution of these texts and their con-texts: the aspects of culture and ideology that are carried along with the text.[30]

One essay representative of this focus on visual texts as a means of cultural critique is written by Joel Foreman and David R. Shumway: "Cultural Studies: Reading Visual Texts." In this essay, the authors advocate for the study of visual texts as a means to bring cultural studies into the classroom. In doing so, students encounter pictures as visual texts, the cultural influence involved in interpreting these texts in the first place, and the amount of ideological information available through the analysis of assumptions and elements constructed in visual texts (245). Not only does this article demonstrate the impact of bringing visual rhetoric into the classroom, but it also demonstrates how visual analysis is a powerful and relevant methodology of analysis: students learn to observe, to see with fresh eyes what they may have been only passively filtering (or absorbing) from the media before. This essay rightly assumes that any student, given the tools of such analysis, could become proficient at reading visual texts and critiquing the assumptions inherent in them (recall my distinction before between visual literacy and critical literacy). Again, this kind of scholarship is valuable because it works to help discount the myths that students might be inherently visual, or, conversely, inherently disinclined toward the image. By emphasizing visual rhetoric as also an analytical *method*, Foreman and Shumway empower students to engage nontraditional as well as traditional texts as a mode of critical analysis under the guise of cultural studies.[31] Though similar to the first category of research which considered images a crucial literacy for students to learn (something I do not dispute but view as too reductive), the problem with visual analysis in cultural studies is that it does not seem to indicate a willingness to directly consider the image as an important aspect of non-discursive symbolization. Cultural distribution, despite its strengths, still seems to advocate the primacy of discursive text over non-discursive text, and as a result, reduces the image to a discursive artifact. Non-discursive elements such as those aspects that evoke emotion, therefore, become subordinated to and perhaps erased by the discursive elements of the image.

As another example of the visual being critiqued by cultural studies as a form of mass cultural distribution, consider "Visual Rhetoric, Photojournalism, and Democratic Public Culture" by John Louis Lucaites and Robert Hariman. This essay works "to explain the role that iconic photography play[s] in American, liberal-democratic public culture" (37). Such photography accentuates the way iconic photos, by the very nature of their status in society, simultaneously place the locus of value on the individual, while the locus of power remains with the collective (40). Power and ideology play a considerable intellectual part in the way cultural studies examines visual rhetoric. By focusing on iconic photography, the authors have in some way identified a kind of historical canon of visual images in an effort to equate nontraditional texts with traditional texts while, at the same time, emphasizing the problematic nature of any kind of canon in a culture, or, even more importantly, the way a canon becomes widely distributed within an culture.[32] In doing so, these scholars shift the image from a level below traditional text to a level that is at least equal to it: in effect legitimizing the image as text in the first place (a claim that has been controversial in the past). Images can be more than eye-catching pictures used for ornament: they become actual objects of study available to cultural analysis.[33]

Other essays attempt to demonstrate the degree to which we distribute cultural ideology through image within a specific culture. In "Ideology and the Map: Toward a Postmodern Visual Design Practice," Ben Barton and Marthalee Barton equate traditional modes of representation, specifically maps, to modernism, citing their tendency to "naturalize and universalize" discourse visually. The modernist ideal, in other words, is in part distributed through our culture by the very way we construct and use maps. As a remedy, Barton and Barton advocate a representational system more like the collage, "with its emphasis on the heterogeneity and discontinuity of representational format," and claim such a system is a kind of "postmodern visual design practice" because it is "noncartographic" and thus not complicit with the "social-control mechanisms" linked to modernist representation. These authors, in a sense, wish to complicate the discussion concerning visual rhetoric by critiquing images in much the same way texts are critiqued by postmodern theorists: as linear meta-narratives which tend to universalize a single truth at the expense of many coexistent truths. In short, such a visual system "privileges complexity over simplicity and eclecticism over homogeneity, an aesthetic that tends toward the fragmentary and the local" (76). Like the other authors in cultural studies category of visual rhetoric, Barton and Barton link ideology with visual text and, in doing so, theorize how verbal text and nonverbal text both provide insight into the culture and its distribution of texts in general.[34]

On the other hand, not all cultural theorists are content with using the visual to critique culture—some wish to critique the culture's preoccupation with the visual in the first place. Clay Calvert's book, *Voyeur Nation: Media, Privacy and Peering in Modern Culture* (2000), sets out to critique a kind of scoptophilia that is endemic in our culture to the point of obsession. In defining "mediated voyeurism" as "the consumption of revealing images of and information about others' apparently real and unguarded lives, often yet not always for purposes of entertainment, but frequently at the expense of privacy and discourse, through the means of the mass media and Internet," Calvert puts his finger on something that seems to be a growing concern among academic scholars, and he rightly criticizes the "all-to-be-revealed" culture very often communicated through the visual realm (1). He identifies four types of mediated voyeurism and he elaborates on the politics of voyeurism (or, more accurately, he elaborates on politics *as* voyeurism, citing examples ranging from Clinton White House scandals to other episodes captured by the paparazzi-type journalism around many political officials). The book spells out the cultural backlash such voyeurism evokes, making "real lives" into "real entertainment." Though he does not situate his argument rhetorically, or show how his observations are themselves voyeuristic, Calvert manages to delineate some of the possible consequences of a culture of voyeurs, and, just as there are abuses present in print literacy, he rightly points to some of the abuses present in the production and dissemination of visual texts.

The cultural studies category of visual rhetoric is currently the most active of all three categories, possibly because it is the most able to pick up any cultural artifact and analyze its non-discursive elements. We hear about how images impact our culture in debates about what children should or should not see in the media, what ads should or should not be put on prime-time television, and even in the way political candidates deliver during public debates. It is an exciting and potentially fruitful area of inquiry, and I know I have personally benefited from the methods these scholars advocate in the way I teach my classes and conduct my own research. But, ultimately, this area of visual rhetoric does not engage the complex nature of *how* images work to historicize or critique discourse, or even inspire and invent future discourse.

Consequently, the taxonomy used in this section—consumption of images and pedagogy, production of images in digital rhetorics, distribution of images and cultural studies—provides a way to look at the limited way composition has taken up the image in its scholarship and pedagogical practice. Compared to the language theorists already discussed earlier, image and the visual are made teachable by focusing on their discursive qualities: readability, analysis, interpretation and limited composition of images in the service of discursive meaning. But what about the non-discursive aspects of image? What is it about image that leads to text generation? The next section attempts to suggest some possible answers to these questions.

Image as Non-discursive Symbolization

This sketch of scholarship demonstrates how most of the work done in composition under the guise of the image or visual rhetoric has been influential and fruitful, yet limited. Most of the scholars continue to investigate their particular view as to why visual rhetoric is important to composition. But it remains true that many scholars *within* our field do not seem as willing to investigate the more intimate connections between the way image works in language and the way image works in the brain and mind—specifically, how image and its non-discursive elements create meaning, and this may be because of the interdisciplinary nature of such work.[35] Though the work done in rhetoric and composition does help pedagogues innovate and respond to current aspects of our cultural demands for composing, it is at least equally necessary to look at the interdisciplinary work being done in order to understand how fields such as art history, philosophy, sociology, psychology, and biology find connections between how we use images to form, to symbolize, and to imagine.[36] If image is to be understood and incorporated into our writing processes, then we must take a new direction in visual rhetoric—a direction that moves beyond the consumption, production, distribution taxonomy mentioned already. Image studies, not just visual rhetoric in compositio, must also account, in part, for the ineffable, the unsayable, and the affective if we are able to take advantage of the non-discursive in our writing practices. To do that, we must investigate and acknowledge the non-discursive elements of image.

One reason for the continued reliance on the discursive elements of image may be due to a superficial split between the rational and the irrational. This is partly due to the way language has been perceived by scholars. Those who posit language as a reflection—or mirror—of reality may hope to keep both the imagination and emotions at bay in order to minimize error—in other words, to eradicate "noise" from the communication. On the other hand, scholars who posit language as epistemic—as the primary way we create, discover and represent knowledge (as in Berthoff's "great heuristic")—find a direct role for image, imagination, and the affective in their theories. Susanne Langer's work on the non-discursive positions her language theory in such a way as to accept the image as more than a means to communicate ideas; Langer's work acknowledges the non-discursive. Ernst Cassirer necessitates "noticing" as prerequisite for the inner tension necessary for language. Just as these and other language theorists have emphasized image in their theories, they have also helped transform the idea of image beyond its pedestrian, representational meaning. Image is not simply a picture of an object, or just a discursive illustration of a known concept (in other words, image is not just discursive). But, because image is a powerful basis to symbolization and cognition, with all the power and ambiguity that implies, image *carries* much more than just the representations of an object or action. As Langer says, it is the vessel as much as it is the cargo. Though meaning does exist in the format of traditional discourse, such texts are also imbued with non-discursive meaning. Therefore, at the level of symbol, when symbol encompasses both discursive and non-discursive forms, image is not simply an ornament but a legitimate, articulate form of meaning.[37] The meaning may not be primarily discursive, however, and that is the major distinction between image-as-meaning and most printed text-as-meaning: image-as-meaning often relies primarily on non-discursive forms, whereas printed-text-as-meaning often relies on discursive forms.[38]

Accordingly, what philosophers such as Langer and Cassirer do for us is de-emphasize the exclusivity of verbal logic as the only form of legitimate articulation by subsuming traditional, discursive text under a larger, more inclusive definition of symbolization. This expanded view of symbolization, then, allows for the displacement of discursive *meaning* as the center or primary function of language—if not the displacement, then at least the exclusivity of discursive meaning. Cassirer's view that we first attempted to resolve an inner tension through metaphoric language necessitates the primacy of image, not discursive meaning, in our language-making. The charged gap, or difference between what we perceive and our thoughts, is first and foremost a function of image and the non-discursive, not discursive meaning. In some ways, our discursive and non-discursive language-making is a bartering of images before a trade of discursive meaning because images can so easily and immediately accommodate the non-discursive, while the discursive must wait. All of this is to say that the center of our symbol-making must derive from image and, therefore, non-discursive symbol-making before it can become discursive. What image does for rhetoric, therefore, is to create a supercategory that subsumes all texts that are discursive as one category and all texts that are non-discursive as another. Rather than discuss and theorize visual rhetorics only to have to also discuss auditory rhetorics, haptic rhetorics, gustatory rhetorics, and/or olfactory rhetorics—or some combination,[39] one main argument of this book is to group these sense-oriented rhetorics all into image rhetorics, or non-discursive rhetorics. All symbolization, then, could be discussed in terms of its discursive or non-discursive rhetoric, and all non-discursive rhetoric could account for each of the ways humans receive information and, consequently, persuasive appeals.

There are several new texts in composition that theorize visual rhetoric through an expanded view of symbolization.[40] These texts address image as a legitimate part of our available symbolization systems, or at least treat image as formidable enough to be considered with equal weight as discursive text. The purpose of setting up a taxonomy and then mentioning texts that fall outside of it is twofold: (1) to first highlight how texts within the taxonomy fail to take up non-discursive elements of language, and (2) to suggest that there are at least a few texts out there that are beginning to take up image and the non-discursive (even if only implicitly) in a way we would consider different from those texts that fit within the taxonomy. Both Roy F. Fox and Kristi Fleckenstein, to name just two, seem to do just that because they both regard image as inherently meaningful, as important to cognition and our culture, and, therefore, important to the field.

Roy F. Fox edited a collection called *Images in Language, Media, and Mind* (1994) in which selected essays from composition—as well as from other disciplines such as photography, clinical psychology, and sociology—underscore both the discursive and the non-discursive aspects of image, not just the way images are consumed, produced, and distributed. The book stands out because it assumes that "the most important kind of meaning is constructed from personal interactions with images," that, like in Langer, "thinking and feeling [are] the same thing," and that images are "highly intertextual" (xi). These assumptions allow for a perspective of the image as a module of meaning-making, something commonly claimed by cognitive psychologists. In its own review of the book, NCTE managed to hit on what is a central point of this section: "the writers advocate that we emphasize images in our classrooms just as much as we do words, that we teach images not only as products or 'texts,' but also **as processes of visual thinking** [. . .] that we must treat word and image equally and simultaneously" (back cover, bold my emphasis). In other words, to treat the image as text to be both consumed and produced is interesting and socially responsible, but to claim that images are integral to thought itself is truly different because thought includes both discursive and non-discursive forms. As I will show later, scientists investigating the way images operate in the brain hold a very similar view.

Another recent book to undertake the relationship between image and text in such a way as to link image and thought is *Imagery and Text: A Dual Coding Theory of Reading and Writing* by Mark Sadoski and Allan

Paivio. The dual coding theory offered by these authors has its roots in the mnemonic techniques known for millennia—a system that codes elements within a scene with various "meanings," thereby relating an image with a verbal construct (3). What Sodoski and Paivio reinforce with their unified theory of literacy is the intimate connection between cognitive functions and image, and the book is testimony to the associational power of "verbal-imaginal" relationships. As a contribution to rhetoric and composition, this book reinvigorates the cognitive theory debates that have gradually waned since Linda Flower and John Hayes published "A Cognitive Process Theory of Writing" in 1981, and it reauthorizes, in some way, the notion that closer studies of the brain are valid sources of knowledge for the practice of textual production. Though Sadoski and Paivio rely heavily on empirical data and methods in order to reach their findings, their effort to align their theories about writing with larger theories of cognition is similar to my project here. Such a study of image underscores its fundamental place within our symbol-making world of language because it starts from the position that writing must "align with a broader theory of cognition" if it hopes to last. For Sadoski and Paivio, their dual-coding theory relies first and foremost on image and its connection to thought.

But focusing on image is not enough, especially if it relies on a conception of language as only communication. Kristie Fleckenstein's essay, "Inviting Imagery Into Our Classrooms" makes a strong argument for the need for image in composition classrooms to hold at least equal status with the word. By integrating imagery into the composition classroom, Fleckenstein advocates the *relational* value images have: there are more to images than just their thing-ness. She refutes the notion that image is a static, atomistic "picture" of something and, in doing so, emphasizes the information embedded in the image from the relationships it carries along with it: "Information becomes meaningful through relationships" (9). Of course, this also allows her to make the argument that images are not simply mirrored relationships between a mental picture and an actual object: each has a social context, and each context is constructed and highly mutable by sociocultural forces. By emphasizing the need to allow images into the classroom, she proposes, like Berthoff and others before her, to allow emotion and intuitive reasoning into the classroom because these elements are carried along by images whether or not they are discussed in the classroom. Therefore, Fleckenstein acknowledges the link between images and emotions, a link that anticipates the work done in neuroscience regarding the way the brain integrates images and emotions simultaneously.

The strengths of Fleckenstein's book, however, are somewhat undercut by what seems to be her theory of symbolization. She does not seem to operate from a broadened notion of symbolization—one that includes and allows for non-discursive text—and so she ends up privileging the discursive over the non-discursive. She separates image from language, claiming that image operates within a "metaphoric *is* logic" and language within an "*as-if* logic"; the essential difference being that image cannot indicate absence, only presence: "We cannot say 'not' with an image, we can only say 'is' " (15).[41] Fleckenstein is in a sense separating image from language because images are crucially non-discursive. Rather than thinking of language as having the ability to be both discursive and non-discursive, Fleckenstein requires language to *always* be discursive and image to *always* be non-discursive. By requiring image to be the same as discursive language in order to be a viable symbol system like discursive language, image must exhibit the sequential, logical structures of discursive language in order for it to maintain its legitimacy. Rather than simply allowing image to be part of non-discursive language as Langer suggests, Fleckenstein would have image become discursive to be regarded as language.

There are two major problems with this view. First, discursive language also relies on what Fleckenstein calls "metaphoric as-if logic" since, at the most basic level, alphabetic or ideographic language must also operate as metaphor: we must equate letters or ideographs as sounds and/or words, and, therefore, even discursive language suffers from the same function of identification. The distinction between image and language, as Fleckenstein explains it, is a false one, precisely because metaphor is central to *both* discursive and non-discursive language. In other words, she would have metaphor be only relevant to image.

Second, Fleckenstein claims that images do not have the ability to indicate "not is," or absence, and this is also flawed. Images do have the ability to indicate absence: if Fleckenstein is suggesting that reading images is simply a matter of digesting whatever our senses provide, then she is overlooking her own argument about the relationships images necessarily carry with them. Images do indicate the logic of what is, but they also indicate what is not through the relationships, the context, of the image (which, of course, is also true of printed text). What Fleckenstein points out here is not a fundamental difference between image and language; she points out a difference in the way image text and printed text are received. It is crucial for us not to separate images from our available symbol systems because doing so delegitimizes the logical and articulate meaning that is possible in images (charts, graphs, illustrations, etc.). At the core of both discursive and non-discursive language is metaphor, and to position metaphor as only a feature or problem of image is simply to buy into the notion that images lead to ambiguity and error more than discursive text does (also relevant is Berthoff's model of triadicity mentioned in chapter 1). The point is that images can be both discursive (as in illustrations and blueprints) and non-discursive (as in the typeface of text, the author's tone in literature, a photo's affectivity, or the scents of autumn), and any separation of image from language leads to a further devaluation of the non-discursive in favor of discursive text.

But Fleckenstein's work remains crucial to my view of multimodality and symbolization. Her edited collection, *Language and Image in the Reading-Writing Classroom: Teaching Vision*, makes an argument about the impact of images and their value to composition in this way:

> Graphic imagery, verbal imagery, mental imagery—we rely on these images, consciously and unconsciously, in every aspect of our lives, and we can trace their influence in our evolutionary and individual histories. Yet when we enter our classrooms and begin to teach composition, reading, and literature, we rarely reference the rich variety of images infusing our worlds [. . . .] We turn our backs on imagery. Yet imagery, from the kinesthetic imagery of muscle and bone to the graphic imagery of girders and stick figures, can not be choked off so easily. Imagery sneaks into our classrooms through metaphor, simile, and description. It erupts from websites, computer icons, illustrations, body language, and student artwork on chalkboards, desks, and margin doodles. It rips through the illusion that words are all, tying us to the immediacy and materiality of the moment, fusing thought and feeling. Because we cannot separate our words from images without wrenching away meaning and meaningfulness, we need to open the door to imagery. (4–5)

What is the most salient about this statement is not just the claim that imagery is important to language. It is not even the idea that words and images are inextricably linked. The most remarkable thing about this passage is how the ubiquitous image is acknowledged as central to our language experience while at the same time relegated to the periphery in writing instruction—presumably in favor of more discursive, printed forms. Image, both what it does for writers and what it does for readers, is rarely theorized in composition *as* a compositional element important to textual production. In general, an understanding of image is critical for writers not just because it can illustrate or exemplify, but because images carry meaning and emotions that help us make sense out of our world—even if that particular meaning or emotion is unutterable or confined to non-discursive forms. In fact, Fleckenstein stresses that we can no longer "separate our words from images" because to do so would be to strip away "meaning and meaningfulness." Specifically, image, as primarily a non-discursive type of symbolization, is *the* form that provides the emotional shading required to make our symbols meaningful and *known* to us. Therefore, it makes sense that our writing theories and forms of textual production must learn to include and account for non-discursive text as well as discursive text. In her book *Embodied Literacies*, Fleckenstein suggests a way to break down the differences between image and word, opting to frame all textual production as a kind of hybrid "imageword":

> This book reframes imagery not as an artifact, although it can be that, but more important, as a process by which we create and respond to that artifact. Simultaneously, it reframes text as image. Within this frame, asking which comes first—image or word, writing or reading, meaning or teaching—is tantamount to asking whether the chicken precedes the egg. The term *imageword* highlights these twisting loops and circular cause-effect relationships, affording us a double vision. Thus, literacy and literacy praxis framed through imageword do not require that we denigrate language and instead glorify the formative and transformative power of imagery. They require that we focus neither on imagery nor on language but on the necessary melding of imageword in meaning. (5–6)

As a result, Fleckenstein is both maintaining the separation between image and language (just as the chicken and egg are separate) while advocating the "melding" of the two. However, although words can create images just as lines, patterns, colors, and arrangements of any number of media can, images carry meaning and emotion to the brain, not words. Just as "all semiotics is multimedia semiotics," all media is multimedia to some degree (Lemke 72). Because all words rely on image and the brain relies on image (we usually even learn words as children though the use of multisensory images), all text is at some level image.

Although I disagree with the way Fleckenstein theorizes the relationship between image, language, and metaphor, she has published widely regarding the importance of image not only because of its exchange value with discursive text, but also because of its inherent connections to emotionality and what she calls the "somatic mind": "mind and body as a permeable, intertextual territory that is continually made and remade" ("Writing" 281).[42] This work on the somatic mind is important and consistent with the physicalist view of body/mind addressed in the next chapter. Clearly, her work has been and remains important to image studies in composition. She was one of the first theorists in this field to take up image in such a way as to move beyond its discursive value, and, in so doing, seriously take up the connections between image, emotions, and the mind.

One main purpose of the work done in this book up to now has been to avoid the problem of delegitimizing image simply because its non-discursive elements do not seem "logical" or "rational." In fact, this book hopes to show quite the opposite: not only is the non-discursive logical in its own way (i.e., Langer's "intuitive logic"), but even what may be considered "ill-logical" and error-prone (i.e., namely emotions and the ineffable in image and the imagination) are also legitimate, even essential. In fact, what I hope to add to the work already reviewed in this chapter is a view of image that is vitally connected to both our symbol systems and our emotions—image and emotions are intractably connected and, in a healthy mind, inseparable. This image emotion relationship is so important, in fact, that it will play a central role in the new composing model theorized by the end of this book. The next chapter, then, explores not only the way affect has been taken up in rhetoric and composition, but it will also highlight some of the new work being done in neuroscience which substantiates this link between affect and image and, thus, symbol-making itself.

CHAPTER 3

Affect and Image— Neuroscience and Symbolization

O ne of the consequences of the last two chapters—of acknowledging the importance of image to symbolization and meaning-making in general—is that it is even more important than ever for writers/composers to become aware of the affective domain: both its history in rhetoric and its place in the everyday classroom. This chapter will emphasize how the non-discursive in general and image in particular most directly carries meaning through its connection to our emotions and the affective. It briefly touches on how other fields (such as neuroscience and philosophy) have come to similar conclusions, implicating a more far-reaching consequence of image to cognition.

Though there have been some attempts in rhetoric and composition to make this connection clear, new research being done in fields such as neuroscience and psychology have made it possible to see to what extent emotions and feelings inform our images.[1] This chapter endeavors to reinvigorate the debate on emotion in composition primarily because image can not function without emotion and composing can not function without image. To address emotion in composition studies, we need to attend to work already being done by compositionists on the affective domain, and the interdisciplinary work being done on the connections between image and emotion. We also need to investigate how the debate between reason and emotion and between body and mind inform the way our field has largely overlooked these connections in the past. Finally, this connection between emotions and image offers yet another justification for the importance and power of non-discursive text in our composing and inventing processes and theories.

To understand the importance of image and emotion to non-discursive textual production more fully, I explicitly investigate the connections between the two. Valuing the non-discursive necessitates valuing the emotions and intuitive reasoning because the two are interconnected. Image, as a vessel full of relationships, carries with it the emotional import that belongs to our understanding of that same image: the two complete each other. Without the emotional connection, there cannot be a full and appropriate understanding of the images we encounter, and this has everything to do with the way we generate text in the first place. In fact, what we mean when we call an activity generative is far more complex than simply saying the activity is productive or adequate. It implies a motivated quality that comes from a certain kind of focus—a pleasure of movement, a centeredness that results in an excited and prolific inventional moment. In short, for something to be generative we must acknowledge the emotional component as well as the resulting text.

Feelings and emotions are often talked about as opposite poles to reason and rationality—a dichotomy this book refutes. The recent redux in the affective domain in composition studies, though a generally positive development in the field, often fails to avoid this dichotomy. Efforts up to this point show how emotionality, and the affective, are just as important as reason, critical thinking, and rational discourse—to this I would agree with one proviso: because of the way the brain functions through image, reason, critical thinking, and rational discourse *are also affective*. What I hope to emphasize is not so much the point that students need emotions to navigate the writing process, or that feelings are relevant to student subjectivity and thus to their identities as writers (these are paramount concerns). Rather, because mentality itself relies on affectivity to operate the brain, emotions are integral to all brands of thinking: critical or creative, social or personal, even objective and impartial. Neuroscience teaches us that the affective is crucial because images carry not only perceptual information but also emotional information: the two are inseparable if meaning is to be possible. If compositionists see the affective domain as integral to both reason and rationality, then the debate and scholarly conversations regarding the affective domain may become a more permanent and important aspect of the fields scholarly endeavor, rather than remain as a somewhat ostracized movement that regains popularity from time to time.

The affective gains and loses scholarly emphasis because of the mounds of criticism it receives in the field's journals and conferences. Much of this criticism has to do with the social turn in composition studies, and as such carries with it the implied notion that focusing on the emotions leads to autistic writing theories and practices (such as the charge against expressivists by Winterowd, for example).[2] In response to this critique, this chapter also emphasizes emotions as having *social* value: they are not necessarily a remnant of atomistic theories of self-expression at the expense of social conscience. Emotions are always present, and our acknowledgement of this facilitates our ability to move out of the false dichotomies, such as mind/body and emotion/reason, that often drive many of the debates in rhetoric and composition. Without a theory of writing that values emotion (and works against these binaries), there can not be a complete and effective rebuttal to the all-too-prevalent privileging of discursive text over non-discursive text so common in writing pedagogies today.

By showing some of the connections between composition and the work done in neuroscience, I hope to underscore the value of the affective domain in rhetorical theory as well as its critical role in writing theory. Rhetors throughout history have often addressed the emotions, but in rhetoric and composition—a discipline that, at least in part, derives itself from this tradition—scholars have largely ignored the work on the affective domain. Recently, however, the number of presentations at the Conference of College Composition and Communication (CCCC) regarding the relationship between writing and the affective domain have increased. A renewed interest may be on the horizon as we ask why it is our discipline as a *human* endeavor strives for cold objectivity (despite our insistence, often, that there is simply no such thing). In the context of this work, however, emotions may not only be an integral part of our writing process but they may actually help to provide meaning because of their connection to image. It may no longer be possible for us to talk about the split between reason and emotions simply because, as others before me have pointed out, such a split does not exist. Recent work done by neuroscientists suggests, for example, that consciousness is "the feeling of what happens,"[3] so for our field to attempt to continue to view the affective as distinctive from reason simply becomes nonsensical: reason is part of our consciousness, and, therefore, reason must be affective. In what follows, I attempt to support this claim by illustrating the value of emotions in logical/rational thought.

Throughout this discussion, the definitions of the words "feelings" and "emotions" change slightly from theorist to theorist. In general, though, there is some consistency regarding the way neuroscience defines the terms. Specifically, Damasio makes an important distinction between emotions and feelings. Emotions can and do generate feelings, "but not all feelings originate in emotions" (*Descartes* 143). Emotion "is a collection of changes in body state connected to particular mental images that have activated a specific brain system," while feeling "is the experience of such changes in juxtaposition to the mental images that initiated the cycle" (145) Feeling, in other words, builds on a collection of emotions and compares them to something else. The complexity and importance of this mental activity leads Damasio to later proclaim that our ability to feel what happens is the definition of higher consciousness itself.

To show even further why emotions are integral to images, let me recount one of the case studies offered by V. S. Ramachandran in his book *Phantoms in the Brain: Probing the Mysteries in the Human Mind*. One particular patient who recovered from a massive head injury after a car accident was able to function normally, yet would *feel* as though his own mother and father were complete strangers, even imposters (all other aspects of his cognitive functioning were quite normal)—a malady commonly referred to by neurologists as Capgras's Delusion (161). After investigating the problem with other neurosurgeons, Ramachandran explained this patient's condition: one of the pathways in his brain that connects images in his memory with emotions was severed in the accident. The brain was no longer receiving the emotional charge usually connected with the image of the patient's mother and father, and, therefore, these people were recognizable but foreign to him (162). In other words, because these people did not *feel* like his parents, the patient explained their likeness to his parents in the only way he knew how: that they must be imposters.

Cases like this illustrate something about how the brain works, but more importantly, they also show how intimately connected emotion is to image, memory, and even "rational" thought processes like identification and description. Every image in the brain has an emotional charge, however slight, and because of this, both image and emotion are indelibly linked to our consciousness. If our emotions are this central to everything we sense, everything we know, and everything we remember, then to continue to regard them as distractions full of error works to propagate the myth that emotions and reason are separate, that body and mind are separate, and that rationality without emotional content is a viable concept. The feeling connected to the image "mother" must be there if we are to be convinced she is indeed *my* "mother": though she looks, sounds, smells, and even acts like mother, she cannot be mother unless the emotional shadings related to these images are also available to the brain for processing.

Our writing theories should therefore account for this intimate connection between emotions and image. Because of the intimate connection between image and thought, and because images themselves operate *primarily* as non-discursive text, then I hope to make a case in this chapter for the value of the non-discursive through the importance of the affective domain in inventing and composing.

Affective Domain in Composition and Rhetoric

Composition studies has theorized the affective domain in various ways before. Nevertheless, few ask why the affective is so important to the act of composing. As Berlin notes, there are historical connections to eighteenth-century rhetoric which explain, to some extent, the positivistic slant in twentieth-century composition studies.[4] This section sets out to link emotions to image and meaning, making the three virtually inseparable (as well as connecting the non-discursive with the affective domain).

Alice Brand and Susan McLeod were perhaps two of the most vocal advocates of the affective domain in composition studies during the late 1980s and early 1990s. Though they are among the first to acknowledge the long history scholarship on the emotions has in rhetorical theory, both Brand and McLeod emphasized the role of emotions in the writing process. They both reinforce the interdisciplinary nature of this work by drawing on research from cognitive science, psychology, and sociology in order to make an argument in favor of the affective in composition theory. Any review of how composition studies has taken up questions concerning the affective domain must include their work, especially since it came at a time when the field eschewed theories that may be interpreted as "expressive" or focused on the individual in favor of the social-epistemic theories dominating the scholarly literature of the time. Brand and McLeod's theories were largely ignored because they seemed to be investigating areas of composition deemed irrelevant or otherwise hostile to a social-epistemic, postmodern conception of writing. Such a reaction was due invariably to the fact that any mention of the emotions evoked several binaries: intellect/emotion, cognitive/non-cognitive, rationality/irrationality, mind/brain, mind/body, individual/social, et cetera. Any conversation in the field on the emotions was seen as a return to favoring the individual over the social or cultural, and though the work attempted at times to refute such charges, research on the affective domain continued to be branded as "expressivist," leaving much of the work done by Brand and McLeod underappreciated.

Let me provide a specific example of how rhetoric and composition treated work on the affective domain during this period. Lester Faigley's essay "Competing Theories of Process: A Critique and a Proposal" attempts to place research on the composing process into three views: the cognitive, the social, and the expressive. The latter category, the expressive, included anything related to emotions and feeling (527–28). Simply put, the work done by Brand and McLeod is far more sophisticated than Faigley's "expressivist" category would allow. "The focus of a social view of writing," according to Faigley, "is not on how the social situation influences the individual, but on how the individual is a constituent of a culture" (535). But this says nothing about how such an individual is an *emotional* constituent of a culture, and both Brand and McLeod attempt to make a case for the importance of emotional content in a culture.

Ultimately, even Faigley's "expressivist" category fails to fit the work done by Brand and McLeod. According to Faigley, the only qualities of good writing that belong to expressivism include "integrity, spontaneity, and originality," none of which are considered specifically by either Brand or

McLeod (529).[5] Rather, Brand and McLeod base their tradition in cognitive psychology and consider questions such as writing anxiety, intuition, student beliefs about writing, and motivation as viable objects of study—elements that do not attempt to qualify "good writing" in any way. It is in this "expressivist" category that Faigley includes the work of Peter Elbow, D. Gordon Rohman, and Albert Wlecke.[6] Among other charges, these "expressivist" scholars were considered "instigators of a 'neo-Romantic' view of process" (529). But Sherrie Gradin, in her book *Romancing Rhetorics*, deems this critique of expressivism as unfounded:

> Perhaps a social-expressivism has not previously been articulated because scholars in composition studies are inclined to make passing remarks about romanticism without much knowledge of what it entailed as a movement [. . . .] Lester Faigley (1986) mentions expressivism's tie to romanticism through his citation of M. H. Abrams and the expressivist emphasis on "integrity, spontaneity and originality." He never explains, however, what these mean in terms of romantic philosophy and expressivist theory and pedagogy. (xv–xvi)

Although Peter Elbow and Linda Flower are both cited as influences for these researchers, McLeod and Brand seem to defy Faigley's categories because they take a little from each of them while—like Gradin—criticizing their limitations. In fact, Brand and McLeod concentrate their philosophical inquiry on the overall concept of emotion in the writing process through a kind of theoretical blend of Faigley's three categorical views: they value the social and cultural impact of language and discourse, they incorporate research from the best cognitive psychology of the day, and they value the importance emotions play in the writing process. Nevertheless, because their work focuses on emotions and feelings, Brand and McLeod are largely ignored for not being part of the larger social movement in composition studies.[7]

Since the definition of words such as "emotions," "feelings," and "affective domain" can be slippery, it is beneficial to first compare how McLeod and Brand define these key terms in their work. McLeod's defines "affect" as a multiple term that

> embraces a wide variety of constructs and processes that do not fit neatly under the heading 'cognition.' Besides the varied use by psychologists [. . .], educators have employed the term to describe attitudes, beliefs, tastes, appreciations, and preferences [. . . .] I also include one phenomenon not listed by [. . .] psychologists, intuition." (*Heart* 9)

Brand, similarly, defines affect "as a high-brow term for emotion. It stands for emotion in its most scientific sense. Affect is also used as a superordinate or umbrella construct, "under which are included concepts imbued with emotion such as moods, interests, sentiments, passions, and so on" ("Valuative" 160–61). McLeod and Brand seem both to agree that the term "affect" is an umbrella concept under which most emotive qualities of the human psyche are grouped.[8]

Both McLeod and Brand also define "emotion" in similar way. Brand defines it as an often misunderstood word: "Acceptable use of the term *emotion* reflects its elusive quality. Emotion may mean excessive arousal at one time, motivation at another, or a specific feeling at still another" ("Valuative" 161). McLeod's definition of emotion seems to also engage the physicality Brand mentions:

> But whatever their particular stance on the number of and names for emotions, cognitive psychologists generally agree that emotions consist of a bodily activation (arousal of the autonomic nervous system involving a visceral reaction—increased heartbeat, a knot in the stomach, a heightened awareness of external stimuli) and a cognitive evaluation of that activation. (*Heart* 10)

Though these definitions are fundamentally similar, they demonstrate how much both McLeod and Brand take up work done by the cognitive psychologists of the 1980s. Brand devotes two lengthy chapters to the evolution of the affective domain in cognitive science (see "Valuation" and "Cool"), while McLeod devotes an entire chapter to the subject (*Heart* 19–42).

In discussing definitions, however, there is a tendency to return to Aristotle and his definition of emotion. In brief, Brand and McLeod dispute the notion that emotions are not simply one leg of the rhetorical appeals triad (*ethos*, *pathos*, and *logos*), and they both contend instead that emotions are an integral and often ignored aspect of cognition. Aristotle's definition of emotion is often cited as an appeal to argument and as a distortion of judgment:

> The emotions are all those affections which cause men to change their opinion in regard to their judgments, and are accompanied by pleasure and pain; such are anger, pity, fear, and all similar emotions and their contraries. And each of them must be divided under three heads; for instance, in regard to anger, the disposition of mind which makes men angry, the persons with whom they are usually angry, and the occasions which give rise to anger. (1378a)

However, as W. W. Fortenbaugh points out, this passage is only part of the definition of emotion. Fortenbaugh references other passages to show how Aristotle eventually defines emotion not as distortion. For example, one passage Fortenbaugh refers to, but never fully quotes, is this one from the *Nicomachean Ethics*:

> one can be frightened or bold, feel desire or anger or pity, and experience pleasure and pain in general, either too much or too little, and in both cases wrongly; whereas to feel these feelings at the right time, on the right occasion, towards the right people, for the right purpose and in the right manner, is to feel the best amount of them (1106b)

The ability to achieve this "mean" is significant to Aristotle because it shows how this particular definition is wrapped in the context of morality and ethics as well as cognition. For Aristotle, a balance of the emotions was not only a crucial cognitive function but an ethical one as well. Fortenbaugh attributes Aristotle's definition, then, to cognition: "Hitting upon the mean is a critical act and therefore properly referred to a cognitive perfection" (73). So when Brand states that "cognitive ability may be measured by moral orientation," and, subsequently, "traced to emotion," she seems to be saying something very similar to Fortenbaugh and Aristotle ("Why" 438).

Neither McLeod nor Brand cite Fortenbaugh's book *Aristotle on Emotion*. Instead, both include Langer, Polanyi and Piaget as prominent philosophical influences, "none of whom was shy about enunciating the contribution of affect to intellectual development" (Brand, "Hot" 6). However, Langer and Polanyi both cite this work by Fortenbaugh, and this becomes relevant to those in speech communication who, like McLeod and Brand, often argue for a more inclusive definition of emotion. Since these philosophic inquiries depend to some extent on how emotion is defined, and because Aristotle approached the subject in a much more complicated way than previously thought, other theorists may also choose to revisit the Western-Classical notion of emotion and its intellectual history.[9]

What Brand and McLeod seem to be suggesting, however, is that the widely held belief that emotion is relegated to the realm of the body—and cognition is relegated to the realm of the intellect—is a false one. In fact, the theory has developmental implications: "As [Susan] Langer pointed out, emotions are not just subjective products of the mind; they actually produce it" (Brand, "Valuative" 158). Specifically, Langer calls the cerebral process an "interplay":

> The dialectic which makes up that life is a real and constant cerebral process, the interplay between the two fundamental types

of feeling, peripheral impact and autonomous action, or objective and subjective feeling. As fast as objective impingements strike our senses they become emotionally tinged and subjectified; and in a symbol-making brain like ours, every internal feeling tends to issue in a symbol which gives it an objective status, even if only transiently. (vol. 2, 342)

This emotional painting of every piece of sensory information is emotionally tinged internally, yet becomes objective through the "symbol-making brain."[10] With this kind of philosophical foothold, McLeod and Brand are ready to confront both cognitive psychologists and compositionists who continually deny (or ignore) the value of the affective domain—or, worse, denigrate it as not worthy of focused study. Langer not only helps to frame the researchers' premise, but she adds language (and a lifetime's body of work) into the debate for consideration.

Brand also investigates the relationship between emotions and reason as she claims that emotions give value to reason. Brand suggests that emotion provides writers with a complete picture, so to speak: "Understanding the collaboration of emotion and cognition in writing is both fundamental and far-reaching. It is in cognition that ideas make sense. But it is in emotion that this sense finds value" ("Why" 43). This connection to ethics, then, becomes not only a justification for the study of the affective in composition, but it also provides a link to the social networks wherein writers exist. In "Hume's Concept of Taste in the Context of Epideictic Rhetoric and 18th-Century Ethics," Dana Harrington underscores this historical connection between emotions and ethics. By revisiting the rhetoric of Hume, Harrington recovers a more complex notion of how emotions impact reasoning: "For Hume, as for the ancients, practical reasoning deals with the way human interact in the material world and thus necessarily involves taking into consideration the emotions" (24). This connection to emotions becomes especially relevant in terms of how a rhetor assigns ethical judgment, and, in turn, social consequence. Emotions, even for many 18-century rhetors, are not simply a matter of individual aesthetics irrelevant to larger social concerns. Emotions, at least in this particular example, form the basis for the ethical standards upholding and defining communities. In this way, emotions have an ethical and, therefore, social function that may otherwise be commonly overlooked.

Although both McLeod and Brand depend heavily on cognitive psychology, they distinguish themselves from the traditional cognitive scientists of the time by asserting that cognitive science, as it is defined by psychologists, does not account for the affective domain—something that is much less the case now, at least in terms of the work being done in neuroscience. In rebuffing the cognitive science of the day, McLeod attempts to extend and enrich the work of Linda Flower and John Hayes by making room for social cognition (the combination of social psychology and cognitive psychology) within their cognitive model.

Another criticism of the work being done in cognitive studies is methodological: the common use of think-aloud protocols. Brand's position on these protocols is that unlike the cognitive domain (or what may be thought of in this context as a kind of discursive domain), emotions are not often easily (and quickly) characterized in words. Such a research method assumes logic to be the normal mode of thought ("Why" 439). Instead, Brand proposes that a fuller account is needed, one that would "reveal imagistic and free associative thinking and connotative commentary" in order to observe "differences in cognitive style and personality" (440). It is only then that researchers can begin to assert they have a description of the underlying mental activities in writing (440). In fact, what Brand calls for here is precisely what the non-discursive image can best offer: "imagistic" and "free associative" language that carries with it the benefit of emotional shading.

Another reason why Brand refuses to ally with the cognitive theory of the 1980s is because it "refer[s] to intuition, interpretation, or goal-setting," all of which are overtly aligned with cognitive concepts ("Why" 439). In the end, then, the cognitive model for Brand fails to "capture the rich, psychological dynamics of humans in the very act of cognizing" (440). The philosophy attempts to completely account for the complexity of human thought by including emotion as a critical aspect of cognition.

Like this cognitive view particular to the 1980s, McLeod and Brand consider social construction as a formative influence on how emotions are communicated and managed, but they also criticize social constructionists for ignoring emotion as an valuable social force; in fact, Brand emphasizes the distance this inquiry has from social construction research, arguing that "the term 'social' is a convenient gloss on and gloss over the emotions" ("Social" 5). Brand argues in "Social Cognition, Emotions, and the Psychology of Writing" that social constructionist theory cannot ignore the affective any longer: "If [. . .] composition studies continues to embrace the social construction of writing fully as it has thus far, then it needs to study *all* its component parts. And that includes emotion" (395). To deny emotions from the social fabric of our culture, according to Brand, ignores far too much of what makes that fabric social in the first place.

That said, in looking at Peter Elbow's work directly it is obvious he asks similar questions regarding emotions and the writing process as Brand and McLeod. In his book, *Writing without Teachers*, Elbow connects the lives involved behind the written word through his awareness of the stress on the emotional state of the writer during the writing process. In fact, Elbow wrote the book in response to his difficulties in dealing with his own writing anxiety. McLeod uses Elbow to explain why she chose certain pedagogical methods in her research (use of portfolios, error-free evaluation, etc.), but she does not address his view of emotions directly. Elbow's concentration is about creating environments that are encouraging, that "coach" rather than evaluate. McLeod borrows this in her study of emotions in the writing classroom, and she uses Elbow's methods while explaining her own philosophic positions concerning motivation, beliefs about writing, and teacher's expectations (*Heart* 60–113). There are similarities between Peter Elbow and Susan McLeod, therefore, that cannot be easily ignored. Like Elbow, McLeod's interests also involve questions regarding writing anxiety. Unlike Elbow, McLeod addresses the entire affective domain, not simply the classroom or the individual confronted with an especially insistent internal critic. For example, in "The Affective Domain and the Writing Process: Working Definitions," McLeod cites cognitivists such as Charles Spielberger to help her provide detailed distinctions within terms such as anxiety ("trait anxiety and state anxiety"), but anxiety itself is only one term among five she defines. Her focus is emotionally more sophisticated than Elbow's because she concentrates on the entire affective domain (feelings, moods, intuition, beliefs, motivation), while he limits his analysis on writing problems due to anxiety and frustration.[11]

Although both Elbow and Donald Murray have essays included in the collection Brand edited (Elbow's "Silence: A Collage" and Murray's "Where Do You Find Your Stories"), Brand rarely cites them in her essays about the affective domain (though they are often in the bibliographic listings). Brand's primary interest seems to be to position these ideas as examples for her premise, but not necessarily extend them. This may be because both Murray and Elbow are so specific in the way they look at emotive aspects of writing, while Brand and McLeod are asking questions that evoke emotion as a cognitive force *along with* the cognitive, or "rational." Again, Elbow and Murray provide practitioner lessons that support, not define, the theories of Brand and McLeod.

In contrast, McLeod does credit the work of Linda Flower, claiming to extend both her early work as well as her later work. She criticizes how much the writing model by Flower and Hayes looks like a flow chart for a computer program, but she does not dismiss it: "In spite of negative critiques from several quarters [. . .], this theory has had an enormous impact on how the composition community views the writing process" (*Heart* 27). She goes on to credit Flower's *Problem-Solving Strategies for Writing* as "an elegant example of cognitive-process theory translated into practical pedagogy," but then continues by saying that "like other cognitive problem solving models developed by researchers at Carnegie-Mellon University, this one did not address affective issues" (28). Like Brand, McLeod admonishes traditional cognitive theory in composition for ignoring how emotions factor into these processes, and for having the same problem as most of the cognitive sciences. In addition, McLeod demands that researchers need "to come to terms with affect, viewing the affect/cognition split not as a dichotomy but as a dialectic" (7).

McLeod's work also attempts to bring cognitive research closer to the composition classroom by suggesting specific ways it may help teachers learn more about their students and, consequently, more about their student's writing process. By specifically locating her methodological antecedent in Vygotsky, McLeod emphasizes the value of no longer ignoring the affective domain:

> the separation of affect from cognition "is a major weakness of traditional psychology, since it makes the thought process appear as an autonomous flow of 'thoughts thinking themselves,' segregated from the fullness of life, from the personal needs and interests, the inclinations and impulses, of the thinker. Such segregated thought must be viewed either as a meaningless epiphenomenon incapable of changing anything in the life or conduct of a person or else as some kind of primeval force exerting an influence on persons life in an inexplicable, mysterious way." (*Heart* 6–7)

Vygotsky's influence in composition authorizes McLeod to invigorate research into the affective domain. McLeod suggests that by ignoring the affective realm on a consistent basis, no real progress in composition is possible. Yet, despite the amount of scholarly and philosophic arguments to the contrary, the influences of the emotions in the writing classroom remain largely outside of the community's conversation. Going back to the origins, back to Vygotsky, is the only way to reinvigorate the discussion and generate further research. By showing how researchers ignore the affective domain, McLeod locates a fundamental problem for composition—a problem that traces its roots philosophically to Langer and Vygotsky.

In his introduction to Brand's coauthored book *Presence of Mind: Writing and the Domain Beyond the Cognitive*, James Moffett states that

> Real cognizing occurs harmonically, at all octaves of our being— physical, emotional, intellectual, and spiritual—in such a holistic way that to single out one discursive activity and to feature even then only a certain range of the abstractive spectrum is bound to defeat itself. (xi)

This statement gets at the practical goal implicit in these theories: to better student writing by acknowledging how emotional states come and go during the process of writing and, therefore, how these emotional states affect the final product. Moffett emphasizes the effect of ignoring the affective domain:

> The futility of a course in which one is supposed to just write, in a vacuum, can be seen in several telltale symptoms, the most notable of which is the headscratching, paper-staring search for something to write about. The instructor resorts to assigning "provocative" essays or other texts (not only supplying subject matter but the same subject matter for all). Other symptoms of stripping down to focus on the "cognitive" are notoriously poor motivation and chronically disappointing results. (xi)

What is especially poignant about this passage is the way it illustrates writing that is ignorant of the emotional and non-discursive elements already present. There is no attempt to help students to become emotionally connected, or motivated, to their topics, or to utilize a more non-discursive form of invention through image—Brand and McLeod also list specific elements that affect the writing process (anxiety, motivation, and attitude), as explained in more detail later in this section. In fact, the situation described above may be familiar to many composition instructors: the expository essay that springs from controversial readings; writing exercises intended to just practice writing as if that function is a skill that can simply be turned on or turned off; and, consequently, a student who does not care to write anything at all. Here, Moffett highlights exactly why studying the affective domain is crucial right now, not just why it *might* be important: writing is taught as if people are in a "vacuum," divorced from their emotional state, coolly and completely. Such an emphasis on student writing outside of this artificial rationality reinforces the need for an expanded view of writing that includes image and emotions through the use of non-discursive text.

Though Moffett, Murray, and Elbow are loosely connected to this view of emotion because of their interests in the affective, Brand and McLeod are the most directly interested in looking at emotion as a cognitive concept rather than as part of the emotion/reason split. Brand and McLeod are valuable as researchers because their work investigates emotion not as an opposite of cognition (or a lesser aspect of cognition), but as an equal element within the mind that is just as essential (if not *more* essential) to writing as is rational, or traditionally cognitive, thought.

Like Brand, McLeod offers three major areas such research may help compositionists understand students' composition difficulties. The first is within the area of writing anxiety. Although researchers have found trends in writing anxiety, no one has answered questions such as, "What causes writing apprehension?," "How does it develop?," and "How is it maintained?"

In "Some Thoughts about Feelings: The Affective Domain and the Writing Process," McLeod suggests that emotions have both a negative and a positive effect on writing: that emotional involvement can help as well as hinder engagement with the writing task (428). By studying this engagement, the teacher can better help students defeat or utilize writing anxiety.

The second research task proposed by McLeod is in the area of writing motivation. By understanding how students become more intrinsically motivated through the study of emotions, "we can design tasks which are challenging and interesting enough to provide opportunities" for motivated writing (429). McLeod states that motivation "refers to the internal states that lead to 'the instigation, persistence, energy, and direction of behavior'—in other words, to the setting of goals and the energizing of goal-directed behavior ("Definitions" 100). She encourages researchers to examine "student attributions of success or failure at writing tasks in naturalistic settings" in order to get at performance-oriented versus learning-oriented motivation (101). She devotes significant energy to the subject in *Notes to the Heart*, and links motivation to the use of grades in the assessment of writing. She cites the work of two cognitivists (Lepper and Greene) who state that "the explicit use of extrinsic rewards (like grades) to motivate behavior brings up the issues of control and volition" which can "influence an individual's perception of an activity's intrinsic value (51–52). Emotion, here, works doubly against composition instructors: students evoke an emotion through motivation to the writing task (working hard to receive a grade), and then emotionally label the entire activity based on how manipulated, or controlled, they feel afterwards (receiving a poor grade and hating writing). This says nothing of how students motivate themselves again after repeated bouts with this cycle.

The third benefit in affective research connects beliefs with attitudes, and attitudes with investment in the writing task. By helping students internalize a belief system that discourages some students from perceiving how much they are controlled "by outside forces, such as luck or the teacher" while encouraging other students to "see the same results as stemming from their own capabilities," students might expect success and, therefore, succeed ("Some Thoughts" 429). The goal is to have the latter students invest more time revising their work, and, possibly, develop in such a way as to improve their own beliefs about themselves as writers.[12]

Brand, in addition, links knowledge of the affective domain in the writing process to critical thinking. She contends that "if cognitive ability may be measured by moral orientation, then it can be traced to emotion" ("Why" 438). Similar to McLeod, Brand takes the concept of critical thinking to belief systems, to attitude, and, finally, to emotion: "We need reminding that the very idea of being both human and impartial is a contradiction in terms" (438–39). Rather than characterize emotions as simply the cognitive noise that distorts judgment and, ultimately, the writing process, Brand puts the affective question directly into the web of connections that, when taken together, help to create meaning.

The work by Brand and McLeod indicates an effective collaboration of emotion and cognition and its possible effects on writing processes. Though the work done by these two theorists is important, it serves only as a basis for new work in the area of emotion and writing. Recently, a few other theorists in the field have taken up the affective debate despite the early resistance encountered by Brand and McLeod.[13] But it remains the case that much of this work is in some way indebted to these two scholars who, for the most part, were among the first to engage in the connections between emotion and cognition in a significant way.

Many social constructionists have also done pioneering work on emotion. Rom Harre's edited volume, *The Social Construction of Emotions*, sets out to untangle and demystify the various social and cultural ties to emotion as evidenced by our use of words in context:

> Instead of asking the question, 'What is anger?' " we would do well to begin by asking, 'How is the word 'anger,' and other expressions that cluster around it, actually used in this or that cultural milieu and type of episode? (5)

By pointing to the way words are or are not used, social constructionists are beginning to understand how cultural variety may lead to emotional variance. Compositionists would do well to remember that any given emotion may or may not translate to anything recognizable, just as words themselves may not translate well even if they transliterate well (e.g., as in the use of idioms): "The extent to which local moral orders are involved in human emotions suggests that there might be considerable cultural variety in the emotion repertoires of different peoples and epochs" (7–8).[14] As with Brand and McLeod, social constructivists emphasize the role of language in the study of emotions.

This work on emotions and the affective domain indicates a fundamental shift not only in the definition and in the value of emotions with regard to the writing process, but acknowledgement of the more far-reaching implications such a consideration might bring. Will academicians ever free themselves from the clear and present stigma that equates emotion to irrational, irresponsible thinking? Where, exactly, do we stand in the debate between reason and emotion?

Body/Mind and Logical/Emotional:
Overcoming False Dichotomies

In order to fully appreciate the level of importance emotions and the affective domain have to meaning, there must be some consideration as to how these two concepts are too often held in false opposition. This section reviews some of the work done on the false nature of the body/mind dichotomy, as well as its corollary, the logical/emotional dichotomy. By the end, it should be clear that meaning, especially non-discursive meaning, is emotional *and* logical, of the body *and* the mind.

A central theme to some of the scholarship talked about already regarding the affective domain falls solidly within the boundaries of the reason-emotion debate, a debate found in many fields across the disciplines.[15] This section underscores the role of emotions to reason in an attempt to collapse or otherwise enrich this dichotomy. Brand and McLeod, for example, both refute the opposition of these two terms, but they do so only fleetingly and as an aside. This research intends to forefront the inadequacy of such a dichotomy while making the related claim that reason is *dependent* on emotions to function in the healthy human brain.

Michael Stocker, in his book *Valuing Emotions*, sets out with a psychologist as a collaborator to better define the value of affectivity. His book argues for two basic claims: "that there are important constitutive connections between emotions and values, and that there are important epistemological connections between them" (1). Stocker, as a specialist in ethics and political philosophy, denies the ability of philosophy or any other discipline to construct evaluative knowledge or theorize about ethics without acknowledging, even stressing, the central role of emotions as *internal* to values in the first place. He also stresses the value of the affective in healthy human interaction and he argues that any claim otherwise is distorting and illusory:

> [W]ithout emotions it is impossible to live a good human life and it may well be impossible to live a human life, to be a person, at all. An absence or deficiency of affect is a characterizing feature of many neuroses, borderline conditions, and psychoses, as well as of such maladies of the spirit as meaninglessness, emptiness, ennui, accidie, spiritual weakness, and spiritual tiredness [. . . .] Any theory of the person that denies, omits, or misunderstands affectivity and emotions will therefore be inadequate, both descriptively and evaluatively. (1–2)

Stocker discusses value in what is generally considered morally "good" or "bad" based on local and/or communal evaluations of the terms. One of the more relevant elements of his argument comes from his discussion of emotions and reason, and, therefore, warrants more discussion here.

Stocker points out that it must first be acknowledged that emotions and affectivity can have a deleterious effect on reason—that extremes or "mountains and canyons," as he puts it, *can* result in "abnormal, overwhelming, misleading, and disruptive" influences on "rational" behavior (my italics, 5). But these extremes, so often cited by scholars as inimical to reason, are relatively rare and, even, necessarily so. When we wish to talk about the relationship between reason and emotion, the more common case is that emotions and affectivity are just as real but not as intense. It is equally disturbing and distorted to idealize the removal of emotion and affectivity, as in the case of many psychoses and mental diseases. So in order to talk about the relationship between reason and emotion, it is perhaps also helpful to acknowledge a spectrum in which, at one end, emotions are unhealthily absent, and at another end, emotions are overwhelmingly present. Such a spectrum has a middle place, the place between emotional extremes, and this place is rarely considered when scholars discuss the affective domain. To talk about emotions only when they are overwhelming or when they are completely absent is to fall within a kind of dualist extremism that, in turn, negates what it means to exist with emotions present during every conscious moment.

Stocker begins by emphasizing the irreducibility of affectivity. First, like Alice Brand, he defines *feeling* as being psychic feeling common to "emotions, moods, interests, and attitudes" (20). He insists that feelings, thus defined, cannot be reduced to desire (as in the behaviorist argument that we feel good when rewarded and bad when punished) or to reason (as in we feel because we understand or believe). He supports this irreducibility by either concluding that the arguments are circular, or that they employ feeling-laden affect or nonaffect. In other words, Stocker rarely disagrees with many of the views that feelings *can* be characterized by desire or reason, but, significantly, they have not accounted for how desire or reason can be nonaffective or nonemotional (50).

Most critical to this discussion, though, is Stocker's account of how rationality is affective. Stocker shows how our critiques to "not be emotional" or to "be rational" are really requests to "remain relevant" or "focus on the task":

> We can see how some find emotionality distasteful, but we cannot see any connection between that, or between emotionality itself, and intellectual error and danger [. . . .] those admonitions express an already formed complaint, a complaint that is expressed by invoking emotionality, not a complaint that is grounded by faults of emotionality [. . .] 'emotional' is used because the activity is independently thought bad: it is not thought bad because it is emotional. (95)

Stocker also points out that when things go bad, and emotionality is obviously memorable, then the emotions are blamed. But when things go as planned, or go well, and emotionality is memorable, then the emotions involved are quickly forgotten or ignored. Therefore, our perception of emotions is similar to the working of superstition and myth: what we notice of emotions during a memorable event we attribute as a causal connection to the event, especially if the event "goes awry" (96). Emotionality, even before any claims about its relationship to reason, is already attributed to disappointment and failure, rather than success, by the very nature we ascribe our attention to it.[16]

But is it even possible to be without emotion? Not according to Damasio, Ramachandran, and other neuroscientists who have researched the way emotions shade everything we know and understand. Without a slight emotional shade to the image of an object, we can not ultimately connect the image with its value, or meaning, or level of familiarity we have with it.[17] Referring once again to the example in which a patient who thought his mother had been replaced by an exact duplicate, the feeling connected to the image "mother" must be there if we are to be convinced she is indeed "mother": though she looks, sounds, and even acts like mother, she cannot be mother unless the emotional shadings related to the image are also available to the brain for processing—otherwise, she becomes a woman you suspect is an imposter. In other words, the observer must have information provided by both pathways in the brain: one associated with the "how" pathway that tells he or she this is an image of mother, and another associated with the "what" pathway that tells he or she that this image of mother also has the emotional feelings that comes with "mother."

Another reason why it makes little sense to separate reason from emotion in the body is that reason depends on emotions from the body to function. Damasio talks about what he calls "background feelings," a concept that changes the way we might begin to understand affectivity and its relationship to cognition and reason. Because our body is constantly being "imaged" by subcortical and cortical structures within the brain, we are able to keep a representational record of our background body states, and it is this image of our "body landscape" *between* memorable amounts of emotion that constitute what Damasio calls our "background feelings" (*Descartes'* 150–51). Because a collection of these feelings remain relatively unchanged over time, we experience a mood, or a sort of default emotional state.[18] Feelings, then, not only help communicate emotional content to the brain but provide background, physiological information about the body and its current state all of the time. Such feelings are never turned off, they are simply interrupted by other, more direct, immediate sensations, thoughts, interests, or situations. In the context of basic brain function, it is nonsensical—even impossible in a healthy brain—to "stop being emotional" because doing so would stop the communication network between the brain and the body. Clearly, this is also central to how Damasio defines consciousness itself, claiming that consciousness is the "feeling of what happens."

Both Stocker and Damasio critique the practices of their own disciplines concerning the way they often avoid the subject of emotions:

> It does not seem sensible to leave emotions and feelings out of any overall concept of mind. Yet respectable scientific accounts of cognition do precisely that, by failing to include emotions and feeling in their treatment of cognitive systems [. . .] emotions and feelings are considered elusive entities, unfit to share the stage with the tangible contents of the thoughts they nonetheless qualify. (*Descartes'* 158–59)

It is not enough to insist on the consequence of image as an essential part of our body state, but feelings are also responsible for the way we process images in the first place. Feelings are processed in virtually the same way images underlying our thoughts are processed; chemical and hormonal influences cannot alone explain how we come to "feel" (160). In order to understand the neurological basis of feelings in general, Damasio offers a description of two basic processes which both operate by juxtaposing images across two separate systems.[19] The role of image to these two systems becomes obvious, as does the value of feelings to cognitive functioning. In the end, Damasio makes the case in both *Descartes' Error* and *The Feeling of What Happens* that feelings and emotions are worthy of study by cognitivists and neuroscientists, no less than vision and speech. He also makes it clear that there is no single center in the brain for processing emotions, rather there are "discrete systems related to separate emotional patterns" (*Feeling* 62).

Stocker openly agrees with Damasio's concept of background feelings, making the case along with Freud and other psychologists that our awareness of feelings can vary. What he is saying, however, and in light of Damasio, is our awareness of these background feelings varies, or the time between interruptions of this background state becomes longer and longer, giving rise to the distinct possibility that our emotional state is "forgotten," or—as psychologists would say—is located in the preconscious or subconscious. Whatever the case, emotions are undoubtedly with us even during our most "rational," nonaffective moments.

Nevertheless, emotionality is often equated with irrationality. We are often judged by how well we are able to control, subdue, or hide emotions: the implication often being that the one who displays a controlled demeanor has a controlled and rational mind (the influences of faculty psychology

and associational psychology are well documented).[20] The more rational
we are, the more we are judged to be sound, true, and capable of making
reliable judgments. Stocker calls these commonplaces "false truisms," and
he claims that they are not mistaken, but "rest on and give expression to
tendentious views of both emotions and cool rationality" (92). These "false
truisms" form the basis of how emotion and reason remain at arms length
from one another, how one methodology becomes judged more rigorous
than another, how exposition is valued over disposition, how print is valued
over image, and how the disciplines themselves view their own epistemological boundaries from one another. At the core is an assumption that unless
emotions are kept at bay, unless we demand thorough, logical reasoning, and
unless the standards of academic scholarship are kept objective, error and
irrationality may run amok through our discourse. It is essential to make
the point here that although extreme states of emotion are generally counterproductive to textual production, there is a lot in between the extremes
worth considering. Affectivity itself must not be automatically disregarded
just because some hold the view that emotions are made up of mountains
and canyons. It is imperative to view emotions as necessary, even essential,
both in terms of process and product. What's more, there is a neurological
basis which encourages the viewpoint that emotion is ongoing, and, in a
healthy individual, undergirds so-called *rational* discourse.[21] If emotions are
to be considered appropriately at all, they must not be considered inimical
to rationality, reason, or even logic.

Stocker makes it clear that emotions may or may not reveal values,
and that it is a mistake to automatically assign content value to an observed
emotion evaluatively:

> even if all emotions that reveal value also contain it, there is a
> distinction between the values an emotion contains and what is
> shown evaluatively about a person—what values the person is shown
> to contain—by having the emotion [. . . .] there is more to caring
> about such values than simply having emotions that contain and
> reveal them. (68)

This is significant not only to Stocker's main claim about the relationship
between emotion and value, but also because it separates the person from
the emotion being exhibited. In essence, Stocker revokes the assumptions
made by associative psychology that emotional reactions belie emotional
content or feeling in any given person: that our actions are associated with
the content of our minds. If this is true, then observing emotions in the
behavior of a person does not necessarily indicate that the same person is
having an emotion.[22] This is significant because if one were to set out to

determine what is rational or not by trying to determine whether or not the discourse is emotional or not, there would be no way to support or defend what was observed.

Having said this, though, how do emotions affect us during what Brand calls cool rationality, and what exactly is the nature of those emotions? According to Stocker, concepts such as intellectual excitement and interest, motivation, and the ability to concentrate on a task in order to make observations, are just three examples of how emotions aid "rational" thinking and reason. In the case of intellectual interest and excitement, emotions play a part in helping (1) to select one idea over another, (2) to develop a research interest, and (3) to discover and consequentially follow relevant facts and discard others. Stocker links these emotions to learning itself, claiming that part of what it means to *learn* a discipline is to become familiar with what it feels like to be excited about what is "relevant, important, useful, and beautiful" in that discipline (69).

In the case of emotion as motivation, an affective aspect both Brand and McLeod include as significant to writing, imagined completion of a long task or even anticipated joy of completing one may help to keep us going, keep us on the right track, and even help to move us forward despite incredible odds. Maintaining motivation can mean the difference between working towards a solution or not, finding a new methodology or not, and collecting data or not. By imagining an emotional reward, we are able to continue to recursively reflect on what and how we compose to meet the expectations of an audience (who, most of the time, are usually imagined as well). In this example, both imagination and motivation team up to aid in the writing process.

Finally, another significant "cool" or rational emotion are feelings associated with attention. For example, the reticular activating system may cause a heightened awareness of the number and frequency of blue cars around because I just painted my car blue. The heightened attention can also come from a sense of awe, or a sense of amazement following a seemingly new piece of information or discovery, and this awe or amazement may naturally lead to a sense of concentration associated with focused attention (Stocker 69–71).[23] All three of these emotional states—interest, motivation, and attention—weigh in heavily during "rational" processes we consider to be so crucial to reason. Clearly, a rejection of these emotions has obvious epistemological ramifications.

Because emotions are so central to both consciousness and images, emotions are critical to both the linearity and the ineffability of discursive and non-discursive language. Rather than constructing a hierarchy or dichotomy between emotions and "rational" discourse, it is clear that emotions exist in one degree or another in both types of discourse—in language generally. What this means, then, is that images relevant to discursive and non-discursive language must also carry with them emotions relevant to discursive and non-discursive language. In fact, because of the inexorable connection between image and language, there must also be a fundamental link between emotions and reason. The link between reason and images may be the most immediately evident in the use of models, graphs, and maps used to convey large amounts of data. Images are also important in the most "rational" language of science and mathematics, such as those found in fractal geometry and chaos theory: they often rely on the use of images to both conceptualize as well as convey the discourse. From Leonardo da Vinci, to Sir Isaac Newton, images have been a necessary conceptual tool for both experimentation (invention), and epistemological understanding. Francis Bacon, in his *Advancement of Learning*, is at least partly responsible for the artificial split between "rational" discursive language and "irrational" non-discursive language. Even so, I would suggest that Bacon was aware of the power of the image in discourse, especially with regard to its role in ideation. He asserts that "the end of rhetoric is to fill the imagination with such observations and images as may assist reason, and not overthrow it" (268–69). That is to say, reason depends in part on the benefits of image and imagination, and, implicitly, emotions are valuable to both as long as they do not "overthrow" or overwhelm them (this is similar to the mountains/canyons discussion above).

Non-discursive textual production, then, must also acknowledge and directly consider the affective domain for the following reasons:

1. Reason and affectivity are not inimical to one another; in fact, emotions make up what are often labeled as "cool" or "rational" affective states—intellectual interest or excitement, motivation, and concentration or attention are just three examples.

2. Language based in image is also necessarily constructed with emotions because every image carries with it an affective charge or emotional component.[24]

3. Emotions are running all the time through "background feelings," a neural and chemical connection to the body landscape running *between* the states of aware emotions. Perhaps similar to a "mood," these background feelings comprise the baseline context for emotions we are aware of at any given moment.

4. It is difficult, if not impossible, to label what we consider emotional behavior as "rational" or "irrational" since emotionality does not necessarily indicate emotional value—one can have an emotion

independently of value (e.g., The ecologist who cringes at the sight of a spider but values them as vital to the ecosystem).

5. Because images carry with them emotional meaning, and since affectivity is central to reason, then images must be central to reason.

These five connections, between emotion and reason, solidify the claim that the affective domain is critical to writing in particular, and rhetoric and composition in general. This section's goal was to remove the false dichotomy between the two and, importantly, show the significance of emotion to reason itself. Consequently, I hope to level the differences placed on discursive language and non-discursive language based on the claim that the non-discursive may be "emotional" while discursive language is considered coolly rational.

Similar to the reason/emotion dualism, the mind/body dualism has also remained a significant shortcoming as to the way emotions, feelings, and image have been discussed and imported into composition studies; just as reason has often been associated with the mind, intellect and objectivity, emotion has variously been associated with the body, the irrational, and subjectivity. Such associations belong at least in part to the larger debate in philosophical discourse concerning what is often called the mind-body problem: specifically, how the mind and body are connected to each other. Although this debate continues in contemporary philosophy, there is hope that by summarizing it here, it will be clear as to why recent work done in neuroscience is so important to this work. What is certain is that it is no longer helpful to maintain the Cartesian dualist notion of mind-body, and what the study of image does is to help solidify an alternative. Specifically, scholarship on the image presents a modified physicalist, or materialist, perspective on the mind-body problem, while, at the same time, accounting for consciousness, emotions, and a sense of self and identity: aspects often traditionally cited as the most egregious downfall of the physicalist point of view. In order to explain this more directly, however, it is first appropriate to consider a brief historical account of the mind-body problem as represented in the philosophical tradition.

D. M. Armstrong in *The Mind-Body Problem* provides one succinct account of the history of the mind-body problem by dividing the philosophic tradition (or story, as he likes to call it) into eight separate arguments which are also somewhat chronological: Cartesian Dualism; Bundle Dualism; Epiphenomentalism; the influence of Ryle; Identity theory; Causal Theory; Eliminativism; and Functionalism, also sometimes referred to as Materialism (3–6).[25] These categories each argue for a different perspective regarding the relationship between the mind and the body, but they can be loosely grouped into two camps: the Dualists and the Physicalists.

The first in the Dualist category is Descartes himself. Cartesian Dualism is Descartes's notion that there are two substances that make up a human: a material substance (body) that works according to physical laws; and a spiritual substance (mind) that is not material and does not work according to physical laws.[26] Cartesian Dualism can be seen as an attempt to break away from the Aristotelian notion that material substances operate differently if they are organic as opposed to if they are inorganic (organic substances having what Aristotle called a "vegetative soul"). Descartes helped science to consider both bodies and non-bodies as subject to the same physical laws (Armstrong 12). Bundle Dualism, after Cartesian Dualism, accepts the dualism Descartes established between mind and body, but attempts to replace the mind as spiritual with the mind as a bundle of perceptions; David Hume's work falls into this category. Finally, the third dualist category is Epiphenomenalism, a position put forward by Thomas Huxley (famous for his defense of Charles Darwin's theories), which keeps mind and body as separate entities, insofar as the mind is considered "a bundle of perceptions" that cannot interfere with the body at all, rather than any kind of spiritual substance. Each of these three dualist accounts works from the position that the body and the mind are indeed separate, but most differ as to their theories of mind. It may be notable here that even at its inception, the mind-body problem struggles with how to define the concept of mind—a struggle that does not get easily resolved by later philosophers.

Armstrong credits the behaviorist Gilbert Ryle with creating the first entirely physicalist solution to the mind-body problem. Ryle's position, influenced by the behaviorists of the time, is to subsume all characteristics of the mind to the body.[27] In a sense, Ryle collapses the two substances Descartes spoke of into one: the body. Such a position, then, initiated another important debate: if the behaviorists are right, then how does one account for individual consciousness, emotion, and "the inner realm of the mental" (Armstrong 4)? In response, identity theorists such as U. T. Place and J. J. C. Smart began to theorize a concept of mind that attributed consciousness and emotions to "physical processes in the brain" (5).[28] Both of the other answers to the mind-body problem—the Causal Theory, Eliminativism, and Functionalism—are all basically further refinements to the physicalist position, attempting to resolve the nature of how the mind deals with these "inner mental processes."[29] All three of these positions are essentially physicalist because they do not maintain a dualist position that separates mind and body; rather, in one way or another, mind becomes body, converting Descartes original notion of mind (an immaterial substance) into materiality.

Other surveys of the mind-body problem seem in large part to be consistent with Armstrong's dualist/physicalist categories. Tim Crane and Sarah Patterson, in their book *History of the Mind-Body Problem*, characterize the history of the relationship by categorizing the mind and the body as distinct, or physicalist:

> [F]or some, the problem arises because of the assumption that mind and body are distinct (essentially, dualism). This assumption then demands that we explain how mental causation is possible, if mind and body are distinct things. But on other views, the problem arises from fundamentally physicalist assumptions. It is because we think that the world is completely physical in nature, that we find it hard to understand how mental phenomena (specifically subjectivity and consciousness) fit into the world so conceived. Here physicalism, the view that the world is fundamentally physical, is not the solution to the mind-body problem, but part of what poses the problem. (1)

The difference here is that Crane and Patterson see the Physicalist view as, essentially behaviorist, limited only by what is observable and external to an organism. Armstrong's survey of the mind-body problem make it clear, however, that aspects such as consciousness and subjectivity *can be* attributed to processes in the brain, and it seems as though Crane and Patterson have overlooked this possibility. In fact, there is an increasing amount of research that in a sense reinforces the physicalist notion of the mind-body problem: recent findings in neurology suggest that the body contains elements of the mind just as the mind contains elements of the body—something I will discuss in more detail later. Mark Johnson, in *The Body in the Mind: The Bodily Basis of Meaning, Imagination, and Reason*, refigures the physicalist notion as an essentially "objectivist" notion of embodiment:

> The key to an adequate response to [the crises in the theory of meaning and rationality] is to focus on something that has been ignored and undervalued in Objectivist accounts of meaning and rationality—the human body, and especially those structures of imagination and understanding that emerge from our embodied experience. The body has been ignored by Objectivism because it has been thought to introduce subjective elements alleged to be irrelevant to the objective nature of meaning. The body has been ignored because reason has been thought to be abstract and transcendent, that it is not tied to any of the bodily aspects of human understanding. The body has been ignored because it seems to have no role in our reasoning about abstract subject matters. (xiv)

Johnson makes the point repeatedly that we are *"rational* animals" and we are "rational *animals."* It is our body that informs our rationality, and is the objectivist perspective of the separation of the two that is problematic (xix). The physicalist/materialist perspective of the mind-body problem is consistent with what neuroscience offers in its latest discoveries about the way the brain works to create images, to form consciousness, and to conduct feelings and emotions.

Another philosophical tradition, namely the feminist philosophical tradition, has also long maintained a perspective on the mind-body problem that is largely consistent with what we will see neuroscience proposing in the next section. Susan James, in "Feminism in Philosophy of Mind: The Question of Personal Identity," introduces her article by claiming that feminist work has long maintained that "the key oppositions between body and mind, and between emotion and reason, are gendered" (29). Specifically, James states that the feminist philosophical tradition has worked "to develop philosophical positions which do not devalue the symbolically feminine" by "unsettling the hierarchical relations between mind and body, and between reason and emotion" (29). The tactic does not necessarily propose that the mind is part of the body (as in the physicalist position mentioned already), but it does help philosophers find *value* in the body and not just the intellect: put another way, it also helps discover the intellect of the body. James points out that this work "aims to question the distinction between the mental and the physical by showing how mind and body interrelate, and how the body contributes to, and is implicated in, thought" (30).[30] What is most evident in this conception of the mind-body problem is the notion that while philosophers may ultimately side with scientists who maintain that the mind is essentially a physical phenomena, they do little to explore in what way the body, apart from the brain, is also a part of who we are—both in terms of consciousness and emotion.[31] In some ways, in trying to solve the mind-body problem, it took the impact of feminist philosophers to ultimately begin the inquiry into the ways our bodies inform our thought, not just whether our thoughts are ultimately physical or not.

In "Embodied Classrooms, Embodied Knowledges: Re-Thinking the Mind/Body Split," Shari J. Stenberg goes so far as to insist on embodiment as a way to counteract the prevailing deference paid to mind and thought in scholarly and pedagogic environments. Here, mind and body enact a kind of dualism philosophy has since rejected. Says Stenberg,

> while feminism has a long tradition of examining the body as a material, political site, 'new' postmodernist scholarship has tended to 'textualize' the body, articulating it as a site that can be altered and even transcended, often at the expense of attention to the concrete and experiential. (44)

That is to say, even if we may acknowledge the fundamentalist position regarding mind and body, the reality is that in our discourse and in our classrooms, we still maintain an illusion of disembodiment. In other words, the mind-body problem tends to *enact* a preference for mind and a deference of body in the way we construct and deliver discourse in scholarship and academia. In Stenberg's example, she admits to being particularly sensitive to being pregnant while teaching her class, acknowledging the possibility that other may see her as anti-intellectual or otherwise too emotional simply because of her physical presence in the classroom. Upon reflection, she realized she was helping to propagate such cultural myths of the mind over the body by, essentially, not addressing in her class the physical reality of her pregnancy. In the article, then, she advocates a position that addresses the body directly:

> I examine critical pedagogy's important insistence that we recognize the lived experience and embodiment of students, and challenge the way this discourse tends to assume a disembodied teacher who seemingly exists above the social relations she critiques. Rather than transcend the body, I contend that we might see its potential to operate transformatively. While I focus most extensively on female bodies—women, after all, have historically been positioned as mere bodies—my call for greater attention to embodiment includes all those "non-standard" (i.e. non-white, male) bodies that are erased to the detriment of critical consciousness. (44–45)

Feminist philosophy, then, often works to emphasize the importance of body, not just the subjugation of mind under body. The mind-body problem expands not only to include the ways in which the body is ignored but also the way subject positions are valuable to both scholarship and pedagogical practice.[32] In a sense, the feminist philosophical tradition expands on the original problem, changing it from a largely autistic question to a larger, socially constructed one, bringing with it the observation that the mind-body problem continues to manifest itself as a dualist concept in sociocultural contexts.

In addition to these social contexts, the mind-body problem forms the basis of many assumptions regarding emotions, identity, and consciousness, so it continues to be an important problem for philosophy. As a consequence, other disciplines are taking up this question with renewed vigor; science, particularly neuroscience, is beginning to seriously examine how the brain constructs these noumenal aspects of mind. Though their assumptions are overwhelmingly physicalist, these neuroscientists are beginning to explore the connections between image, emotions, and consciousness in order to answer for themselves the following question: Where is the mind within the brain's pathology? In a sense, these scientists are addressing what many philosophers have critiqued as the central problem of the physicalist/materialist perspective on the mind-body problem: the presence of sentience, of the mind, within the brain. Tim Crane, in his book *The Mechanical Mind*, frames the critique this way:

> Some—materialists or physicalists—think that despite our feelings to the contrary, it is possible to demonstrate that the mind is just complex matter: the mind is just that matter of the brain organized in a certain complex way [. . . .] the brain is just a piece of matter, and how a piece of matter can represent anything else seems just as puzzling as how a mind can represent something—whether that mind is a piece of matter or not. (45)

It is telling that Crane uses the phrase "despite our *feelings*" because the work being done in neuroscience actually suggests that it is feelings that give rise to consciousness: that consciousness is actually the feeling of what happens to us. Crane's critique of the physicalist/materialist stance on the mind-body problem is largely answered by the way neuroscience has come to theorize consciousness as emotion through image. They answer, in fact, how it is a "piece of matter can represent anything else."

Perhaps the mind-body problem is more complicated than the two categories—dualism and materialism—allow. One scholar who attempts to avoid these two categories is John Searle—a philosopher who has been consistently sympathetic to the work being done in cognitive science over the years. In *Mind, Language and Society: Philosophy in the Real World*, Searle starts from the position that "the mind affects the body and the body affects the mind" (59). He attempts to complicate the debate by examining assumptions:

> Both dualism and materialism rest on a series of false assumptions. The main false assumption is that if consciousness is really a subjective, qualitative phenomenon, then it cannot be part of the material, physical world. And indeed, given the way the terms have been defined since the seventeenth century, that assumption is true by definition. The way Descartes defined "mind" and "matter," they are mutually exclusive. If something is mental, it cannot be physical; if it is physical, it cannot be mental. I am suggesting that we must abandon not only these definitions but also the traditional categories of "mind," "consciousness," "matter," "mental," "physical," and all the rest as they are traditionally construed in our philosophical debates. (50–51)

Searle confronts the problem by going back to definitions and assumptions inherently contained in the problem, and then he borrows on the work currently being done in cognitive science and neurobiology to help gain another perspective. In addition, Searle works to address the mind body problem by simply refusing to see the two as dichotomous. In doing so, his philosophy of mind no longer allows for a view of language mired in emotionless, bodiless, positivist, and objectified theory. Searle rejects the traditional binaries and, in doing so, much of the traditional labels associated with those binaries, and he seems to do it with the hope that neuroscience will eventually address the connections between mind and body by investigating consciousness, emotion, and our subjective experience as humans if it is to continue investigating the mind.

Neuroscience, Image, and Affect

The reason that the affective domain is so important to composers is because images provide the very basis for language and meaning. Many working in the fields of neuroscience and cognitive science agree that image—the multisensual, multimodal, multiexperiential snapshot held in our neural cortex—is fundamental to thought. As such, those who compose in several modes are more likely to be rhetorically appropriate for any given audience (by simple ratios of likelihood, never mind any concerted efforts to know the audience well). Rhetors who understand how to compose with image (and, consequently, affect) also understand how to reach an audience.

Other disciplines are currently investigating images and the consequence of our ability to manipulate them. By working with patients with damage to their brains, neuroscientists and cognitive psychologists have begun to fully recognize what some philosophers and rhetors have long claimed: that the image not only is a basic unit of thought in the brain—the progenitor of language and a component of reason—but also that the image *shapes* the brain, constructs pathways and nodes within the various elements of the brain which make up such potentialities as personality, health, and acumen. Cognitive science, a field once trapped by a more computational theory of mind, has now begun to ask some of the same questions that used to be regarded mostly as philosophical regarding consciousness, emotions, self and identity—including the role of image in thought. Subjects, in other words, that were often thought to be far too subjective for empirical, scientific study. Partly through the advances in real-time brain imaging, and partly through the careful study of people and animals who suffer from different forms of brain abnormalities previously considered too anomalous to warrant serious study, neuroscientists are now theorizing about subjects that intersect with areas of direct importance to rhetoric and composition. It is particularly crucial to any writing theory that image, emotions, and consciousness are considered and, when appropriate, reflective of whatever new advances are made in neuroscience.

This study focuses on three neuroscientists—Antonio R. Damasio, Steven Pinker, and Vilayanur Ramachandran—who have published studies on image, consciousness, and language acquisition in journals such as the *Journal of Experimental Psychology, Cognition, Communication and Cognition, Language, Principles of Behavioral Neurology,* and *Society for Neuroscience.* These are reputable journals in scientific discourse, to be sure. But these three scholars also publish their findings in books written for the general public—as public intellectuals and citizen scholars—in order to make their discoveries accessible to an audience larger than those in scholarly journals. Publishing for the layperson, among other benefits, also allows them to theorize more broadly than perhaps their own scientific methodologies and discourse conventions usually permit. Ironically, the result is that these scientists advance theory in books written for the larger, more public audiences and tend to report experimentation according to discourse conventions in the more formal journal article. The work of Damasio, Pinker, and Ramachandran does not exist exclusively within the confines of popular publications; their work is meticulously documented within scholarly medical and scientific publications. It is in this sense that these scientists are also philosophers; they develop theories of the mind derived from both their life's experience with patients and the specific data collected from their formal experiments. As a specific example of this, Antonio Damasio published an article in the journal *Behavioral Brain Research* in 1990 that provides most of the scientific substance addressed in his much more narrative, much more accessible book *Descartes' Error,* published in 1996.[33] I found many other links such as this between the journal publications and the claims made in the books later written for the general public for all three of the scientists discussed here. Because there is somewhat of a bias in rhetoric and composition against scholars who publish for a mainstream audience (as if their work is somehow less credible or less subject to peer review) and because there is an equal amount of distrust in our field concerning scientific rhetoric in the first place, the use of this material by some may seem controversial or, at the very least, inconsistent with the remainder of the work being done here. But, to those critics, it is important to emphasize the fact that there is little question as to the credibility of these "general public" sources, especially because they function as a kind of translation, eliminating as much as possible the jargon of neuroscience for the more narrative approach easily digestible by others not in that field.

These general publications are also a way to share their work with other theorists who are not as steeped in the formal medical and psychological terminology associated with neuroscience—they are a reaching out, so to speak, to other disciplines and other scholars working in intersecting fields. Kristie Fleckenstein, for example, references Antonio Damasio specifically in her edited collection *Language and Image in the Reading-Writing Classroom*, especially regarding his work on human emotions and consciousness, as do other authors within that collection.[34] Clearly, this work is not only becoming increasingly relevant to our work in composition, but it may also be an essential step forward as we begin to unlock more of the mind's secrets through scientific methodologies. The most astonishing thing about this work in neuroscience, however, is simply how well it reinforces earlier, more philosophical work done by Langer, Cassirer, Vygotsky, and others, giving these theorists a new relevance to our field.

On the other hand, though Damasio, Ramachandran, and Pinker may translate their work credibly from scientific journals, they also are part of a dialog within their field, and as such there are dissenting voices. In fact, these neuroscientists are often considered mavericks in cognitive science, venturing into subject matter that is on one hand at the forefront of neuroscience, but on the other has typically been eschewed as too "subjective" to be worthy of serious, scientific analysis. Even as this neurological moves into a larger audience, many within cognitive science regard theories of the consciousness, image, and emotions skeptically.[35] But as the work being done concerning such difficult topics becomes more public, and more independent experimentation replicate the same results, the findings discussed here are becoming more and more established. In addition, if our field is interdisciplinary, then it must be able to balance its criticism of outside methodologies with the potential knowledge other fields provide.[36] In sum, the work from neuroscience and neurophilosophy adds significantly to our knowledge about the brain and our own relationship to image and emotions, and I would make the argument here that we in rhetoric and composition can benefit from this research.[37]

I am not only trying to make the case that this kind of research is valuable to rhetoric and composition studies: I am also asserting that cross-disciplinary study in language and image is inevitable and healthy to our field. As these theories regarding the centrality of image and emotion to language and consciousness gain currency, so too does the claim of interdisciplinarity in rhetoric and composition. In addition, these authors are not exclusively using scientific sources for their arguments—in fact, cognitive science is said to be a combination of psychology, computer science, linguistics, philosophy, and neurobiology (Pinker *Language* 3). This interdisciplinarity in cognitive science is evident even in the works of these authors: Damasio cites Langer in his book, *The Feeling of What Happens*; Ramachandran disputes Freud; and Pinker cites and adapts work from Noam Chomsky. The main point is that this work, by its very nature, is interdisciplinary, and attempts to be exclusionary to any one discipline amputates far too much valuable discourse. Appeals for the interdisciplinarity in rhetoric and composition are commonplace, but we must be more vigilant in insuring that credible voices are not silenced due to disciplinary snobbery or territorial line drawing. These scientists make their findings more public, more accessible, and invite the larger academic community to take part in their conclusions—all of which are elements we ought to emulate in rhetoric and composition.

The most relevant contributions by neuroscience, as regards this book, are the connections between image, emotions, and consciousness in general. Some of what these authors claim is supported by scientific study of brain damage as part of controlled studies. Other claims are supported through anecdotal information and informal studies conducted by these scientists and derived in their everyday work with patients. In terms of methodology, I am not attempting to lend credibility to this research by borrowing the ethos of the scientific community. On the contrary, this book largely touts historical philosophers and humanists whose ideas are now demonstrated empirically by science. But current work in neuroscience provides a fresh perspective on old ideas while adding new insight at the same time. In other words, it is not so much that neuroscience is validating the conversation regarding image, symbolization, emotions, and consciousness; instead, neuroscience is joining the conversation and, despite its empirical proclivities, ought to be heard as well.

Neuroscience, Consciousness and Symbolization

The previous section summarizes some of the false dichotomies often constructed regarding the relationships between mind and body, and in a sense, the work in neuroscience continues that line of inquiry as it investigates consciousness and the relationship between mind and the brain. As a term, "consciousness" evokes confusion right from the start, especially because it is used in so many different ways by so many different disciplines. Some equate it to sentience, to the soul, to an act of awareness, to the ability to *know* we know, or to the difference between wakefulness and sleep. In short, studies of consciousness point to the difference between the brain as an organ and the mind as a reflective, characteristically human individual. As a subject, consciousness may be the most difficult to research no matter what methodologies are applied—yet, it is no less crucial. Antonio Damasio and Stephen Pinker both venture into the subject in an attempt to understand the difference between the mind and the brain, to defy the myth of the homunculus,[38] and to open science up to studying what had previously been considered too individual and too subjective for rigorous study:

> The organism's private mind, the organism's public behavior, and its hidden brain can thus be joined in the adventure of theory, and out of the adventure come hypotheses that can be tested experimentally, judged on their merits, and subsequently endorsed, rejected, or modified. (Damasio *Feeling* 15)

I want to point out some of the most significant contributions concerning consciousness by neuroscience in order to make connections to image and emotions already mentioned in previous chapters.

Damasio begins by separating consciousness into two parts, one built upon the other: core consciousness and extended consciousness. He defines the former as having a single "level of organization" which is stable throughout life and which is not exclusively a human phenomenon (16). Core consciousness provides a sense of self, a sense of "here and now," yet it does not provide a sense of the future or the distant past. It is akin to the "old brain core" (hypothalamus, brain stem, and the limbic system) that "handles basic biological regulation" (*Descartes'* 129).

Damasio's extended consciousness, on the other hand, consists of many levels and grades, providing a more "elaborate" sense of self, or identity. It provides a complex sense of time, making the organism "richly aware of the lived past and of the anticipated future" (*Feeling* 16). Unlike core consciousness, extended consciousness continues to evolve throughout the lifetime of the organism, continues to be enhanced by language, and ultimately requires memory. Like Vygotsky, Damasio defines the mechanism of consciousness not as a *thing* but as a relationship:

> The organism in question is that within which consciousness occurs; the object in question is any object that gets to be known in the consciousness process; and the relationship between organism and object are the contents of the knowledge we call consciousness. Seen in this perspective, consciousness consists of constructing knowledge about two facts: that the organism is involved in relating to some object, and that the object in the relation causes a change in the organism [. . . .] The process of knowledge construction requires a brain, and it requires the signaling properties with which brains can assemble neural patterns and form images. The neural patterns and images necessary for consciousness to occur are those which constitute proxies for the organism, for the object, and for the

relationship between the two. Placed in this framework, understanding the biology of consciousness becomes a matter of discovering
how the brain can map both the two players and the relationships
they hold. (20)

Obviously, then, consciousness requires not just awareness, but awareness
of three main aspects: a sense of self, a sense of objects and people in the
world (images), and a sense of the relationship between them. Consciousness pulls together these three things through neural patterns that act as
proxy representations of each.

Damasio is careful to emphasize another aspect to consciousness,
though, that is akin to Cassirer's idea of *noticing*: low-level attention. In fact,
Damasio asserts that "a theory of consciousness should *not* be just a theory
of how memory, reason, and language help construct, from the top down,
an interpretation of what goes on in the brain and mind," and he posits
that the "natural low-level attention proceeds consciousness, while focused
attention follows the unfolding of consciousness" (18). The amount and
manner of attention correspond to the ability for consciousness to evolve
and individualize. While attention and noticing are absolutely necessary
to forming images in the extended consciousness, they are not the same
as consciousness.

Like Damasio, Stephen Pinker also separates the consciousness into two
parts: access-consciousness and sentience. Access-consciousness acts as the
director of the brain, pulling together information from different sites in the
brain in order to become "aware" of it. Pinker lists four major features of
access-consciousness: (1) the perceptual field, including an "intermediate-level
awareness" which simultaneously limits as well as highlights and integrates
what we perceive; (2) attention, short-term memory, and deliberative cognition; (3) emotional shading to sensations and thoughts; and (4) the self, an
executive, who serves as the controller and "selects a plan from the hubbub
of competing agents" (*Mind* 138, 144). Even these individual parts—perception, attention, emotion, and self—make the mind no less complex. This
theory of consciousness, like Damasio's, relies on aspects of the mind not
traditionally studied within neuroscience, receiving the appropriate amount
of attention only recently. In fact, Pinker's theory of access-consciousness is
so close to Damasio's that Pinker credits Damasio for much of it.

The second part of Pinker's theory is concerned with sentience, an
aspect he willingly concedes may be part of access-consciousness. In fact,
Pinker's account of sentience is vague, but it refers most to the quality of
what makes humans unique, what makes them different than, say, a computer
or a series of microchips filled with information and the ability to connect

and/or represent that information to others. Clearly, sentience is that aspect
of consciousness that is most difficult to define and understand:

> But in the study of the mind, sentience floats in its own plane, high
> above the causal chains of psychology and neuroscience. If we ever
> could trace all the neurocomputational steps from perception through
> reasoning and emotion to behavior, the only thing left missing by
> the lack of a theory of sentience would be an understanding of sen-
> tience itself [. . . .] The concept of sentience underlies our certainty
> that torture is wrong and that disabling a robot is the destruction
> of property but disabling a person is murder. (148)

Whatever sentience is, it seems to concern itself with the ethical aspects
of consciousness, not necessarily the cognitive aspects. In terms of this
research, sentience only reminds us that there is a lot more to learn about
consciousness, especially as it relates to the more holistic identification of
what it means to be human.

In sum, consciousness is now an object of study in science, and it is
often characterized as the relationship between self and the world. Perhaps
most relevant to this study is the fact that consciousness is made up of images
(a point both Damasio and Pinker emphasize), and that the making of symbols works to extend consciousness away from the core consciousness of our
evolutionary ancestors to the more refined, self-aware consciousness located
in higher brain functions (such as the cortex and neocortex, as well as areas
connected to the frontal lobes). This is not to say that images do not exist
for animals other than humans. Damasio and Pinker both are careful not to
make the forming of images exclusive to the human brain. But the difference
between the brain and the mind might very well be the difference between
perceiving images and knowing and manipulating those same images.[39] As
such, these images provide a powerful link to not only our environment, but
to our very own consciousness. What is the nature of this link, and how does
this association connect to our own sense of self and identity?

Although perhaps criticized by postmodernism as an attempt to create a
grand narrative through science, the work being done in neuroscience today
is nevertheless very important to how we may come to theorize identity in
rhetoric and composition.[40] My intent throughout this discussion is to stay
consistent with the postmodern view of multiple selves, though for ease of
discussion I may refer only to "self" or "the self." In talking about self and
identity, neuroscience is attempting to address what it means to have sentience: what higher consciousness really is. As such, the postmodern critique,
though valid, must be suspended until the work can present itself.

An obvious question, then, arises about the way a theory of writing based in image affects notions of self and identity, especially given the view of the non-discursive proposed in this study. It is not enough to say, in other words, that language and identity are inextricably linked, nor is it enough to propose that identity is formed through the social nature of an individual's experience in a collective. In fact, our brains maintain a sense of self based in images that change, that shift from moment to moment, *and* by memory and imagined recollections of past selves. Damasio makes this point this way:

> The neural basis for the self, as I see it, resides with the continuous reactivation of at least two sets of representations. One set concerns representations of key events in an individual's autobiography, on the basis of which a notion of identity can be reconstructed repeatedly, by partial activation in topographically organized sensory maps [. . . .] In brief, the endless reactivation of updated images about our identity (a combination of memories of the past and of the planned future) constitutes a sizable part of the state of self as I understand it. The second set of representations underlying the neural self consists of the primordial representations of an individual's body [. . .] not only what the body has been like in general, but also what the body has been like lately, just before the processes leading to the perception of object X [. . . .] Early body signals, in both evolution and development, helped form a "basic concept" of self; this basic concept provided the ground reference for whatever else happened to the organism, including the current body states that were incorporated continuously in the concept of self and promptly become past states [. . . .] At each moment the state of self is constructed, from the ground up. (*Descartes'* 238–40)

What this definition of the "neural self" offers to our field is not only biological explanation as to why there is no such thing as the stable, singular self, but a notion of identity *based* in image, just as language is based in image.[41] In Damasio's third book, *Looking for Spinoza: Joy, Sorrow, and the Feeling Brain*, this point is reiterated in a kind of reflection between Damasio and Spinoza's *The Ethics*: "Spinoza's solution no longer required mind and body to integrate or interact; mind and body would spring in parallel from the same substance, fully and mutually mimicking each other in their different manifestations" (209). Similarly, Damasio underscores this point by stating that "without mental images, the organism would not be able to perform [. . .] the large-scale integration of information critical for survival," and "without a sense of self and without the feelings that integrate it, such large-scale mental integrations of information would not be oriented to the problems of life" (208). The consequence of such a view is to not oversimplify and state that self depends on image (thereby mixing the notion of image I have defined for this study with the alternative, media-based notion of image as in a celebrity's *image*), rather it is to show the connection between language and self as located at the same level in the mind: our impulse to form language through image is identical to our impulse to form self through image. We write or compose our sense of self, both biologically and autobiographically from moment to moment, and we are also writing our own memory of self-image and past selves right along with it. Conventional writing, then, is in some ways a mimicking of this process through text. To *inscribe* ourselves, as it is so often referred to in contemporary theories of self, is perhaps more accurate than we ever knew: we *scribe in* ourselves as we continuously update our own sense of identity. This connection between the composing of image and the composing of self has direct ramifications for writing theory because it highlights the compositional processes that are ongoing biologically in all of us, all the time.

Image and identity are critical to writing in another way: as we create images of our self based on autobiography and biology, we also create our worlds, our subjectivity, our notions of real and unreal, perceived and unperceived. Damasio explains how images begin to form our subjectivity:

> As images corresponding to a newly perceived entity (e.g., a face) are formed in early sensory cortices, the brain reacts to those images [. . . .] The end result is that dispositional representations in nuclei and cortical regions are activated and, as a consequence, induce some collection of changes in the state of the organism. In turn, those changes alter the body image momentarily, and thus perturb the current instantiation of the concept of self [. . . .] When the organism's brain generates a set of responses to an entity, the existence of an representation of self does not make that self know that its corresponding organism is responding. . . . Having an image alone is not enough [. . . .] Having both images and a self is not sufficient either [. . . .] In other words, imagine that the third-party ensemble is building a dispositional representation of the self in the process of changing as the organism responds to an object [. . . .] I propose that subjectivity emerges during the latter step when the brain is producing not just images of an object, not just images of organism responses to the object, but a third kind of image, that of an organism in the act of perceiving and responding to an object. I believe the subjective perspective arises out of the content of the third kind of image. (241–43)

Damasio calls this third type of image the image created by the "metaself": a notion of self that is not just autobiographical or biological, but one that establishes and maintains images of *relationships* with the world: he is theorizing a biological basis for subjectivity. Perhaps such a view of how this kind of neural subjectivity gets written can also help compositionists find ways in which writing (or any experience for that matter) can help to rewrite or revise notions of self for some student writers, or, conversely, how some writers may affect the way in which text may alter (for good or ill) an other's sense of self, even if momentarily. Like a stream or river, self is constantly being made and remade. Any encounter or any experience may change the content and/or direction of such a river, but it may do so with varying affect. No longer is it feasible to talk only of the self and other; both are rewritten continuously.

The relationship between images and selves, then, is based on the same basic process that image and symbolization—and image and mind—is based. By not accounting for the way selves change during writing processes we may be neglecting both the process of self as much as the process of writing. As the two continue, both are continually revised. As self manifests in writing as style, voice, diction, mood, tone, or other means, both writers and audiences are changed at the level of self through the metaself, through our own subjectivity. Relationships to worlds and objects in those worlds manifest through the imagination of a social, variously constructed rhetor.

Identity and the subjective self are stepping stones for scientists to create a larger theory of consciousness based in biological processes. It is also important to understand how image functions within consciousness because images hold the key to how students can move from non-discursive to discursive text. Consciousness, like emotions, has long been considered too subjective or too individualistic to warrant sustained academic study (especially in science), but that is changing. Specifically, as neuroscience joins the interdisciplinary discussion on consciousness, there seems to be renewed interest in many other disciplines as to what consciousness is and how it functions.[42] I want to first sketch some ways consciousness has been talked about, and then suggest how image and the theory of consciousness and language provide a concept of emotions and feeling that is significant to the field.

In *A Universe of Consciousness: How Matter Becomes Imagination*, Gerald M. Edelman and Giulio Tononi describe a theory of consciousness that significantly influences the work of Damasio and Ramachandran. Through various advances in brain imaging techniques, as well as the long-term study of various brain anomalies and disease, Edelman and Tononi make the following conclusions about human consciousness:

> By highlighting several observations, ranging from neurophysiology to neuropsychology, we argue that (1) neuronal processes

underlying conscious experience involve groups of neurons that are widely distributed; (2) these distributed groups of neurons engage in strong and rapid reentrant interactions; and (3) for consciousness to appear, such rapidly interacting neuronal groups must be able to select among a sufficiently large number of differentiated activity patterns. (52–53)

In order to appreciate this definition, we must first understand what "reentrant interactions" are in the brain and their usefulness. Edelman and Tononi explain it this way:

> Reentry [. . .] is the ongoing, recursive interchange of parallel signals between reciprocally connected areas of the brain, an interchange that continually coordinates the activities of these areas' maps to each other in space and time. This interchange, unlike feedback, involves many parallel paths and has no specific instructive error function associated with it. Instead, it alters selective events and correlations of signals among areas and is essential for the synchronization and coordination of the areas' mutual functions. (48)

This concept of reentry allows the brain to integrate in countless ways what are often very specialized areas, and it is the "basis for the integration of perceptual and motor processes" (48). The consequence of such a system is no less than what makes humans and other advanced vertebrates different from the rest of the animal kingdom. It is through reentry that we are able to categorize, discriminate objects and events, and filter what is important from what is not (48–49). Reentry is quite simply the ability for the brain to be its own master, its own coordinated behavior—in short, it provides the functioning of conscious activity previously afforded to a homunculus.

According to Edelman and Tononi, consciousness must have systems that allow for both integration and differentiation. As soon as the neural activity patterns become repetitive and insufficiently diverse, consciousness is lost, as is evidenced by the brain waves during sleep or during epileptic seizures (though brain activity is high, in the latter case it is not sufficiently diverse to be conscious (72).[43] Consciousness is present to the degree that brain activity is not uniform or homogeneous; the brain relies on both complexity and integration in order to be conscious. Edelman and Tononi's "Dynamic Core Hypothesis," then, states the following):

> [A] cluster of neuronal groups that are strongly interacting among themselves and that have distinct functional borders with the rest of the brain at the time scale of fractions of a second a "dynamic core," to emphasize both its integration and its constantly changing

composition. A dynamic core is therefore a process, not a thing or a place, and it is defined in terms of neural interactions, rather than in terms of specific neural location, connectivity, or activity. Although a dynamic core will have a spatial extension, it is, in general, spatially distributed, as well as changing in composition, and thus cannot be localized to a single place in the brain. (144)

Consciousness, then, is a process, not a "thing or a place," and it is present through both the complexity *and* integration of neural activity. This indicates that consciousness, like image and language, is internal and external, social and communal, and integrated and differentiated. By making consciousness a process, Edelman and Tononi emphasize the comprehensiveness as well as the difficulty inherent in researching the complexity of conscious activity.

This emphasis on the social is reminiscent of another theorist who asks hard questions about consciousness, and who also makes the case that consciousness must be a viable area of study: Vygotsky. Like Edelman and Tononi, Vygotsky's theory of consciousness includes the social realm, and he seems to anticipate much of the recent research being done in neuroscience. In his essay "Consciousness as a Problem in the Psychology of Behavior," Vygotsky takes up the question of consciousness and insists that it become central to psychology:

> The denial of consciousness and the attempt to construct a psychological system without this concept [. . .] have resulted in a situation in which method has been deprived of the most vital means and instruments for studying latent responses not observable with the naked eye, such as internal movements, internal speech, somatic responses, etc. In studying only those reactions that are visible to the naked eye, one is totally powerless to explain even the simplest problems of human behavior. (6–7)

Such ignorance, according to Vygotsky, casts both a methodological shadow on the discipline of psychology, and it casts an epistemological shadow on the (perceived) differences between humans and other animals. Vygotsky even goes so far as claim that without some attention to consciousness theory, "it is impossible to undertake a critical revision of the accumulated scientific knowledge in this area," rendering not only present research but also the possibility that past research may become questionable (12).

What Vygotsky actually contributes is a theory of consciousness that provides a historical as well as a social complexity to the overall intricacy and context of human activity. Without taking into account consciousness, we miss not just the biological but the environmental and historical dimension of behavior as well. Similar to what neuroscience has already postulated, Vygotsky actually anticipates Edelman's concept of reentry:

> Our awareness or ability to be conscious of our deeds and states must be seen primarily as a reflection of a system of transfer mechanisms from one set of reflexes to another, a system that is correctly functioning at every conscious moment. The more correctly every internal reflex, as a stimulus, elicits a sequence of other reflexes from other systems or is transmitted to other systems, the more we are capable of giving account to ourselves and others of what we are experiencing and the more consciously that experience is lived (sensed, formulated in words, etc.) [. . . .] Consciousness is the experiencing of experiences, just as experience is simply the experience of objects. (19–20)

Just like Edelman and Tononi, Vygotsky requires consciousness to be integrated as well as complex, with reentry mechanisms reaching a diverse set of "systems" in the brain. Vygotsky goes a step further than Edelman and Tononi, however, by also insisting on the *primacy* of social consciousness over individual consciousness: "the individual dimension of consciousness is derivative and secondary, based on the social and construed exactly in its likeness" and that "consciousness of speech and social experience occur simultaneously and completely in parallel with one another" (30–31). That is to say, consciousness manifests itself in language and, perhaps, expands and enlivens itself though language interactions within the social sphere. Not uncharacteristically, Vygotsky's privileging of the social aspect of consciousness has direct consequences for language, and, therefore, as in psychology, writing theory can benefit from being aware of how it fits within the study of consciousness. Vygotsky's claim that language and consciousness are parallel to one another, and that social networks provide the integration necessary for such interaction, echoes this suggestion.

As Vygotsky warned psychologists of the impact theories of consciousness have to methodology, scholars in rhetoric and composition should be equally warned. These integrated theories regarding consciousness are vital not only because of what they may offer to composition studies, but also in what they offer methodologically to research in general. For example, external methodologies (as in empirical observation and formulation) based on practical, observable behavior and internal methodologies (as in narrative, introspection, and reflection) based on intuited, subjective behavior, benefit from not only their respective theories on language, but also their respective theories on consciousness (as well as their *relationship* to consciousness). It suffices to say, then, that views concerning consciousness may also affect research methodologies—both in theory and in practice.

Damasio also considers what essential qualities are required for consciousness, especially as human consciousness is different from the consciousness of other animals. Damasio distinguishes between reflex and action, instinct and behavior, and he postulates what characteristics of thought indicate consciousness, or the presence of a mind:

> Brains [of any animal] can have many intervening steps in the circuits mediating between stimulus and response, and still have no mind, if they do not meet an essential condition: the ability to display images internally and to order those images in a process called thought. (The images are not solely visual; there are also "sound images," "olfactory images," and so on.) [. . .] My view then is that having a mind means that an organism forms neural representations which can become images, be manipulated in a process called thought, and eventually influence behavior by helping predict the future, plan accordingly, and choose the next action. (*Descartes'* 89–90)

Thus, the impact of images, language, and emotion becomes immediately apparent to any theory of consciousness. All three work to create an environment in which text generation and imagination engage the mind and its consciousness to produce text—to write.

If Damasio and Vygotsky are correct, if consciousness is indeed the "feeling of what happens" and the "experiencing of experiences," respectively, then it must also be the case that consciousness exists within a complex milieu of emotional complexity not easily relegated to reason or logic. In fact, many theorists, such as Damasio and Vygotsky, dispute the ability of consciousness to be anything but comprehensive of both body and mind, intuitive and logical, real and imagined.

How then does such a view of consciousness lend itself towards a theory of writing based in image and the non-discursive? The answer is that theories of consciousness, along with theories of affect and language, help to clarify the *relationships* between body and mind, mind and identity, and emotions and reason. Specifically, consciousness is both differentiated and integrated, and it relies on images to help plan for the future and "choose the next action." Because of the make-up of consciousness and its reliance on images, it is clear that our use of non-discursive text—a language form rich in image—must hold a more intimate connection to our mental processes than found in our use of discursive text. Perhaps because consciousness relies on feelings and images, so must writing. However, to make this claim, we have to understand the role of image within consciousness.

The work being done in neuroscience, especially by Antonio Damasio, suggests that as we theorize consciousness the importance of image and emotions become increasingly apparent. This section focuses on the relationship between image and consciousness in order to make these connections clearer. In doing so, image becomes central to most, if not all, our cognitive processes and, as such, must carry more importance to composing and inventing than was previously thought.

Damasio, characterized the relationship between image and consciousness this way:

> In a curious way, consciousness begins as the feeling of what happens when we see or hear or touch. Phrased in slightly more precise words, it is a feeling that accompanies the making of any kind of image—visual, auditory, tactile, visceral—within our living organisms. Placed in the appropriate context, the feeling marks those images as ours and allows us to say, in the proper sense of the terms, that we see or hear or touch. Organisms unequipped to generate core consciousness are condemned to making images of sight or sound or touch, there and then, but can not come to know that they did. (*Feeling* 26)

This understanding has vast implications for visual rhetoric and composing. Damasio is essentially asserting that it is precisely *because* we associate feelings with images that we are able to reach higher consciousness. Any organism with its primary systems "on" and the ability to respond to stimuli exhibits a "core consciousness." It simply stipulates activity. Higher consciousness, according to Damasio, is more than that; the organism "can come to know" that it is "on," and that it can then be aware of itself and its environment in a way that reaches beyond what their immediate senses provide (90). When we are conscious, we are able to feel what happens to us, but we are also able to direct what we sense through attention. To say consciousness is the "feeling of what happens" is to also say that everything that happens in our consciousness is also a feeling, a sense of *what is*.

What this most directly implies is the centrality of image to consciousness, cognition (or thought), and emotion. Damasio makes it clear that mental images are not "mirror copies" of the "real" image:

> Images are not stored as facsimile pictures of things, or events, or words, or sentences [. . .] there seem to be no permanently held pictures of anything, even miniaturized, no microfiches or microfilms, no hard copies [. . .] whenever we recall a given object, or face, or

scene, we do not get an exact reproduction but rather an interpretation, a newly reconstituted version of the original. (*Descartes'* 100)

Though he makes the point that we can conjure up approximations of images, it is imperative to remember that mental images are just that, approximations:

> images are momentary constructions, attempts at replication of patterns that were once experienced, in which the probability of exact replication is low [. . .] These recalled images tend to be held in consciousness only fleetingly [. . .] they are often inaccurate or incomplete. I suspect that explicit recalled mental images arise from the transient synchronous activation of neural firing patterns corresponding to perceptual representations once occurred. (101)

Recalled images are just one aspect of the role of image in consciousness. Nothing less than thought itself is also reliant on image: "The factual knowledge required for reasoning and decision making comes to the mind in the form of images" (96). It turns out that the use of recalled images and the use of mental images function in similar ways in the brain: a pattern of neural "firings" topographically located in various parts of the brain. Damasio calls this recall a "topographically organized representation," which is controlled by what he terms a "dispositional" system of synapses located in "convergence zones" (102). Image, then, occurs when synapses within a convergence zone stimulates a dispositional representation, which, in turn, orchestrates a topographical representation of the requested image:

> What dispositional representations hold in store in their little commune of synapses is not a picture per se, but a means to reconstitute "a picture" [. . .] What I am calling a dispositional representation is a dormant firing potentiality which comes to life when neurons fire, with a particular pattern, at certain rates, for a certain amount of time, and toward a particular target which happens to be another ensemble of neurons [. . .] The firing patterns result from the strengthening or weakening of synapses, and that, in turn, results from functional changes occurring at microscopic level within the fiber branches of neurons. (104)

As such, images are the building blocks of cognition. These dispositional representations store for us images that make up our knowledge, both innate and acquired. Damasio links them closely to thought itself, claiming that without images, we could never come to know anything (106). Images become central to not only *what* our brains store, but *how* it is stored in the first place. Images, in short, become the lexicon of thought.

Language, then, is made up of images stored in these dispositional representations as well. Damasio explains discursive language in the brain this way:

> It is often said that thought is made of much more than just images, that it is made also of words and nonimage abstract symbols. Surely nobody will deny that thought includes words and arbitrary symbols. But what that statement misses is the fact that both words and arbitrary symbols are based on topographically organized representations and can become images. Most of the words we use in our inner speech, before speaking or writing a sentence, exist as auditory or visual images in our consciousness. If they did not become images, however fleetingly, they would not be anything we could know. (106)

In reference to Fleckenstein's assertion that image operates within an "*is* logic" (and language operates within an *as-if* logic), Damasio makes it clear here that even "nonimage abstract symbols" require an image in order to be known by the brain. He also notes that there seems to be no way for us to form a dispositional representations without first forming topographically mapped perceptual representations: "there seems to be no anatomical way of getting complex sensory information into the association cortex that supports dispositional representations without first stopping in early sensory cortices. (This may not be true for noncomplex sensory information)" (106–07). In other words, if knowledge is to come from experience, then experience comes in the form of images stored in the various networks of the brain: experience is in effect "interpreted" by a dispositional representation that may then later be recalled and repeated. What this implies is extremely relevant to composition studies: the better our compositions of symbols can create a holistic experience through image, the more efficiently the brain can then create a means to recall, or repeat, that experience. This reinforces educational theorists who advocate experiential learning, but it also suggests why it is necessary we help writers elaborate, reinforce, and provide sensory cues to abstract ideas as they compose. A request for more detail in any given section of writing, for example, may also be a call for a better *image* of the idea being expressed.

To better understand this "topographically organized representations" it helps to visualize the various layers of the brain within the cortex. Though the connections Damasio talks about between various areas of the brain may be located within different areas of the brain (front, back, etc.), these areas are also connected through various layers *within* the cortex. The cortex itself, the convoluted surface of our brain, is made up of six columns of cells:

> Cells both large and small within each column share a common purpose: the computation of a certain pattern of output from a given pattern of inputs. They communicate intensely with one another, more sparingly with cells in neighboring columns. Numerous columns with a single region of cortex can be active simultaneously, in parallel. They are the modules of cortical anatomy, exemplifying the order which underlies variety within every part of the nervous system. (Zeman 50)

Each of these columns operates in slightly different ways, partly due to the way the nerve cells themselves are structured. Similar to having six layers of traffic in a metropolitan area, these layers accommodate different kinds of signals depending on the sensory information being processed. The topography, in other words, is three-dimensional. One topographical representation may activate cells in different columns of the same area, leaving other cells in nearby areas unaffected. As the nature and physiology of these layers are studied, the complexity and sophistication of this architecture becomes ever more apparent. Once again, given this complexity of the topography Damasio refers to, these "topographical representations" are actually accessing areas both within these layers and among different areas of the brain in order to form an image. This also reinforces the idea that that images do not "reside" anywhere in the brain: they are called up through the activation of different layers and different sites of different brain areas.

Such a view of image and consciousness indicates a need for a new writing theory, one that places a sufficient degree of emphasis on the image—on the non-discursive. Image becomes much more than simply a handy heuristic, or a way to incorporate more of our senses in the learning environment. Image becomes a building block of language and consciousness, of emotions and reason, and of thought and imagination. Images are integral to every part of our cognition, from memory to future planning. Consciousness itself depends on them, in connection with emotions, to help us shape and compose our knowledge of the world.[44] Such a focus on the role of image does more than illustrate or exemplify; such a focus on image becomes the basis of a non-discursive writing theory.

Theories of Will

The will, or what Aristotle termed the soul or anima, must be at the heart of rhetorical theory because of the rhetor's proclivity towards praxis. However, much of the history regarding scholarship on the will is interspersed with spiritualism and religious dogma *as appropriate* to whatever the dominant view of rhetoric and epistemology was at the time. As theories of will and consciousness favor external, even social or collective sources, so too does the responsibility of action and reform. As theories of will and consciousness favor internal, exclusively mental sources, action and reform become possible insofar as individual action and reform are possible. By emphasizing image in our symbol-making practice, and by insisting on the role of emotions and consciousness in writing theory, human will does both: like consciousness, it integrates and differentiates as it becomes more complex and diverse. The will to compose text, whether discursive or non-discursive, must rely on an integrated consciousness connected to social complexity. It is important to remember that the opposite of *to be willing* is not *to be unwilling*—both of these are, after all, acts of will; rather, the opposite of *to be willing* is *to not have a will*, or to be without volition. Put in this way, it is easier to see why the concept of the will is important to rhetorical study: the absence of will is the absence of rhetoric; the opposite of will is the opposite of rhetoric. In sum, rhetorical theory implies the absence of coercion and the absence of consciousness because the absence of will is the absence of conscious choice.

Theories of the human will move between what Vygotsky calls two poles:

> At the first of these poles, we find the conception of will as something primal, something that is foreign to the conscious aspect of human personality. Here, will is represented as a kind of primal force that moves both the material and the spiritual aspects of life. At the other pole, we find the theories of the spiritualists. Historically, these theories are associated with Descartes' philosophy and, through Descartes, with the Christian philosophy of the Middle Ages. Cartesian theory takes as its foundation a spiritual beginning that directs the entirety of man's spiritual life, and, consequently, all his behavior. (*Collected* 354)

But this dialectic is too easy, and one that Vygotsky suggests is too far removed from our use of language. He avoids the dichotomy between what can be summarized as evolutionary determinism versus spiritual fatalism by making will, like consciousness, a process developed in time first by children and then by adults: "The development of the child's will begins with primitive voluntary movements, then moves to verbal instruction, and is completed with the emergence of complex volitional actions. This development is directly dependent on the child's collective action" (357). In other words, we develop, exercise, and improve our will as time allows.

It is not am inherent characteristic of our personality, or a mental faculty or flaw; it is a developmental process always and already associated with our acts of symbolization.[45]

Like Vygotsky, E. C. White focuses the will-to-invent on the desire to use language; in fact, specifically on the desire to rely on improvisation during and through language. White sometimes uses terms like "desiring energy" to describe will (perhaps as a way to underscore the importance of emotions to will), and he insists on the regenerative powers of the will to create new knowledge:

> If knowledge is to be more than the simple amplification of tra-
> dition, then the self must always be willing to forgo its present
> understanding of reality in order to return to the world in its
> indifferent specificity. Only by opening itself to an encounter with
> the unforeseen spontaneity of the immediate occasion can the
> interpreting subject produce an interpretation saved from obsessive
> repetition. Instead of forgetting the irreducibly specific character
> of the present, the interpreter must constantly recur from a self-
> serving fantasy of meaning to the suchness beyond and enclosing
> the realm of fantasized satisfaction. Desiring energy would then be
> invested in newly improvised interpretations rather than a suppos-
> edly permanent truth. The mind would involve itself in an endless
> process of *beginning again*, continually adjusting its trajectory as new
> points of departure suggest themselves in the course of interpretive
> invention. (86)

Here, White emphasizes the importance of (1) the role of image and consciousness in writing, and (2) the role of the will in the creation of new knowledge. What is fascinating about this description of a rhetor in the moment is that the will is necessary to "forgo its present understanding of reality" as well as open "itself up to an encounter with the unforeseen spontaneity of the immediate occasion"—to wrestle with the ineffable, in other words, and struggle with symbol-making again and again. The rhetor, in short, must be willing to begin again. Therefore, this is why addressing the will is so important in any kind of comprehensive writing theory. Writers must be willing to begin again to contend with the blank page, the blinking cursor, the lens, and the unuttered phrase, to find and convey new knowledge (defined in the broadest possible way). Without the will, no future action makes sense, words become mere placeholders (and not very good ones at that), and our ability to wonder, to inquire, diminishes as our use of the imagination atrophies or explodes beyond the present moment.

Anthony Kenny, in *Will, Freedom and Power*, postulates that there have been two dominant conceptions of will in the philosophical tradition: introvert and extrovert (12). The introvert conception, as seen in the theories of Descartes, Hume, and William James, is a view of will as "a phenomenon, an episode in one's mental history, an item of introspective consciousness" with volition as "a mental event whose occurrence makes the difference between voluntary and involuntary actions" (13). The extrovert conception, best represented by philosophers such as Wittgenstein, Austin, and Ryle, regards "the volitions of the introvert tradition as mythical entities" and "starts with the observable behaviour of agents and asks for the external criteria by which to distinguish between voluntary and involuntary actions" (13). Kenny illustrates just why it is so important to theorize consciousness before talking about the will. These very same false dichotomies are often evoked by consciousness theorists, and, for the same reasons, theories of will ought to be released from the constraints of internal/external, collective/individual dualisms. The view of consciousness supported by this theory necessitates a view of will that is not wholly internal or external, collective or individual. Will, like consciousness and symbolization, is a key operator in rhetoric.

How does the will relate to multimodal writing? A theory of will must also be consistent with symbolization theory and consciousness theory in order to be integrated and differentiated into our collective and individual lives. The will relates to writing theory because it embodies the actions of consciousness, from state to state, moment to moment. Consequently, will and consciousness also fluctuate with emotions, imagination (i.e., through image) and, finally, in what we compose—whether that textual production is discursive or non-discursive. Will is both mental and physical, collective and individual, specialized and diverse; it develops as we develop, collecting experiences and newly discovered plans.

Kenny later insists that the most important defining characteristic of will is based on practical reasoning, or "rational appetite." Derived from St. Thomas Aquinas's view that defines will as the "ability to have reasons for acting and to act for reasons," Kenny presents a third possible way between the introvert and extrovert poles regarding theories of the will already mentioned:

> Like the extrovert tradition the [rational appetite] view I have defended defines the will as the capacity for a certain kind of action; like the introvert tradition it defines the kind of action which the will is the capacity to perform as action issuing from a certain kind of *thought* (conceived, though, not as an item of consciousness but

as a mental state). Like the extrovert tradition it approaches the nature of the will via the nature of voluntary behaviour; but as the introvert tradition implicitly did, it assigns a very special place to linguistic behaviour, and in particular to the agent's sincere account of what he is doing and why. (20)

What is compelling about this third conception of will is the way it stresses the connection between will and language. Nevertheless, such a theory pits reason versus emotion, rationality versus irrationality, and body versus mind. In this conception, the will is too narrowly defined, restricted to what can be reasoned or rationalized. Kenny concludes that will, or volition, is not "motions of the mind" but a "state of the mind," meaning that the will works to change larger patterns of mind over individual acts of mind (26). What is needed is a theory of the will that is not defined in terms of rationality or reason, but in terms of consciousness and, perhaps, the neural functions of the brain itself. In fact, the will has much to do with the role of emotions in language, as well as the role of emotions in argument, and we must look closely at how will relates to our brain's physiology and neural processes in order to make some connections between will, consciousness, image, and emotion.

The connection between will and consciousness is never clearer than in the research on prefrontal and frontal lobe damage Damasio reports in *Descartes' Error*. One famous example of a railroad worker named Phineas Gage who in 1848 survived the trauma having a tamping rod shot completely through his head: "The iron enters Gage's left cheek, pierces the base of his skull, traverses the front of his brain, and exits at high speed through the top of his head" (4). Though he survived, Gage—and other patients with similar damage to the frontal lobe—then underwent a drastic change in personality and demeanor. Patients with this kind of brain damage often become unsociable and misdirected, lacking any solid direction in the choices they make on a day to day basis: "[I]t was selective damage in the prefrontal cortices of Phineas Gage's brain that compromised his ability to plan for the future, to conduct himself according to the social rules he previously had learned, and to decide on the course of action that ultimately would be most advantageous to his survival" (33). Curiously, many other functions, including memory, learning, and basic linguistic skills, remained intact.[46] But Damasio reports that Gage and similar patients demonstrate how the slow accumulation of poor decisions, inappropriate social behavior, and emotional numbness begin to wreck their lives. Left on their own, patients eventually become self-destructive, even suicidal. In short, what is damaged or missing in these patients is nothing less than their own will.

After some research into the matter, Damasio suggests this is indeed the case. Damasio finds that the prefrontal cortices are important to consciousness and the will in four important ways: "[T]he prefrontal cortices [. . .] are ideally suited to acquire a three-way link among signals concerned with particular types of situations; the different types and magnitudes of body state, which have been associated with certain types of situations in the individual's unique experience; and the effectors of those states" (183). This area of the brain, then, seems to help to describe if not define the essential characteristics of will in context with an integrated view of consciousness: this damage caused interruptions in the integration of information including body state (which is linked closely with a sense of self or identity, as mentioned already), the use of knowledge gained from past experiences, and "effectors," or agents, of various states of consciousness (such as knowledge about one's own sensitivities and preferences). Taken together, these signals aid the prefrontal cortices to plan and take action according to such an imagined plan. According to Damasio, our ability to effect change due to the future is perhaps the most important feature of human will:

> Willpower draws on the evaluation of prospect, and that evaluation may not take place if attention is not properly driven to both the immediate trouble and the future payoff, to both the suffering *now* and the *future* gratification. Remove the latter and you remove the lift from under your willpower's wings. Willpower is just another name for the idea of choosing according to long-term outcomes rather than short-term ones. (175)

First there must be evaluation, and as I suggested in chapter 3, evaluation can be, even must be, based in emotion and feeling—something largely denied these patients with prefrontal brain damage, except in extremes. As we grasp for a future and evaluate the present in terms of past experience, we imagine, organize images into thoughts, and from those imaginings, we intuit a possible end. Imagination works as a conceptual tool for will just as it does for language and consciousness. The importance of will becomes even clearer, then, as we see the effects of its absence: it directs attention, provides a context for personal experience, and, possibly, helps us to, as White suggests "recur from a self-serving fantasy of meaning to the suchness beyond and enclosing the realm of fantasized satisfaction" (86). This "suchness" is nothing less than a notion of a possible future.

What Damasio and White suggest, then, is that will as energy can not exclusively rely on logic, reason, or even hope to attain some kind of unemotional or nonaffective objectivity with the world in order to function. Of course, as writers, we know this to some extent already: anyone who has found what they are looking for through prewriting or even meditation may readily subscribe to this idea.[47] Yet, so many theories of will rely on a nearly exclusive connection with reason that any outright suggestion that will exists separate from reason would otherwise have been easily discredited. What I hope to have shown through this survey of scholarship regarding will, though, is simply that (1) study of human will is important to writing theory; (2) human will is not entirely within the domain of reason—it also includes intuition; and (3) will is learned through experience and integrated into our ever-changing states of consciousness. Again, to be unwilling is not the opposite of will—being unwilling is, after all, an act of will; on the contrary, the opposite of will is the absence of will. Phineas Gage was not unwilling to integrate his past experience with his "effectors" and his future plans: he simply did not will anything at all, relying on baser, more primitive instinctual responses to stimuli to get him from moment to moment with no regard for consequences or what lies ahead.

The next section attempts to pull together the concepts of consciousness and will in order to make clearer my claim that non-discursive text provides a bridge between the ineffable and the discursive. Scholarship on the will may in fact be the important link between pedagogy and theory, one that is comprehensive without neglecting the specific, differentiated characteristics of the writer during invention, memory, arrangement, style, or delivery of text.

The Role of Consciousness and Will in the Non-discursive

If, as suggested, consciousness and will are integrated and differentiated concepts that avoid the common dualisms of physical/mental, rational/ irrational, and communal/individual, then the enactment of language itself is always a non-discursive act: thoughts are based in image, language is based in image, consciousness is based in image, and the ability to plan and or *intend* a future action is based in our ability to imagine. Image, then, rules our psyche. Without image, we would not form typographical dispositions that make up one thought or memory versus another. Without image, we would not form primary or secondary feelings used to form core consciousness or relegate reason and logic. In sum, the workings of our language require non-discursive thought, as does our consciousness and will.

This is not to say that discursive thought, reason, and logic are not important. On the contrary, they provide structure, scaffolding, a skeleton, if you will, to the fleeting, dynamic, always fluid sense of identity and self, states of consciousness, and emotional tides we constantly experience. If this metaphor is correct, then the muscles, tissues, and fat making up the majority of our bulk, the shape and character of our features, is like non-discursive text: it is our surface, our connection with others, our history and our present. Langer reminds us of the importance of discursive text this way:

Because the prime purpose of language is discourse, the conceptual framework that has developed under its influence is known as
'discursive reason' [. . .] any appreciation of form, any awareness
of patterns in experience, is 'reason'; and discourse with all its
refinements (e.g. mathematical symbolism, which is an extension
of language) is only one possible pattern [. . .] but [. . .] there are
whole domains of experience that philosophers deem 'ineffable.' If
those domains appear to anyone the most important, that person
is naturally inclined to condemn philosophy and science as barren
and false. To such an evaluation one is entitled; not, however, to
the claim of a better way to philosophical truth through instinct,
intuition, feeling, or what have you. Intuition is the basic process
of all understanding, just as operative in discursive thought as in
clear sense perception and immediate judgment [. . .] But it is no
substitute for discursive logic in the making of any theory, contingent or transcendental. (29)

Discursive text, then, makes books such as this one possible, and—as stressed
already in the first chapter—provides important linkages between knowledge
and communities who value knowledge.

However, non-discursive text is not just the neglected half of symbolization—it is more than that. The non-discursive provides a path for
the discursive because it is so intimately connected to consciousness and
will through image itself. This is why theories of the will and consciousness are so important to writing theory: the non-discursive provides *a way
into* the discursive, even when the *end product* intended by any writer may
be discursive. Because the central feature of language is image, language is
first non-discursive before it is discursive: this is why prewriting, so-called
"freewriting," and even calls to allow for writing to be "messy" are effective as textual production strategies.[48] When writers confront an empty
page, unconstructed web site, blank canvas, unchiseled stone, unmolded
clay, unphotographed event, unchoreographed dance, and/or unvocalized
speech, they necessarily also are confronting their own imagination within
their own consciousness, and they do that not through linear, stepped logic
and reasoning, but, as this research has tried to show, through the use and
interaction of non-discursive images within language. In citing Cassirer,
Langer reinforces the importance of the non-discursive to the discursive
though Cassirer's notion of noticing and naming:

The naming process, started and guided by emotional excitement,
created entities not only for sense perception but for memory,
speculation, and dream. This is the source of mythic conception, in

which symbolic power is still undistinguished from physical power, and the symbol is fused with what it symbolizes. (236–37)

From the onset of language, then, "emotional excitement," "speculation," and "dream" all work together to help fuse a symbol with its referent: the act of non-discursive processing through image and emotions (which are also images) creates a beginning for discursive text.

The role of consciousness and the will is to further integrate our experiences into our language. This is done, as shown already, through the centrality of image in the brain through neural processes which rely on a combination of past experience and memory, of present states of self and identity, and on "present future" plans and intent.[49] Such integration, however, is not done at the expense of the differentiation also necessary for consciousness to function. Instead, images that lead to symbolization adapt and create new pathways just as consciousness and will adapt: new discursive and non-discursive methods, structures, genres, expectations, and evaluations develop as the fluidity of consciousness and emotions continue to create new topographically organized representations (or images). These new images then create new convergence zones for calling up those images, construct new reentry pathways to allow for the parallel integration of body and mind, and, ultimately, new knowledge.

The next chapter offers a specific composing model that integrates theories of image and imagination, language, consciousness, and will in such a way that is applicable to writing instruction and writing theory. Consciousness and will are important to writing theory because they provide the context in which our emotions, imagination, and language create text. In moving toward a writing theory comprehensive enough to handle multimodal texts of all kinds, we must first imagine the intricacies and inner-relationships between image, consciousness, and will. What is clear is just how important these concepts are to composing non-discursive text.

CHAPTER 4

Non-discursive Textual Production and Multimedia

*U*p until now, four key concepts have been needed to contextualize a theory of non-discursive rhetoric: (1) the difference between discursive and non-discursive text; (2) the centrality of image to symbol-making; (3) the necessary connection between image and the affective, especially in non-discursive text; and (4) the connections between image, consciousness, and will in symbol-making. Non-discursive rhetoric, then, is a term that is useful to describe the rhetorical practices of non-discursive text: a theory of rhetoric that relies on image (made up of all the sensual inputs) and non-discursive meaning in order to persuade, move, and/or create unsayable (or word-independent) meaning for an audience. It is not reliant on the rigor and sequentiality of discursive texts; rather, it is often copresent with discursive text in either direct or indirect forms: the tone of an essay, the body language of an orator, the color of the background of a web page, et cetera. Non-discursive rhetoric, in sum, include all the extra-communicative elements of any kind meant to construct consensus, praise and/or blame, or encode ethical and moral behavior, all the while remaining completely separate from the discursive text commonly purported to be the exclusive purveyor of meaning. As argued already, discursive bias is in part due to the way symbolization is thought of as primarily word-based, primarily nonaffective, and primarily monomodal. But a new perspective of symbolization can yield a view of textual production that no longer fails to reiterate the importance of composing non-discursive text. Each of the key concepts covered in this book up to now points to how a non-discursive theory of textual production will work against the discursive bias and provide a way for pedagogues to encourage non-discursive textual production in the classroom—a mix of multimedia text that is increasingly multimodal.

Students composing in digital environments simply cannot ignore, or worse, be ignorant to the importance of non-discursive rhetoric. Whether they are instructed about it or not, they need to deal with image: whether it is the graphics and digital photos used in a web page, the animated faces of avatars in a 3-D virtual reality environment, or even the choice of font on a resume. Each of these choices requires that the student understand the rhetorical situation, the audience, and even the larger context of such choices as they are made in a social domain. For example, a rhetor may decide to use a particularly controversial image on a placard while protesting at a local community event, and if that rhetor is not practiced at considering the use of that image in that particular forum at that time and place, then the rhetor may fail to be convincing at best, or succeed to sway people against that rhetor's purpose at worst. The broader social and cultural context may have nothing to do with the discursive message on that placard; on the other hand, the non-discursive messages on the placard may be ineffective. How does a rhetor learn to consider these issues? How do we teach students of non-discursive rhetoric how to compose non-discursive text?

Writing Theory/Invention Theory

This section provides the way in which the four values of non-discursive text (image, non-discursive text, affect/emotion/intuition, and multimodality) and the four values of multimodality work together to encourage textual production. Other invention theories are considered briefly, but I will concentrate on how non-discursive invention can be an important aspect of all textual production, even discursive textual production. This research presents a conception of writing that is an alternative to other writing theories prevalent in the field reliant on dualist or dichotomous constructions of discourse. In no way does it attempt to supplant or otherwise usurp existing theories primarily because such a position would be inconsistent with many positions this theory values: namely that discursive text based in reason is also important to writing and writing instruction. In addition, I do not wish to create a new "grand narrative" or authorized metadiscourse that would, in the end, tip the scales too far the other way.[1] In fact, I would rather promote plurality of theories rather than imply a need for a single theory of writing. However, the intent of this chapter is to construct a writing theory consistent with this research on image, imagination, emotions, consciousness, and will, and, at the same time, to point to the importance of ambivalence, ineffability, and the non-discursive in the creation of new knowledge. Before proceeding, here are some of the main concepts discussed so far:

1. Symbolization is based not in discursive meaning but in image. It is by its very nature communal *and* it constructs reality for individuals.

2. Because image is central to symbolization, imagination is also central to symbol-making. Without our imagination, we cannot only create images of the unknown, but we also cannot create apperceptions of the known. Image and imagination define rhetorical invention in part because audiences are imagined, the rhetor's content is imagined, and non-discursive text is conveyed primarily through image.

3. Because imagination and image are central to symbolization, and because emotions exist *along* with topographical representations of what we know and experience, emotions are central to language. If, by one definition, core consciousness is the "feeling of what happens," then emotions are as important to language as they are to reason, ethics, and evaluation. Because image and feeling are neural processes intertwined with conceptions of body state and memory, emotions are also integral to self and identity. As such, symbolization and identity are also intertwined.

4. Consciousness exists as an integrated neural activity that is also differentiated, and it fades as diversity and breadth of experience fades. Consciousness is not a place or a thing; rather, consciousness is a fluid, constantly dynamic repetition of states that can alter—or be altered by—image, language, emotions, and will.

5. Because consciousness is integrated and differentiated, because it requires emotions as one "vortex of energy" important to creating structure where no structure normally exists, then will becomes the self-directing agent of consciousness to enact change. Will is learned and developed, not inherent. Theories of will can move beyond the internal/external, mind/body, voluntary/involuntary dichotomies that so often reduce it to "reason" or volition. The opposite of will is the absence of will.

6. Because symbolization, imagination, emotion, consciousness, and will all rely on image, and because image is primarily non-discursive, then the non-discursive can provide a way into the discursive from what is ambivalent, intuitive, unutterable, or ineffable.

These assumptions suggest a proposed writing theory and they do so by suggesting a unique composing model that contrasts with other composing models already mentioned in this study. The aim is to theorize a model of composition that is compatible with these assumptions and that is applicable to writing instruction in rhetoric and composition, but to do so without attempting to master the subject or hold it within an exclusive domain.

Like Aristotle, these theoretical assertions are based upon and asserted by a comfort with probable, not absolute, knowledge.

Non-discursive Theory of Writing

Current process theory and post-process theory offer writing instructors valid, if incomplete, composing models from which to base pedagogy.[2] Few theories, however, attempt to associate themselves overtly with theories of language or consciousness, beginning instead with answers to questions such as "What is good writing?" and "How do we teach rhetoric as epistemic and culturally relevant?" These are good questions, but these are not questions that lead to writing theory as much as they are questions that lead to writing practice. Rhetorical theory, it seems to me, must answer questions such as these as well as others, but rhetorical theory is different than writing theory: the former best answers questions about *what to do* with writing and why, the latter best answers questions about *how to do* writing in the first place.

For too long, writing theory was simply a matter of functional literacy. Then writing theory became about all literacies. In contrast, the point of this project, and the impetus for its creation, was to show how such a view reifies writing, reduces it as a problem or a kind of solution to a problem. Writing, the creation of both discursive and non-discursive text, the symbolization of what is noticed, named, and then connoted and historicized, the management of semblance and image, the constant revision of selves and identities, the fusion of knowledge and the unknown: all of this indicates the larger picture writing inhabits, irregardless of any particular literacy or a particular "cultural reproduction." What we need, and what we currently do not have in rhetoric and composition is a comprehensive writing theory that acknowledges the non-discursive not only as important in and of itself, but also as a possible bridge to creating discursive text.

To put it more directly, I propose a theory of non-discursive writing made of the following five values operating through and with texts, in accordance to the assumptions listed above:

1. **Will-to-Image**: this includes, as a minimum, images of past events and selves, as well as the inclination to move between several disparate worlds: what exists and what does not exist; what is real and what is not real; who the audiences may or may not be; what is or is not expressed; what is material and immaterial, relevant or not, et cetera. The closest to imagination itself, the will-to-image

differs in that it *allows*, or creates a space, for experience to be encoded as topographical dispositions.

2. **Will-to-Improvise**: derived from White's *Kaironomia*, this conception includes not only how to invent in connection to the kairotic moment, but also how to confront failure and play within the dark spaces of the unknown, the unuttered, the ineffable.

3. **Will-to-Intuit**: precisely the ability to disregard reason, this value insists on allowing the power of intuition to dominate over intellect (which, of course, is a false dichotomy). It encourages the role of emotions and feeling. It is the basis for inquiry and investigation. This is the curiosity maker, the hunter, the provisional experiment, the willful accident.

4. **Will-to-Juxtapose**: this value is able to contrast images and thoughts with one another, put them against one another, let them interact with one another, cause them to conflict, agree, disrupt, or collapse. This is the Bakhtinian centripetal force of language, the power of metaphor and simile, the magic of abstraction, the breaking-apart of analysis.

5. **Will-to-Integrate**: the final value is synthesis, connection, parallelism, functionality, materialism, and the ability to coalesce. As the beginning of the transition into discursive text, this is the Bakhtinian centrifugal force in language, the power of development and organization, the strength of concretization, the meaning-making power of unity and coherence.

These values work to create non-discursive text that may or may not be explicated and converted into discursive text. The primary motive here is not exposition or even meaning-making; rather, the primary motive of this theory is disposition, the making of *what is* within a world of becoming. If there is an actual textual product, then there is no need for that product to *do* or *say* anything in particular; rather, at best, these values lead to text that may be translated into discursive representations of meaning. Until then, these values function to generate pure non-discursive symbolization: multimodal, multigenre, and kinesthetic. The purpose of such writing could be to discover or invent the discursive, to create art, to enliven or depict, or any other purpose as appropriate to audience(s). There are no truth claims, no denial of self or emotion. Finally, connections to image, consciousness, and will are nearly direct connections, making any attempt at discursive translation a poor paraphrase, an imposter, a simplification, a dimension shift, a denial of ready explication, and/or a possibility for further non-discursive or discursive text to be in response or in conversation.

These values, then, are not simplifications or a kind of procedural manual for the creation of non-discursive text: rather, they all emphasize their common element, the will. Without will, symbolization becomes a behavioral display, much like the aquatic antics of an otter or the hunting prowess of a lion. Will, through both a collective (or social) and an individual (or historical) consciousness, *guides* and *produces* our symbols toward an end, even if that end is ineffable. These five values are not meant to be taken in any particular order, or as distinct units, or even within a logical framework of any kind. They are provided *discursively* even though their content is obviously non-discursive; this is a shape to a *plan* for non-discursive composing, not the substance or even the comprehensive praxis of such a theory. Much like the five canons of traditional Hellenistic rhetoric, these values come in and out of favor, become stressed with different emphases, and even become interpreted differently as cultures and discourses weave themselves in and around them. The most important ramification of such a theory, then, is to spell out more specifically how non-discursive text intimates with image, emotions, consciousness, and will. In turn, the non-discursive can then move beyond the ambivalences, ambiguities, and failures of discursive text, leading to new inquiry, new theory, and new knowledge.

Will-to-Image

Easily one of the most important values, the will-to-image is, in a sense, the will to experience: this includes both phenomenal as well as noumenal experience. The will-to-image differs from the imagination proper in that it is specific to our ability to construct and deconstruct images at will, whether perceived or not. The imagination proper, as suggested in chapter three, is required for all conscious mental processing and can be said to be the work force behind all the values of this theory. Because image encompasses so much more that simply perception, and because image is a vehicle for more than simply discursive information (including emotional shadings and connections to self and identity), the will-to-imagine works to relieve the inner tension between subject and object. Our will-to-image nourishes observation just as observation nourishes the images we store, recall, and continually revise.

We begin to cogitate because we put images to work, though we may not know what the thoughts mean or how they are connected. Goals are envisioned, plans are made, but the imagination keeps up with the fluidity of consciousness. When partnered with will, imagination is limitless (despite the common cliché "you are limited only by your imagination"), just as the possibilities of language and symbolization are limitless. Rhetors are not just rhetors for an imagined audience; rather, rhetors are rhetors for the imaginations within an imagined audience. This just reiterates why scholarship into non-discursive text is so important.

Because language often puts into matter what it hopes to symbolize, it may be a common understanding that matter comes from the imagination. But such a conception halts what is normally a dynamic cycle: matter into imagination and imagination into matter, etc. Images are integral to this process, and the will-to-image is a baseline requirement for the creation of non-discursive text. One requires the other, even when "matter" is nothing more than the firing of images within our neural cortices. The subtitle to *A Universe of Consciousness* by Edelman and Tononi is *How Matter Becomes Imagination*, and though they never expressly declare it, I interpret this to mean that investigations into consciousness are not unlike investigations into the non-discursive: the content of the imagination becomes the morphed, highly dynamic character of whatever "matter" that presents itself. The conversion of matter into imagination is, in the simplest terms, the process of consciousness. The will-to-image, then, fuels that process.

Images also collect and categorize memories, including memories of past and future events and identities. Since memory is not a playback of images but more a construction of new images based in the current context of consciousness, the will-to-image operates with a backdrop of emotion. The will-to-image, consequently, implies a will to write and rewrite self and identity, continually challenging any notion of a static or single self. As we

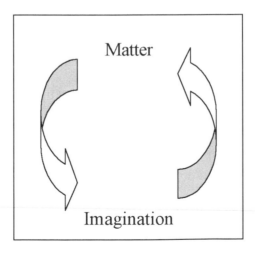

Fig. 4.1 Diagram of the Matter-Imagination Cycle

pull from memories in creating non-discursive text, those memories bring with them emotional images as well as physical or "recollected" images, and then these images come into contact with whatever the content of consciousness happens to be at that moment, altering them. The idea of a "true" or accurate memory is no longer a viable (or even important) one.[3] Imagination is always fused with experience through the reentry pathways that connect past experience with current body maps and present-future possibility. Consequently, the will-to-image may be more difficult or traumatic than it sounds: it risks not only the use and alteration of our experiences with our conception of our experiences, but it also risks challenging our representations of our own memory due to how images exist in the near-present.

Finally, the will-to-image suggests a possibility of alternate worlds of experience and becoming. Rather than will-to-master, as Lynn Worsham suggests, the will-to-imagine is roughly equivalent to the will-to-become:

> Writing brings forth a world, a world of possibility, and opens up a space in Being in which we are invited, not compelled, to dwell along with others, other beings and other things. Moreover, if it is writing and not on the way to some other thing—like a solution figured as knowledge or self—it re-members our connection to the earth. To paraphrase one of Heidegger's most quotable aphorisms on the nature of genuine thinking, writing cuts deep furrows into the soil of Being. (227).

The will-to-image, then is the will to inhabit other worlds of symbolization and ideas, to "dwell with others, other beings and other things." It is a world full of language, and it is also a world waiting for language to be. In concert with consciousness, the will-to-image satisfies our need to symbolize.

Will-to-Improvise

E. C. White's book *Kaironomia: The Will to Invent* makes a strong case already for the use and purpose of the kairotic moment. I want to append to his argument two important distinctions: improvisation is key to non-discursive text just as much, if not more, as discursive text; and improvisation can rely on rules, formulae, even boundaries to keep the energy of the language act moving. As White is quick to often remind us, it is the ability to confound and even avoid the obfuscation caused by reality that renders improvisation so powerful:

> If all knowledge is unforeseeably one-sided, then acceding to the desire for a permanent state of equilibrium would actually preclude

the self's successful adaptation to its environment. Forewarned, then, of the deluded nature of the desire for final truth, the mind must seek constantly to displace itself from its customary centers of meaning. Instead of seeking permanent rest, it must resign itself to a never-ending activity of discharging the desiring tension provoked in the organism in the course of its interaction with its environment [. . . .] Tradition should be understood not as a repository of privileged meanings but as a reservoir of topoi or points of departure for an endless process of improvisation and experiment. (85–86)

This improvisational desire, or will-to-improvise, is exactly what reiteratively seeks, outlines, and attempts to overcome the inherent ambiguity in language. The moment comes and goes, but the will-to-improvise uses each moment as an advantage as consciousness and emotion guide us to possible outcomes, logical or not, discursive or not.

Another important aspect of the will-to-improvise is to cope with the confrontations of feelings, moods, and emotions that are inevitable in language and inquiry. Writing does not guarantee any affect or result. Failure is inevitable if not common: in fact, even in normal discourse, we are so used to having to reword, rephrase, repeat, and even start over that we hardly notice we do it at all. Meanings can be elusive when they are known, so they are especially slippery when—as I the case of non-discursive text—meaning is not the goal at all. The will-to-improvise (coupled in part with the other values) becomes, metaphorically, the will to stare at an abyss and jump. The abyss is the ineffable, the place where language fails, and the leap is the willful undertaking of non-discursive symbolization to generate text even despite the full knowledge that failure may be imminent again.

The second important appendix to White's *Kaironomia* is in the use of rules and structure to aid improvisation. Jazz musicians rely on a progressive cord change they know through experience and practice, and these "changes" allow for a kind of boundary that is useful in improvisation. Though any improvisation is not (nor should it be) always faithful to these rules or boundaries, they can be useful: some work with the guidelines, some work against them, but either way, they provide the will-to-improvise a structure, loose as it is. In discursive writing, the first and most obvious boundary, our set of rules that prove useful to improvisation, is the particular language rules and meanings inherited from generation to generation, all with their own denotations, connotations, and intonations, and many others relating to genre, discipline, and so on. In non-discursive writing, however, the will-to-improvise may work within much looser parameters, using an entire stage or a blank canvas in the shape of a circle, or a particular meter in a poem to guide the improvisation. The point here is that the will-to-improvise might exist within a conceptual structure that serves to create discursive or non-discursive text.

Will-to-Intuit

Intuitive reasoning privileges, if not depends on, the primary and secondary emotions present in consciousness during writing. It is the value of the hunch, the guess, the unsayable, the incommunicable, the kind of reasoning not tied down to logic, rationality, or even relevance: the art of trial and error. Within the world of writing, intuitive reasoning is also connected with desire, with the ability to will yourself into curiosity without the necessity of fanfare or acknowledgment.[4] Intuitive reasoning, as discussed already, depends on the images we form as we navigate in consciousness and emotions. It is a preamble to knowing, a prescience for perception, and a limitless source for transcending time and space within the imagination.

Langer's intuition, as quoted above, is the basis for "all understanding," and this speaks to not only non-discursive text but also discursive text. As texts become discursive, *understanding* text becomes more of a process, a hermeneutic whose operant is more like intuition than enthymemic or syllogistic. Repetition, as a discursive activity, cycles the hermeneutic process toward understanding and attempts to move it out of intuitive thinking and into reason. But in non-discursive text, intuition is the primary means of understanding; repetition only serves to change the amplification of such text, not move it closer to reason. The will-to-intuit, then, is also the will to understand, but not understand in any kind of rational, unemotional sense. If anything, the will-to-intuit works as a clarifying measure, a notation of what has passed and what has yet to come. Intuition, in this way, serves to move our non-discursive text into the emotional tide already present in consciousness. Emotions rule our intuitive image making.

Intuition also incorporates play, or the willful intent to engage the emotions just to see what transpires, what happens. Play is the willful accident; it is the will-to-intuit without the need to justify, defend, or reason. This is why there are strong objections with the conception of will that posits it is a function of having reasons for what we do, reasons why it was done, or reasons for possible consequences. Though such reasons may exist, playful activity in language through intuition is one of the most important aspects of will that does not rely on reason. Consequently, the will-to-intuit becomes similar to the content of dreams: images and emotions guide such a world free of the otherwise learned boundaries and rules associated with "intellect," though it is clear that intellect could not function without intuition and language play.

Finally, the will-to-intuit fosters meaning-making out of seemingly complex or meaningless content. As symbolization occurs, the will-to-intuit anticipates, moves ahead, and avoids conclusion simply by positing infinite alternatives. It has yet to be named or observed, in the past, present, or future. "Suchness," as described earlier by E. C. White, is the way around reality or a problem. The will-to-intuit confers with the will-to-improvise, in order to continue without meaning realized, without an end realized—even without realized purpose.

Will-to-Juxtapose

As texts of either discursive type become realized, they are in themselves self-generative, self-dispositional, and self-explicating. Juxtaposition, the comparison of two things no matter how alike or unlike they are, creates the inner tension Cassirer posited to as the impetus for the origin of language itself. More specifically, the will-to-juxtapose is similar to the function of metaphor: our brains have an uncanny ability to compare anything to anything else, and it can do this non-discursively better than it can do it discursively. As an example, asking a student to write an essay about the south after reading Faulkner is, in a sense, asking the student to make a non-discursive juxtaposition of the two and then convert—or translate—that juxtaposition into discursive text. Through the will-to-intuit, the student may instantly have a felt sense or an intuitive idea of what the comparison is *like*, but no discursive means as of yet to explicate it.[5] The student arrived at that intuitive sense not through a rational compare/contrast topoi, but through an intuitive reaction to a juxtaposition of two very complex images: the image of the South as it exists in that student's consciousness, and the image of Faulker's writings as it exists in that student's consciousness. Non-discursive texts, therefore, generally precede discursive texts, and this is most evident in the will-to-juxtapose.

But comparison is not the only benefit of this canon: it also allows language to fly apart, divide, even collapse as it grapples with its new collaboration of images and thoughts. By juxtaposing two topographical dispositions, new neural connections are made. The brain literally changes composition as it "rewires" itself to accommodate the newly willed semblances.[6] In addition, the very *experience* of such an activity may cause new memory and emotions, new intuited inquiry, even new knowledge. In fact, the scientific method relies a great deal on juxtaposition in order to categorize and classify, just as in non-discursive text juxtaposition is used to conflate or differentiate, subsume or overpower.

Above all, the will-to-juxtapose becomes a way around paradox, the unknown, even the routine. It heightens consciousness because consciousness, as we have seen, relies on both a diversity of neural connections as well as an integration of neural pathways. We begin to abstract, speculate, and confer possible meanings even if none of them sticks for very long. Abstraction, as Berthoff reminds us, is itself a speculative instrument:

Abstracting by means of generalizing goes by many names, of which "reasoning" and "concept formation" are the commonest. Abstracting by means of apprehending gestalts—non-discursively—is characteristic of what Cassirer calls "mythic ideation," in which parts stand for wholes, images bear conceptual significance, and spatial or temporal contiguity represents causality [. . . .] But the essential point is this: generalization requires abstraction, but we can have abstraction without generalization. Abstraction seen as the recognition of form; as the symbolic representation of our recognitions; as enabling, but not requiring generalization—this is the conception of abstraction which can help us think about the composing process and composition dialectically. (*Barricades* 229)

That is to say, as we create juxtapositions, as we make abstractions, we are then on the path to generalization. It becomes clear that as we hover within abstraction without the immediate ability or desire to generalize, we are experiencing the non-discursive in favor of the discursive; as abstraction becomes generalization, especially the kind of generalization Berthoff is talking about here, our text becomes more discursive.

The will-to-juxtapose can vividly present a puzzle the brain is used to grappling with every day as it surveys familiar and unfamiliar faces, even presenting the unknown quickly and easily to the known.[7] In order to write non-discursive text, the will-to-juxtapose contributes to our will-to-intuit in order to grapple with language itself. Keep in mind that these juxtapositions are composed primarily of *images* within language, and images carry with them histories, connotations, emotions, and a diversity of perceptions and open potential. They are not an answer, nor are they necessarily a question. They reside as *what is*, and the will-to-juxtapose opens up myriad possibilities. The will-to-juxtapose is therefore similar to Bakhtin's notion of the centrifugal forces in language: the force inherent in language which works to create ambivalence and confusion as it emanates, propagates, and dissipates into connotations and ambiguities.

Will-to-Integrate

Finally, the will-to-integrate is that feature of non-discursive symbolization that allows for the making of connections and the synthesis of what the text is and what we intend. Integration is a key feature of human consciousness. The reentry systems, or parallel pathways, which connect every portion of our cortex to itself provides a system of self-integration *while at the same time* allowing for differentiation of systems. The will-to-integrate, then forces non-discursive text back towards its center, back to a kind of recursiveness that creates a whole. Without integration and synthesis, non-discursive text may not ever materialize *as text*. We must will ourselves to integrate non-discursive symbolization into textual form if there is to be a manifestation of symbols at all.

However, I do not want to conflate the will-to-integrate too closely with physicality: integration is itself a function of consciousness, and therefore happens all the time *whether or not* we will it into text. It is a natural, fully automatic process that helps to integrate in consciousness the body-state—and, thus, our identity—with the "feeling of what happens." Our will-to-integrate, then, is a mirror of that process, but it is also part of the larger set of processes within symbolization.

Non-discursive text, in particular, may not require integration in terms of audience, however. Though audience is a constant and formidable concern for discursive text, it fades as one among many background moods or experiences consciousness draws upon during image recall or formation. Non-discursive integration is a form of generalization, however, in that it requires connections be made between various worlds, not just comparisons, and then those comparisons are *integrated* into consciousness. Damasio puts it this way:

> Creatures with consciousness have some advantages over those that do not have consciousness. They can establish a link between the world of automatic regulation (the world of basic homeostasis that is interwoven with the proto-self) and the world of imagination (the world in which images of different modalities can be combined to produce novel images of situations that have not yet happened). The world of imagery creations—the world of planning, the world of formulation of scenarios and prediction of outcomes—is linked to the world of the proto-self. The sense of self links forethought, on the one hand, to preexisting automation, on the other [. . . .] I would say that consciousness, as currently designed, constrains the world of the imagination to be first and foremost about the individual, about an individual organism, about the self in the broad sense of the term [. . . .] In short, the power of consciousness comes from the effective connection it establishes between the biological machinery of individual life regulation and the biological machinery of thought. (*Feeling* 303–04)

Damasio is highlighting the action of connection here: the connection between images of self with images of consciousness, or, said differently, the connection between imagination and the world. What Damasio calls the "proto-self" is the images of self that come directly from the body: body states, background feelings, heart rate, level of biological contentment, et cetera. The importance of this passage cannot be fully realized until we consider how often debates in rhetoric and composition, as well as other disciplines, hinge around the question of self and society.[8] What the will-to-integrate suggests, however, is that there must be an intent to connect self with the world, even see the self as *part of the world*, in order for integration to take place. In order for the proto-self and the self to become integrated with consciousness, it must first make these linkages.

Scott Dewitt, in his book *Writing Inventions: Identities, Technologies, Pedagogies*, underscores how important making connections and linkages can be to invention. He explains that linkages or connections create "a mental text of sorts, a link between two or more moments, that begins to pull together their fragmented experience" (23). This "mental text" is, in some ways, the non-discursive text so readily created by the will-to-integrate, and it is this text which may most quickly help writers move from non-discursive thinking to discursive textual production. Damasio's role for consciousness is to put limits on the limitless, to "constrain the world of the imagination" at the level of the "proto-self" in order that we integrate, or as Dewitt says, "pull together" imagery into textual production.

The next section addresses explicitly the way this non-discursive theory of writing can be applied to a composing model for discursive text. As should be abundantly clear by now, the composing model I suggest derives from the assumptions delineated at the beginning of this chapter, and it is but *one* possible composing model among many that may be equally valid.

A Non-discursive to Discursive Composing Model

In order to more clearly suggest how this theory of non-discursive writing can be used as a composing model, it may be necessary first to suggest that a shift in composing models has been underway in rhetoric and composition over at least the last twenty years or so. Genre pressures brought on by changes in technology—and the requirements of professional and civic writing—are actively suggesting changes in the dominantly held composing models within the field, some with more success than others. Unfortunately, much of the groundwork needed for such changes has somehow been neglected, especially in terms of how these composing models reflect changes in writing theory and, consequently, language theory. The main effort of this project has been to reverse this trend, and it is important to begin with language theory before constructing a writing theory and the subsequent composing model.

Like Berthoff's composing model, this model for composing relies on a dynamic conception of composing. This non-discursive/discursive model is a snapshot of what would normally be two independent, continually gyrating

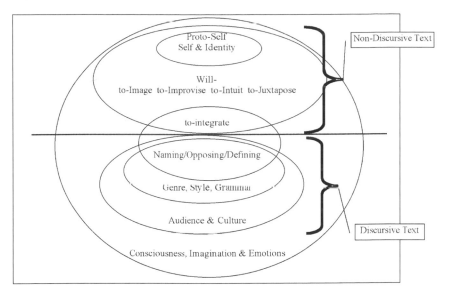

Fig. 4.2 Non-discursive-Discursive Composing Model

spheres. The top half of the diagram illustrates how—within consciousness, imagination and emotions—the non-discursive works with the will to create an epistemology; the bottom half illustrates how—again within the greater sphere of consciousness, imagination, and emotions—the discursive works within rhetorical constraints to create its own epistemology. In this model, the non-discursive and the discursive work together in text generation.

This figure represents the composing model as it moves from non-discursive text to discursive text: from the largely noumenal processes of the sociolinguistic self to the phenomenal processes of the sociolinguistic world. The bridge between these two worlds, as I have suggested earlier, lies in the will-to-integrate found within the non-discursive half of symbolization. It is here that the work of the non-discursive begins to coalesce into a form meaningful (though never an identical translation) to the discursive. The bridge, as represented here by the dotted line, is itself dynamic, shifting up or down as appropriate to the will of the writer.

This composing model provides a conception of writing that is not driven by product *or* process—though, like consciousness, composing remains a process that leads to a product. The main difference between this model and other composing models is that it not only acknowledges the role of image, emotions, will, and consciousness in the writing process, but it centers on them. This model not only suggests a method for moving from the non-discursive to the discursive (or vice versa), but it is also a hermeneutic model which overcomes the classic hermeneutic circle: as we compose (and visit time and again the canons of will illustrated earlier), we also learn how to make discursive text itself rely on image just as our own consciousness relies on image. Technical writing, narrative, poetry, professional writing, hypertext: all these genres of discursive text require, to some extent, images from the writer: pictures, video, graphs, fonts, layout, tables, as well as emotional mood, tone, and voice are only a few of the more obvious examples. Though discursiveness may vary within each of these images, they all become part of the non-discursive image production and consumption within the brain as they are processed, recalled, and "thought" about ("thought" being just one other manipulation of image). This composing model suggests, then, not only a model for process, but also a model for product, and it does so without suggesting the primacy of either one.

No part of this model makes sense, however, outside of the socialpolitical reality of writers as they commune within cultural networks. From the very first discussions about language, it has always been an assumption that language is social, and, what is more, consciousness and will are social. No special attention needs to be given to the social in this model because it is steeped in it: composing requires a social milieu, and as such, every element of this model is touched by it. Material conditions and any other hard "reality" of the writer are reflected within *and* outside the writer's consciousness. One of the areas where the material, historical, and social reality of the writer may affect this composing model the most is in the area of will and identity: constraints caused by hierarchic, paternalistic, imperialist, and any other hegemonic force (structured or not) have a direct impact on will. As already discussed, will is developmental and relative to culture: anything that alters or otherwise changes the way will is learned also affects the way non-discursive and discursive text becomes generated (or not). One challenge and possibility for future research on this composing model is to investigate more closely the connections between culture and will; I maintain that though the method and manifestation of will changes from culture to culture, marginalized group to dominant group, the will itself remains. Perhaps what changes are the amount and the consequences of the shift from the non-discursive to the discursive.

This model does not encourage a particular genre, nor does the model insist on the movement from non-discursive to discursive text. What it does do, however, is clarify the relationships in language between consciousness, image, emotions, and will, and it does so in the effort to suggest a bridge, through integration, between the non-discursive and the discursive. That is not to say, however, that this bridge is crossed once. In fact, the energy in this model relies on the suggestion that the bridge is crossed constantly, in parallel, not as a feedback loop but as an independent cycling of recursive information. Composing models familiar with the benefit of reflection might see some similarity with this movement, but reflection itself is not the goal. As a composer moves from the non-discursive—through identity, the omnipresent image, and the values of will—into integration and the discursive act of naming, opposing, and defining, the composer might continuously be looping back to the non-discursive for each additional image or concept. Like consciousness, this model depends on the *constant* and *varied* interaction of diverse action in order for it to work. The movement from non-discursive to discursive stops as soon as the composer finds reason to dwell in one or the other. For example, a mathematician may be able to compose text (equations and numbers representing only a specialized vocabulary and symbology) *entirely* discursively without the need to cross into the non-discursive, that is until the rational, logical rules of discourse are exhausted and the only way forward is through the will-to-intuit or the will-to-image, etc. At that point, the mathematician is generating text through the *alternation*, the movement back and forth, between the non-discursive and the discursive.[9]

Such independence from genre may be considered a limitation by some: namely in that it does not lead to a specific genre of writing (such as academic discourse), nor does it *necessarily* guarantee features that any particular culture, subculture, or discipline may value in "good" writing. What it does do, however, is posit a model of writing that opens up the connections between image, self, and emotions not as properties of "expressivist" or "creative" writing, but as necessary components to *any* genre of writing. For too long, genre issues have been conflated with compositional issues, so much that separating the two may seem at times impossible. This model sidesteps that issue by simply allowing a composing model that does not privilege the "rational" or the "logical" as the way to create worlds through language. Instead, it opens up possibility unencumbered by dichotomies that have proved divisive and unhelpful in past notions of writing and, especially, consciousness. Reason and logic still have their place, but this model does not *require* discursive text, much less a particular disciplinary genre.

Though any model is open to criticisms on the basis of structuralism, I want to preempt such a critique by repeating three claims: (1) this is only *one possible* model among many possible models derivative of the non-discourse theory of writing; (2) there is no real "structure" or hierarchy here because the model is organic and fluid—it is a snapshot of what could in an instant be altered by consciousness or culture; and (3) inasmuch as this model might suggest a hierarchy (say non-discursive over discursive, or vice versa), the assumptions made at the beginning of this chapter preclude the possibility because they attempt to make it abundantly clear that neither ineffability nor perspicuity is valued over the other in this model: in fact, it might be said that each depends on the other. Any account of this theory as structuralist or "expressivist" or other commonly held dichotomies fails to take into account the assumptions used to create both the theory and the composing model.

The final point regarding this composing model is that it is not a heuristic: a procedural or mechanistic "manual" for generating text. Like any theory essentialized or distilled into its key elements, it may be *used* as a heuristic, but I caution against such an effort. In an article entitled "The Question Concerning Invention: Hermeneutics and the Genesis of Writing," Lynn Worsham reminds us how heuristics often attempt to will us towards mastery rather than towards Being:

> Writing, the work and play of writing, does not happen first of all as a cognitive act of problem-solving, as an act of self-expression, or even an act of creation or discovery of knowledge, though at times can be made to take on all these guises. Writing happens first of all as a hermeneutical process, as an event of disclosure. Writing is a techne, an art, understood in its original sense of 'a bringing forth,' and it brings forth *how*, not *what*, things are and how things *might* be. More subtly, it brings forth allusions to what is conceivable but unrepresentable: The impossible, the other. (236)

As instructors of writing, it is easy to forget how reified a concept of writing is when it is looked at as a skill or something requiring mastery. Writing, the composing of discursive and non-discursive texts, is above else a "bringing forth" because consciousness is a "bringing forth": images into memory, images into identity, images into emotions, images into language. It can point to exposition and explication, but it never *is* because language is multi-layered, multi-modal, and multi-mediated. To reduce such a model to a systematic procedure would be to undo all that the model tries to do for composers: integrate and differentiate.

I would like to suggest that this model serve as a theoretical basis for classes in any number of writing genres: rhetorical analysis and theory, historical research, creative writing, hypertext[10] and cyber-composition, auto-biography, literacy, narrative, work-place writing and professional writing, civic and community writing, film, collage, music, et cetera. It is precisely because of the ability for this theory to be applied to so many modes that I see no benefit in constructing any particular pedagogical practice—there are simply too many possibilities. However, in thinking about texts of all types and modes, and as a precursor to the next chapter on composing multimodality, there are six lessons to take forward as we focus on composing with this new model:.

1. Image is at the center of all symbol-making practice, and symbolization includes both discursive and non-discursive meaning-making.

2. Consciousness and will are tied with image, resulting in the *necessary* presence, acknowledgement, and application of feelings and emotions.

3. Will must be taught and developed, not assumed. In order to get authors to symbolize—whether symbolize through discursive text, non-discursive, or, as in most cases, some combination of the two—rhetors must be taught how to will themselves to symbolize with a particular audience in mind.

4. The social is omnipresent in composition, just as consciousness is omnipresent. Inquiry and invention may be halted because the will-to-intuit, or any other value of non-discursive textual production, may not be valued. All writing can affect change, just as social change can affect consciousness.

5. Audience is as much of a concern for non-discursive rhetoric as it is for discursive rhetoric. All writing requires alternation between the non-discursive and the discursive as the will makes connections between self and the world.

6. The will-to-integrate is a key value available to writers and learners useful in the bridging between non-discursive and discursive text. As we integrate, we compose, and consciousness is always integrating. The act of integrating is similar to the act of composing discursive text once it becomes based in sequential experience.

As an example, a course that utilizes linked communities or community learning environments may decide to begin reading the non-discursive text produced by their respective communities as a way to understand the discursive text produced by that community. Another course focused on research writing may begin to explore the ways images help writers move back and forth between non-discursive text and discursive text in order to discover new paths of inquiry and new ways to integrate archival material. Obviously, some courses currently in existence do this work already, so the only change necessary by writing instructors may be in the way discursive texts are written (i.e., becoming multimodal, multilayered, or multigenre, etc.).

These values are not exhaustive or complete, but they do provide some key features of this theory in context with pedagogical practice. What needs to happen now is the development of specific curricula and syllabi that adopt the non-discursive texts as viable objects of analysis and goals of student production. As new rhetors are required to compose multimodal, multimedia texts, they must become aware of how non-discursive texts carry emotion as much as discursive content with them. Just as the Internet has changed the way texts are distributed, so too has the realization that image, the core of textual production, also carries emotion. Consequently, images always distribute emotion.

Image Consumption, Production, and Distribution

One of the most often cited influences of the importance of image in composition studies comes from the glut of images in cultural texts all around us: from the number of images reproduced on advertising and packaging to the ability to instantly and globally distribute them. This sort of fixation on consumption and distribution does little to help students produce rhetorically astute texts, however, except inundate them with examples and standards.[11] Like textual production of the print era, textual production of the electronic era must take into account consumption and distribution while simultaneously helping students analyze these images as cultural artifacts: texts produced by a culture for a particular audience. Rhetorical analysis becomes ever more important in this context, but traditional, discursive rhetorical analysis can only scrape the surface of these globally produced, globally distributed, and globally consumed images. Students, in short, must be able to become critically aware of the non-discursive elements of these texts; they must also learn how to produce and distribute non-discursive text as well. Just as we teach students to become more critically aware of discursive rhetorics as we have them analyze essays, books, speeches, and dialectic in general, we must also help students become more critically aware of the non-discursive rhetorics that both accompany and, very often, supplement multimodal texts that come in the guise of film, music, photos, food pavilions in shopping malls, and even the design of the spaces they travel through at school, work and home. These rhetorical images have always been consumed, but we have not always asked students to be aware of and critique that consumption; these images have always been produced, but we do not always ask our students to produce them; and these images have always been distributed, but we have not always asked our students to be critically aware of and then participate in the distribution of these images.[12] The only way these students could have the tools they need to do this work is if they understand the importance of non-discursive text, the importance of the emotional charge that accompanies these images, and the way these images are composed to affect a particular audience at a particular time and place (given the correct material resources).

Often, in the context of creating multimodal and multimedia texts, the issue of computer literacy becomes the dominant focus of attention. No doubt, literacy concerns are nearly emblematic of writing concerns: one usually evokes the other. Stuart Selber's book, *Multiliteracies for a Digital Age*, also makes the case that students need to critically consume, produce, and distribute these kinds of multimodal texts. He does this, though, by emphasizing computer literacy specifically, and multiliteracy in general: that computer literacy must engage in a "tripartite framework" that includes "functional literacy, critical literacy, and rhetorical literacy" (28). In turn, these literacies translate into specific kinds of practices in the classroom, notably the "tool metaphor that stresses effective computer use" as functional literacy, the "informed critique" that results from critical literacy, and the "reflective praxis" stressed by rhetorical literacy (24). Taken together, Selber claims that these literacies can help guide a responsible computer literacy program. But such a focus on computer literacy plagues the scholarship on multimodal texts because, as Selber suggests, the conversation too quickly becomes all about the tools of technology and not about the texts themselves: the writing. Gunther Kress's book, *Literacy in the New Media Age*, acknowledges this problem directly:

> It is no longer possible to think about literacy in isolation from a vast array of social, technological and economic factors. Two distinct yet related factors deserve to be particularly highlighted. These are, on the one hand, the broad move from the no centuries-long dominance of writing to the new dominance of the image and, on the other hand, the move from the dominance of the medium of the book to the dominance of the medium of the screen. These two together are producing a revolution in the uses and effects of literacy and of associated means for representing and communicating at every level and in every domain. Together they raise two questions: what is the likely future of literacy, and what are the likely larger-level social and cultural effects of that change? (1)

For Kress, writing is only about creating squiggles on paper (this book refutes that assumption), but his questions about literacy do echo at this particular time in history. The dominance of the image is now acknowledged by semioticians (such as Kress) as well as rhetoricians, and as such, image becomes the central focus of literacy. In order for this to happen, image literacy cannot simply be thought of as a transfer of discursive textual literacies. On the contrary, we must be able to understand and inform our students about image literacies as non-discursive text: the value of emotions in composing, the importance of intuitive logic, the basic forces imbedded in design that are themselves, as Langer says, *articulate*. Kress also emphasizes this in his own way: "In the new making of signs the sign-maker 'supplies meaning' so to speak, whether in the outward production of the sign—in articulation—or in the inward production of the sign—in interpretation" (*Literacy* 170). As images are produced, whether internally or externally, rhetors must be able to manipulate them. Our volition, or activity, in writing these images may or may not result in the intended reaction, but we must be able to enact our will-to-invent, to be active in the rhetor's plan to manipulate the emotions and connotations of meaning that are carried along with these images. Producing image, then, is key to understanding how images are consumed and, to some extent, how they are distributed (or delivered).

In *Multimodal Discourse*, Kress and Van Leeuwen emphasize the consumption, production, and distribution of texts through their "four domains of practice" or "strata": they first divide text into the two strata "design" (which is very much like the non-discursive type of symbolization), "discourse" (which is basically the same as discursive text), and then "production and distribution"—all the while stressing the connections each strata have to the social context (4–7). One of the most interesting consequences of these strata (which are not meant to be hierarchical) is the way in which production itself can be semiotic, as can distribution.

> We want to sketch a multimodal theory of communication based, not on ideas which naturalise the characteristics of semiotic modes by equating sensory channels and semiotic modes, but on an analysis of the specificities and common traits of semiotic modes which takes account of their social, cultural and historical production, of when and how the modes of production are specialized or multi-skilled, hierarchical or team-based, of when and how technologies are specialized or multi-purpose, and so on. (4)

This emphasis on "social, cultural, and historical production" traits distinguishes Kress and Van Leeuwen because they wish to link their strata to previous modes and media. Specifically, in the case of production, performers in music and dance often add their own meaning to what is considered a reproduction of the original composition. Kress and Van Leeuwen correctly emphasize that the performance itself is not just a reproduction of the original score or choreography: that each musician, each dancer interprets and then *performs* meaning into these texts (7). But this meaning is not a function of the production or the composition of these texts. In some cases, they may be interpretations, but just as readers create their own texts when they read a story or a poem (which, I maintain, is another example of the performance of these texts), these musicians and dancers are actually creating their own texts in their performance. At best, we acknowledge the extent to which these texts are intertextual with the composer and the director (and other musicians), or the extent to which the dancers are intertextual with some influences from the choreographer or musicians (or other dancers). In the production of text, then, the "original" discourse and design (to use terminology from Kress and Van Leeuwen) are not pristine layers (or strata) that undergird production layers. Instead, these layers are all changed; the text is changed. It is no longer the originally layered act of meaning-making: it is an entirely new one. What have changed, in part, are the non-discursive texts that make up that production.

The same can be said of distribution: not only is distribution semiotic (according to Kress and Van Leeuwen), but distribution also *changes* the text itself and, thus, its ability to make meaning. In the case of digital technology, distribution may affect the quality of video and audio that accompanies the text due to various compression algorithms. As a consequence, the technologies themselves may become non-discursive symbols used in future textual production: the grainy texture of Super-8 film reproduced in a digital film in order to give it a sense of age; the smeared typeface of a letter to give it a sense of informality or the rebelliousness of underground printing techniques. Kress and Van Leeuwen mention how distribution imparts its own level of meaning this way:

> Just how different the reproduction is from the original, just how many dimensions of sensory experience it lacks, and how many elements of "noise" it adds, is then conveniently forgotten—until the next technical improvement comes along, and we can suddenly no longer disattend the scratching of the record or the absence of colour which, only yesterday, did not trouble us." (88)

The troubling symbolization is actually a tool for non-discursive symbolization to encode various shades of meaning to the distribution of any given text. Not only is the text, to use Bolter's term, "remediated" from an older technology, but the identifiable character of the older technology becomes a tool for textual production.[13] It is therefore the case that distribution is not meaningful because it just adds a layer, or strata, as a "domain of practice": distribution is meaningful because it adds non-discursive text.

But what about adding non-discursive meaning through consumption? It might not be entirely obvious how consumption creates meaning, much less how consumption itself may be written as non-discursive text. Walter Benjamin's essay "Unpacking My Library" might help to explain how the act of collecting, or the collection itself, can be read:

> [T]here is in the life of a collector a dialectical tension between the poles of disorder and order. Naturally, his existence is tied to many other things as well: to a very mysterious relationship to ownership [. . .] also, to a relationship to objects which does not emphasize their functional, utilitarian value—that is, their usefulness—but studies and loves them as the scene, the stage, of their fate [. . . .] Everything remembered and thought, everything conscious, becomes the pedestal, the frame, the base, the lock of his property. (60)

Benjamin's focus on the collector emphasizes the affective connections the collector has to the objects: the memories associated with each member of the collection. If a text is a collection of symbols to be read, then the collections of things we consume are also texts.[14] Like all texts, some are more ephemeral than others, but the collection holds meaning both for and about the collector:

> [T]he phenomenon of collecting loses its meaning as it loses its personal owner. Even though public collections may be less objectionable socially and more useful academically than private collections, the objects get their due only in the latter [. . . .] for a collector—and I mean a real collector, a collector as he ought to be—ownership is the most intimate relationship that one can have to objects. Not that they come alive in him; it is he who lives in them. (67)

The collection becomes a textual representative for the collector. As such, we imbue in any collection meaning about the collector, as well as the culture in which the collector lived.

Perhaps the non-discursive meaning a collection imparts is the most obvious in archeology and architecture. The artifacts that archeology uses to infer the lives of people and cultures long gone are basically the remnants of the collections of things in their lives. Some of those things were made by the people being studied for very practical purposes (as in the case of pots and tools), while others things uncovered by archeologists were made for less practical, even ceremonial purposes (art, burial clothing, masks).

Still, even other artifacts shine a light on the habits and customs of the people in question. It is the collection of what endures that presents a text for archeologists to read, interpret, and come to know. These texts survive only because they were once objects of consumption, and they teach us even divorced from millennia of context.

Similarly, architecture is text; cities and towns are collections of these texts, and they produce and distribute non-discursive meaning. Not only do individual houses say something about the way people live (or lived), so too is it the case that it must accommodate what people are likely to bring into the house. Today, for example, we build houses to accommodate cars, computers, entertainment systems, dishwashers, and the entire "hidden" infrastructure needed to support these items. A blueprint, in other words, can not only reflect the values and living practices of those who consume, but also indicate what consumables are more or less important based on what is given some measure of priority in resources (cost, space, complexity, etc.)—even the white space in web pages can be read as rhetorical.[15] Historians have used maps of cities to "read" the histories of those cities, just as a city itself can represent a collection of architectural texts. Michel de Certeau's "Walking in the City" observes the cityscape of New York is a similar fashion:

> To be lifted to the summit [. . .] is to be lifted out of the city's grasp.
> one's body is no longer clasped by the streets that turn and return
> it according to an anonymous law; nor is it possessed, whether
> as player or played, by the rumble of so many differences and by
> the nervousness of New York traffic. When one goes up there, he
> leaves behind the mass that carries off and mixes up in itself any
> identity of authors or spectators [. . .] His elevation transfigures
> him into a voyeur. It puts him at a distance. It transforms the
> bewitching world by which one was "possessed" into a text that
> lies before one's eyes. It allows one to read it, to be a solar Eye,
> looking down like a god. (92)

For Certeau, the act of walking down the streets and alleys of the city is an act of writing: "they are walkers, *Wandersmänner,* whose bodies follow the thicks and thins of an urban 'text' the write without being able to read it" (93). That is to say that the city itself becomes a text in our viewing of it as well as in our experience of it. The collected buildings, even the icons to mass consumerism itself, become non-discursive texts, as do our paths through them.

Images are produced, consumed, and delivered in an increasingly astounding variety. It is fallacious to think, however, that we somehow encounter more images now than before, and it is also misleading to think of text as having a static set of layers, or strata, when in fact what is really at issue is the non-discursive text itself and the meaning it makes as text. Multimodality is a realization of the complexity of text among these three cultural realities: all texts are produced, delivered, and consumed, therefore all texts are multimodal (never mind the ubiquitous presence of non-discursive texts among and between even the most discursive texts).[16] Since this is the case, and since non-discursive textual production is so often eclipsed by discursive textual production, then the question remains: How do we teach students to value non-discursive text while composing multimodal texts? Is there a composing model, or map, that can represent the relationships between symbolization practices, image, consciousness, and will?

CHAPTER 5

Composing Multimodality

*A*nne Cranny-Fancis, in *Multimedia: Texts and Contexts*, reinforces the cultural and spatial aspects of multimodality by describing the landscape of multimedia as the "cartography of contemporary meaning-making" (5). What I like about this description is the locus it creates in space around meaning-making. Creating texts made of several modes and media is nothing new, but thinking of writing and composing as a kind of cartography implies just how much contemporary writing is not simply the alphacentric literacies of verbal language on paper: not just the application of an alphabet on paper. Cartography acknowledges space and the graphical metaphors employed in that space. Cartography acknowledges writing in the recent era of multimodal composition.

Up to this point I have tried to emphasize how image is at the center of everything we do with our symbol systems: image drives composing just as it provides the mechanisms the brain needs to compose thought. Our sensory systems do many things for us, not the least of which is to provide the input and output for our symbol systems. I realize this metaphor is extremely mechanistic, but it must be remembered that, if we are to teach multimodal composition and multimedia, we must be able to also broaden our notion of writing to the kind of composing done in and among any set of modes and media.[1] No longer can writing remain as merely the enactment of alphacentric literacies because it is no longer the case that monomodal, alphanumeric texts encompass the entirety of textual production. The map itself is made up of sounds, textures, visuals, smells, and tastes—all in increasing combinations, all in increasingly instantaneous delivery. This book establishes image and its various sensual constituents as the main compositional element for all textual production because once image is understood as any type of mental formulation based in our available senses in this world, it can become the most important rhetorical tool to any kind of textual production. Instead of breaking rhetoric up into visual rhetoric and aural rhetoric, et cetera (rhetorics based on their modes and media which, ultimately, are usually always already mixed or hybrid), we can talk of discursive rhetoric and non-discursive rhetoric: the former concerned with those modes and media that create discursive meaning; the latter concerned with those modes and media that create non-discursive meaning. Both are used in composition, both become exhibited to one degree or another in most forms of textual production. Because discursive meaning and discursive rhetorics are already, for the most part, well established and exhaustively discussed (partly due to disciplinary boundaries in the academy), it falls to this book to help establish composing practices for non-discursive texts (or elements) relevant to multisensory texts.[2]

It is now possible to suggest ways that image itself can become important to composing multimodality. This chapter establishes some basic guidelines for designing text of various modes while emphasizing image as the rhetorical touchstone. It differs from the last chapter in that it does not directly address invention; rather, the purpose of this chapter is to help practitioners encourage students to produce multimodal texts: to encourage the process of composition using textual modes that are, themselves, nonverbal: pictures, words, colors, drawings, sounds, et cetera.

Naturally, there may be resistance to this notion of the writing classroom. Some might oppose the goals of such assignments based on image on disciplinary grounds (i.e., we do not teach the visual arts, etc.). But implicit in this book is a breaking down of such artificial barriers: asking students to begin composing image is, on the one hand, not too different than what we already ask of students—asking students to write so that they form "clear" sentences so that they might construct a "clear" argument in the hope that it will form "clear" images in the mind of the reader is also a type of composition through image. Many of the pedagogical and process-oriented steps we ask students to undergo in writing traditional, discursive texts are in fact a type of composition that helps the reader form images related to claim-making. To value interdisciplinarity is to value the work of other disciplines, and this includes art. To claim that only art deals directly with the visual is as obviously shortsighted as to claim that only the empiricism of the scientific method is epistemic, or that only the social sciences can effectively research cultures and societies. Writing and rhetoric scholarship has long been interdisciplinary, but the discursive bias among writing teachers may be our most difficult challenge in encouraging multimodality in writing classrooms: too many teachers insist that writing the essay (itself a relatively anomalous textual mode) is the only way to get at critical analysis, close reading, research praxis, cultural criticism, and the principles of rhetoric. Not only can multimodal composition exercise these laudable goals, multimodal composition can do much more: acknowledge and build into our writing processes the importance of emotions in textual production, consumption, and distribution; encourage digital literacy as well as nondigital literacy in textual practice; and develop rhetorical skills that are more closely aligned with the rhetorical methods students experience on a daily basis. As Stuart Selber notes in the Epilogue of *Multiliteracies for a Digital Age*,

> If students are to become agents of positive change, they will need an education that is comprehensive and truly relevant to a digital age in which much of the instructional agenda seems to be little more than indoctrination into the value systems of the dominant computer culture [. . . .] such an approach simply replaces one literacy for another; it fails to expose students to the wide array of literacies they will need in order to participate fully and productively in the technological dimensions of their professional and personal lives. (234)

This agency is a goal for all compositionists, and by bringing multiliteracies into the composition classroom, the full complexity—rather than a reductionism or simplicity—of writing rhetorically becomes more available to students.[3]

Other than instruction in the mere mechanics of print-based writing, writing teachers are already suited to ask students to compose rhetorically, and students must learn to do so using any type of textual symbolization that is effective for academic, civic, and workplace environments. Anne Frances Wysocki, in her excellent book *Writing New Media: Theory and Applications for Expanding the Teaching of Composition*, also makes this point—a point worth repeating at length here:

> This, then, is why it matters for writing teachers to be doing more with new media: writing teachers are already practiced with helping others understand how writing—as print-based practice—is embedded among the relations of agency and extensive material practices and structures that are our lives. Writing teachers help others consider how the choices we make in producing a text necessarily situate us (or can try to avoid situating us) in the midst of ongoing, concrete, and continually up-for-grabs decisions about the shapes of our lives. Writing teachers can fill a large gap in current scholarships on new media; they can bring to new media texts a humane and thoughtful attention to materiality, production, and consumption, which is currently missing. (7)

Writing and rhetoric teachers are indeed the perfect place for this kind of instruction, as long as they take into account the unavoidable, and powerful, use of non-discursive text as well. As Cynthia Self states in her contribution to the same book, we must teach new media texts also because "students are doing so—and their enthusiasm about reading/viewing/interacting with and composing/designing/authoring such imaginative texts percolates through the substrata of composition classrooms, in direct contrast to students' *laissez faire* attitudes toward more conventional texts" (44). Writing teachers are suited for this kind of work and writing students are excited about this kind of textual production.

The Rhetorical Image

There can be no controversy in asserting that photos, typefaces, colors, spaces, or soundtracks are rhetorical. Each of these could all be experience by a single movie trailer advertising the next box office oriented film: the quick succession of scenes and character shots, the exaggerated typefaces with dripping animations and color, the darkness of the theater and smell of popcorn, the chest-thumping surround sound of the soundtrack and sound effects, et cetera. Each of these is composed, each of these is intended to persuade, each of these are images, each of these (and their collective) is rhetorical.

As implied earlier, image studies is currently gaining ground in composition, though it seems to be doing so without a comprehensive theoretical framework specific to writing or any specific attention to non-discursive text. Steve Westbrook's article, "Visual Rhetoric in a Culture of Fear: Impediments to Multimedia Production" emphasizes just how much rhetoric and composition has seemingly embraced the image without enacting pedagogies that ask students to produce multiliterate texts:

> Ten of the more popular textbooks concerned with visual rhetoric— *Beyond Words* (Ruszkiewicz, Anderson, and Friend); *Seeing and Writing 2* (McQuade and McQuade); *Frames of Mind* (DiYanni and Hoy); *Picturing Texts* (Faigley, George, Palchik, and Selfe); *Practices of Looking* (Sturken and Cartwright); *Ways of Reading Words and Images* (Bartholomae and Petrosky); *Everything's an Argument* (Lunsford and Ruszkiewicz); *Reading Culture* (George and Trimbur); *Writing in a Visual Age* (Odell and Katz); and *Designing Writing* (Palmquist)— contain a total of 2,620 prompts. of these 2,620 prompts, only 143, or roughly 5 percent, require students to engage in multimedia or visual production [. . . .] Only *Writing in a Visual Age* offers students consistent and flexible opportunities to produce visual texts in the majority of its large-scale assignments. (461–62)

One text not mentioned here, Robert Atwan's *Convergences: Message, Method, and Medium*, takes a more rhetorical look at the relationship between image and word in popular culture by stressing the rhetorical methods involved *and* the various media used. Like Westbrook's comment that many of these new textbooks stress reading over producing, so does this one. But I am not altogether convinced that asking students to become more adept at reading texts of various media is not worthwhile, as long as students also get a chance to produce multimodal texts (which is the case in *Convergences*). What is important here is that rhetoric and composition is changing not so much because we are doing anything very different (we are still teaching rhetoric and textual production); rather, what continues to change most dramatically is the interaction acknowledged between diverse modes of text, both produced and consumed. Even so, we can do more as writing teachers to ask that students produce these diverse and interactive texts all the while remaining centered on the rhetoricity of the image.

There has also been a remarkable increase over the last few years in the number of presentations at CCCC dealing directly with image, or multiliteracies, in addition to a few conferences specifically focused on image and image studies.[4] Journals in the field such as *Computers and Composition* and online journals such as *Enculturation* and *Kairos* both have featured issues dedicated to the visual domain, image and text, and multiliteracies. In addition, there seems to be a recent increase in scholarship on image within the field, especially how image is related to multimodal rhetoric and multimedia.[5]

But what seems lacking in this trend in scholarship is a theory of composing that frames work on the image in a way as to not limit or sacrifice the complexity and inherent legitimacy of non-discursive symbolization for a reduced view of textual production. In the end, one of the most vital roles for images is that they thrive in the domain of the unutterable or unsayable; consequently, composing using discursive text at these moments may actually be more difficult than composing using non-discursive text. Such a view of symbolization would then be capable of accounting for both the discursive and non-discursive aspects of human activity—one that responds to current demands that writing pedagogy include the multisensory, multigenre, and multimedia composition practices.

Specifically, image studies might provide a response to a challenge Lynn Worsham voiced in 1987. Specifically, she calls for a "new" writing experience, one that is limitless and complex:

A new theory or a new system, or even a meta-system accounting for a multiplicity of theories and systems, at this point of our history, is nothing particularly new. What would be new is an experience of writing, of "literacy," if you will, that brings to pass an awareness of the limits of literacy, an **awareness of the non-discursive elements** in the event of signification. Such writing would tend to contradict or, better yet, seriously complicate, our conventional or stereotypical notions of literacy: It would be the kind of writing that seeks not so much the conceptual and abstract but the sensuous and emotional. It would seek not the truth of propositions but the rigor of possibility and the nuance of the impossible. It would seek not the distance of generalization and objectivity but the nearness of involvement. (236, bold my emphasis)

What Worsham seems to be requesting here is a paradox: she acknowledges that a "new theory" or "new system" would only reproduce the problems of invention experienced to date, while at the same time describing "what would be new" in terms of a theory: one that is "non-discursive": one that is "sensuous and emotional." This book on image attempts to work through this paradox by describing just this kind of nonsystematic theory that captures the "experience of writing," one that points to image and the non-discursive as crucial to the act of writing (and thinking), while, at the same time, authorizing the affective domain as integral to the "sensuous and emotional" aspect and content of the symbols themselves. This book, therefore, attempts to answer Worsham's call by uniting image and emotions through non-discursive rhetoric.

In order to write the "nuance of the impossible," as Worsham put it, the first thing we must do is allow the rhetorical image to become the center of our pedagogical practice. *Eloquent Images*, an anthology edited by Mary Hocks and Michelle Kendrick dedicated to the importance of image to writing, weaves together image, new media, and the importance of "design practice" in this way:

> [A]s each chapter in this volume outlines specific forms of design and practice, it delineates part of that complex stratification of functioning that constitutes new media's "play" in our digital machines. By looking at new media theories and instances of practice within the stratified, conflicting networks of interpretation, the authors in this volume present important new ways to be nonmodern. Specific instances can move us beyond the merely theoretical to interpret and to create with a fully hybrid eloquence, and the examples offered in the chapters that follow become those everyday practices that enact the verbal and visual complexity of new media. (14)

This effort towards "hybrid eloquence" is reminiscent of Langer's insistence that visual forms are also articulate: eloquence is not a term owned by discursive text, nor is it necessarily monomodal. Eloquence, especially in this anthology, may actually come from the hybridity characteristic of multimodal texts: various media interacting in individually incomplete or incoherent ways that, when taken as a whole, become articulate.[6] Obviously, such a perspective would require the field to stretch its boundaries, a process that has often taken place in the past. In doing so, new knowledge gets integrated while making room for even more. Amy Ione, in *Innovation and Visualization: Trajectories, Strategies, and Myths*, suggests how such stretching works:

> Initial boundaries, I would propose, take form to help us define what is known. Then, as we learn to know more about what we are exploring and what remains unknown, we can once again design a map to bring a tangible quality to emerging information. The beauty of this exercise of stretching our boundaries is that it shows that newly conceived maps can display quantitative and qualitative perspectives, can help shift our understanding of the boundaries and can allow us to bracket information as we inquire—over and over again. Each time we do so we perceive what is "known" and what remains "unknown." Thus the maps are flexible forms. And, as the twentieth-first century unfolds, it is clear that human consciousness has filtered through many maps over the centuries. Our process in effect indicates that boundaries are useful, but they are not static. They also retreat and change location. (154)

Boundaries in discipline identity, boundaries in textual production, boundaries in language and writing: all of these are being stretched by image studies. Like rhetorical theory, it can seem as though "everything is image" in theorizing about non-discursive text, and that may very well be the case. But in stretching these boundaries, vast and newly available areas become apparent: theoretical explorations of new and potentially revolutionary maps shift us into unknown potential. For the rhetorical image to become the center of our pedagogical practice, our current boundaries must stretch.

Another reason image production must become the defining characteristic of what we do as writing teachers is because image, as already discussed, in chapter 3, is not just a visual object to be perceived by the eye. Not only is image primarily non-discursive, it is also a vehicle for the emotions and a building block of imagination and thought. Ron Burnett's book, *How Images Think*, underscores the connection image has to neuroscience and to culture:

As more knowledge is gained about the human mind, embodied
and holistic, the role of culture and images has changed. Images
are no longer just representations or interpreters of human actions.
They have become central to every activity that connects humans
to each other and to technology—mediators, progenitors, interfaces—as much reference points for information and knowledge as
visualizations of human activity [. . . .] In particular, the issues of
how images are used to explain biological processes needs to be
framed by cultural argument and cultural criticism. (xiv–xv)

Burnett is addressing image both as a methodological tool and image as a
rhetorical tool: image may function as a set of topographical representations
(as Damasio maintains), but when these images are connected with human
behavior, Burnett's book insists that they must be contextualized in culture.
This only reinforces the insistence that humanists attend to images even as
we compose with them. If we do not, other disciplines will.

In his pivotal work on the changing nature of English studies and the
encroachment of electronic texts into the humanities, Richard Lanham's *The
Electronic Word: Democracy, Technology, and the Arts* makes the point that new
technology demands change in English studies:

So far as I see it, our instinctive posture has been defensive, based
on the book and the curricular and professional structures that issue
from it. We conceive the humanities as a pickle factory preserving
human values too tender and inert for the outside world [. . . .]
The harsh world wants to imagine a finer world and we pretend
to dwell in it. But our students and the society from which they
come will not permit this illusion to continue unchanged; nor will
a technology that has volatilized print; nor will our own thinking,
our "theory," about what we are and do. All these are asking us to
think systemically about literary study, to model it from kindergarten
through graduate school [. . . .] We are being asked to explain how
the humanities humanize. (25)

The field of rhetoric and composition also seems to suggest its own kind
of "pickle factory," one that places printed, discursive text in the center of
everything we do. Clearly, students and the world we live in (that includes
blogs, podcasts, modular community web spaces, cell phone messaging, and,
soon, electronic paper) demand otherwise. We must not only encourage
our students to think rhetorically about these new and not-so-new texts,
but we must ask them to produce them with deliberate rhetorical aims in
mind. Cultural changes, as Lanham suggests, refocus writing theory toward
the image: "electronic writing brings a complete renegotiation of the alpha-

bct/icon ratio upon which print-based thought is built," adding "[w]e can detect this foregrounding of images over written words most clearly in the world of business and government communications, but it is happening everywhere" (34).

The emphasis on image and culture requires a kind of non-discursive rhetorical analysis: the parsing and translating of non-discursive textual products and elements into focused claims of argument. For Burnett, this means rhetorical images become "both the outcome and progenitors of vast and interconnected image-worlds" (3). Just as Scharfstein links ambiguity and the ineffable to worlds which are too complex and layered for discursive logic, Burnett admits that "the challenge" with images is converting them into discursive versions of themselves: "to map the experiences of interacting with images into a process that is discursive, intellectual, and emotional so that it can be understood and applied to the viewing process" (7). But as students must interact with these "image-worlds," they must learn how and why images work the way they do: they must learn to read images, sure, but they also must learn how to compose with image, to create their own "image-worlds" that are rhetorical:

> spectators have "evolved" beyond the parameters of viewing in the sense of distance and separation, "the images over there"—to living within the confines of a world where images in the broadest sense intersect with the real at all times. (42)

Burnett also links image to the imagination in that "[t]o be within images is not to be suffocated by them; rather, images are vistas on the brilliance of the human imagination and perhaps this is why images are simultaneously loved, desired, and feared" (42–43). The rhetorical image can become a keystone to all forms of textual production: whether discursive or non-discursive. Image, in short, works at the elemental level of the mind/brain and, as a consequence, at the elemental level of all textual production.

As image and non-discursive rhetoric become applied to more traditional forms, questions about how image can create arguments are inevitable. In truth, no type of text can construct arguments without some knowledge of the targeted audience—whether that text is discursive or non-discursive. Moreover, by virtue of the fact that non-discursive texts are defined as nonlinear and independent on the text that precedes it, argument thought of only as a set of enthymemic or syllogistic propositions is difficult to imagine. But argument is bigger than a set of propositions: images can construct arguments because images carry with them much more than objectified text—emotional connections and connotations pervade image, and given the tendency towards hybridity, image functions well among all textual modes. Because, as Richard Fulkerson suggests, "it is crucial that students learn to participate effectively in argumentation as cooperative, dialectical exchange and a search for mutually acceptable (and contingent) answers," and given enough information about audience and what constitutes "mutually acceptable," image is an ideal conveyor of informal logic, especially in terms of how argumentation relates to digital media and non-discursive texts (17). Locke Carter's article, "Argument in Hypertext: Writing Strategies and the Problem of Order in a Nonsequential World" addresses the problem of order in hypertext, and the problems such a nonlinear structure poses for constructing arguments:

> Syllogisms and analytic rules might be well-suited for certain sciences and pure math, but common sense will show even the most brazen skeptic that the vast majority of arguments are conducted successfully day to day based on something else. Everyday argument must be based not on the rules of formal logic, but on a kind of informal logic. This reasoning is always dependent on the audience to whom arguments are addressed. (6)

What exactly this "informal logic" is has been variously theorized, but I like how Langer talks about this idea using the term "intuitive logic" mentioned in chapter one—a kind of logic based not entirely on abstract symbols but also on lived experiences. In the end, the term argumentation itself is constantly blurred with exceptions and adaptations that conform more closely to our lived experiences of discourse.

Different modes used in composing multimedia benefit rhetorically from the non-discursive, emotionally charged image. If text could be purely discursive (a questionable notion all by itself, but such text might be said to exist as computer code—though even computer code is eventually translated into to machine code which later becomes electronic representations of voltage), then such a text becomes a *doxa* reflective of its programmers rather than an *episteme* tested and validated by the polis. Discursive text must rely on what comes before to construct meaning; non-discursive text is already articulate, creating meaning all at once. I argue here that the rhetorical image is not only a valuable tool in textual production but also the vehicle from which belief becomes lived experience. Image alters our brain, both in the pathways it constructs and the topographical representations it assembles. Non-discursive rhetoric actually makes knowledge *livable* in that it places knowledge in the realm of the senses rather than just in the realm of increasing abstraction. Further, when it comes to make the case of justice and ethical behavior, doxa alone is rarely sufficiently convincing. It is not so much the case that images are more or less imbued with rhetoric to be effective: rather, it may be the case that rhetoric is more or less imbued with image to be effective.

Values of Multimodality

By no means intended to be exhaustive, this section sets out to derive a few general values of multimodality implied by the four values of non-discursive text listed in the previous chapters. Some values—such as unity, juxtaposition and perspective—seem closely related to discursive practices already well-known and familiar to compositionists. Other values—such as image and layering—are less well-known and are closely related to non-discursive practices. Once established, these five values provide a way for teachers to integrate multimodal composing with their learning objectives.

Though textual production in multimedia is often composed of several modes (i.e., different types of text such as audio, video, print, texture, image, color, etc.), there are some values that become important to an author (or composer) because they hold particular importance and produce various options. These values of multimedia are not principles or rules or dictums or anything very solid or procedural for a very good reason: they produce meaning, but in no way can any particular application of these values produce predictable results. In the end, these elements are "values" because, as authors, we value what they can do for us during textual production. They can be metaphorical, or synecdochical, or simply sensual, but they are only tools from which we carve meaning using many different modes of production. Just as support and elaboration are values of print-based texts because they employ the defining characteristics of discursive text, so too are these five values valuable to non-discursive text.

Though most of these values may seem to be most relevant to visual forms of image and multimodal text, I must emphasize that I intend them here to be relevant to all forms of images: to multisensory textual production. The term "design" has come to mean many things in recent years: from engineering design to sound design to bedroom design. We often think of the word in disciplinary terms, such as graphic design or architectural design. John Heskett's book, *Toothpicks & Logos: Design in Everyday Life*, underscores the difficulty with the term:

> To suggest that design is a serious matter in that sense, however, is problematic. It runs counter to widespread media coverage assigning it to a lightweight, decorative role of little consequence: fun and entertaining—possibly; useful in a marginal manner—maybe; profitable in economic sectors dominated by rapid cycles of modishness and redundancy; but of no real substance in basic questions of existence [. . . .] Design sits uncomfortably between these two extremes. As a word it is common enough, but it is full of incongruities, has innumerable manifestations, and lacks boundaries that give it clarity and definition. As a practice, design generates vast

quantities of material, much of it ephemeral, only a small proportion of which has enduring quality. (2–3)

What should be clear by now is that design is just another word for composition. All denotations and connotations aside, design is the act of putting together with intent, and that is exactly what students must do no matter if they are writing the most traditional type of academic essay, or if they are creating a poster for a local event. Heskett says it best:

> Beyond all the confusion created by the froth and bubble of advertising and publicity, beyond the visual pyrotechnics of virtuoso designers seeking stardom, beyond the pronouncements of design gurus and the snake-oil salesmen of lifestyles, lies a simple truth. Design is one of the basic characteristics of what it is to be human, and an essential determinant of the quality of human life. It affects everyone in every detail of every aspect of what they do throughout each day. As such, it matters profoundly. (3–4)

What we are doing as writing teachers is effected by design—it always has been (anyone who has ever taught Modern Language or American Psychological Association formatting guidelines knows this has been the case). Composing, or designing, multimodal texts requires writing teachers to stress design issues that have otherwise been dictated to them by editors, printers, or disciplinary guidelines. Therefore, what follows is a brief list of those values we must teach students if they are to explore non-discursive textual production, and, consequently, become rhetors of multimedia.

Image

As I have suggested already, image is central to textual production. But in terms of composing non-discursive texts, students need to be taught how to use image in their rhetorical practice. Just as any creative writing workshop will necessarily instruct students, by example as well as through specific exercises, the importance and value of constructing images using printed text, so too must multimodal teachers instruct students how to read and write images. Even students, who are long-time camera users and have taken photographs for years, few of these students actually learn to *compose* these photographs, through the lens, darkroom, or image editing software. The composition of a photo is a good place to start talking about image because students need to learn how images are constructed, altered, realtered, and rhetorically invented. Photographs are by no means new to students, but thinking about how they might be used to create an argument probably is new. Web texts, hypermedia, advertisements in newspapers and magazines, icons, even charts and diagrams: visual image as a textual product is ubiquitous. But it is also important to have students think about all the multisensory images that are out there: the smell of a popcorn booth at a carnival, the texture of a glossy magazine, the swell of strings during a romantic scene in a film, the combination of flavors during a meal of fine cuisine. All of these image rhetorics can be persuasive, and the operative rhetoric doing the persuasion is non-discursive. Burke's *identification* is especially at work in such cases:

> You persuade a man only insofar as you can talk his language by speech, gesture, tonality, order, image, attitude, idea, *identifying* your ways with his. Persuasion by flattery is but a special case of persuasion in general. But flattery can safely serve as our paradigm if we systematically widen its meaning, to see behind it the conditions of identification and consubstantiality in general. And you give the "signs" of such consubstantiality by deference to an audience's "opinions." For the orator, following Aristotle and Cicero, will seek to display the appropriate "signs" of character needed to earn the audience's good will. (55–56)

For students to identify with their audience, to build consubstantiality (or rapport) with them, they need to see how images are themselves part of the rhetoric: the clothing and grooming of the speaker, the banner in the background, the elegance of the speakers gesture: all forms of non-discursive text. David Blakesley, in *The Elements of Dramatism*, points out that Burke's, "primary aim of rhetoric is identification":

> Burke believes that in any rhetorical situation there is always a dialectical struggle between the forces of identification and division. People can never be identical or divided in the absolute sense. We have bodies and experiences and a common language, each of which can help us identify with each other. Yet we also have unique experiences that we may interpret differently from others, keeping us divided. (15)

If identification and division are the two forces central to rhetoric, then it is obvious that image may function in either capacity, depending on the rhetor's intent. Each image carries with it a package of emotions, histories, and experiences, and as such, may function for one audience as identification, and for another, division. Either way, images are powerful symbols no matter what sense organs perceive them.

Blakesley also points out how images are themselves, like any type of symbolization, a kind of "terministic screen." In *Language as Symbolic Action*, Burke defines a terministic screen as the use of language to "direct the attention": "Even if any given terminology is a *reflection* of reality, by its very nature as a terminology it must be a *selection* of reality; and to this extent it must function as a *deflection* of reality" (45). Putting aside for a moment the definition or nature of the term "reality," Burke is obviously pointing out the opportunity costs of language: that to notice or attend means that we are also not noticing and not attending the other. Burke uses photography as an example: the same object photographed several times with different filters provides a metaphor for how selection and composition are themselves meaning-making activities. Blakesley suggests this function of image to be an interpretation of reality:

> [A] photograph functions much like a terministic screen. It is a distillation, a selection of the photographer's visual field that may or may not be entirely representative of the whole panorama or of its subject. A photograph can help us see a subject in new ways, but it cannot help us see it in *all* ways [. . . .] An image is a subjective phenomenon, conjured in the interface between the object and the viewer. An image involves an act, in other words. It is common to think of the imagination as that process of mind chiefly responsible for making images out of experience, words, emotions, and even the visual world. An image is the end result of an act of perception, which itself is more than just looking. Perception involves what we believe and know at least as much as it does the physiological process of seeing. Perception also involves language, which provides the grammar and meaning that direct our attention (our "glance") and help us interpret what we see. (109)

Like any type of textual production, working with images means working with student interpretations, and this is why it is so important that students practice reading and interpreting images as they learn to compose with them. Blakesley and Burke are both referring mostly to visual images here, but the need to understand how perception is itself a type of composition must carry over to any of other sensual rhetorics.[7]

It is too tempting for students to consider image (or most textual production for that matter) only in terms of discursive meaning. Too many times I have asked students to include images in their essays, and too many times students interpret that to mean they should illustrate their essays with images that are primarily discursive. For example, students who mention a telephone in their essay often choose to include a cartoonlike drawing of a telephone (usually clip art); if they mention the frustration of a public debate, they might include an image of a stick figure with a question mark over its head. It takes some explanation and practice for students to see how a *composed* image does more than represent or illustrate something in an essay or hypertext; an image can itself be articulate of its own meaning, can persuade on its own merit, and be comprised of complex layers of meaning and emotion as long as it is composed to do so. In other words, students often will choose images that are largely discursive, rather than choose images that are more non-discursive unless prompted to do so.

Another point to emphasize with image is to change the questions students might ask from "What does the text mean?" (in other words, the student wants to translate the text from non-discursive to discursive text) to "How does it feel?" (a more difficult analysis of the emotional content carried by the images involved in the text). The former is a question of denotation, or discursive meaning; the latter is affective and filled with non-discursive meaning. We are not accustomed to asking students how texts make them feel, except occasionally in a writing workshop. In fact, many might consider the question irrelevant. But as textual producers, students need to have some idea of how their audience is going to respond affectively to the images they construct, and so knowing the context and proclivities of their audience is as paramount as ever. Students must consider how a lavender background to a web page effects not only the overall tone of the other textual modes that are there, but also the overall feeling of that web site. Though such a change is only a change of color, it affects the entire image and tone of that particular text.

By far the most important of the values listed here, image is the lexicon, the purveyor of meaning.[8] Printed text might even be considered in this context a remediation of image (one of the oldest), and to the degree printed text itself occludes image is also the degree to which it is "unclear" or without substance. Words become "mere rhetoric" when they do not promise a vision of change or consensus. In the strictest sense, visual images must be composed, and they often must be composed out of several media or modes. Ultimately, students construct rhetoric by inventing, styling, arranging, storing, and delivering images.

Unity

Just as in traditional written composition the thesis provides unity for an essay, multimedia compositions must also use elements to provide unity. Unity can be the second most important element to composing in multimedia because it helps a viewer understand (or interpret) how to focus their attention. Though it is possible to have several unifying factors in a multimedia composition, unity alone can carry significance, social action, or even clarity. This is the concretizing effort of symbolization, or Bakhtin's centrifugal force of language. In the case of multimedia, unity provides *expogesis* by providing coherence, even if it is only applied to one small element. In terms of most printed texts, unity of the design was often a result of monomodality. Alex White, in *The Elements of Graphic Design*, characterizes the importance of unity this way:

> Because they had very limited resources, the earliest design prac-titioners achieved visual continuity rather easily: it was *externally* imposed on them by lack of materials. Today, with the abundant resources available as digital information, giving designers the capability to replicate with near exactitude the work of any era, we must exercise *internal* restraint to achieve harmonious, unified design. (51)

Rhetorically, unity indicates many things, not the least of which is coherence between the various elements. Visually, White suggests that proximity, similar-ity, repetition, and themes with variations all contribute to the overall unity of a design (59). Of course, as will all things, unity can only be achieved if the audience is taken into consideration. Academic audiences, not surpris-ingly, will expect clear unity just like they expect (usually) a clear thesis; the local music scene in a specific community may not expect much unity at all, preferring a design that functions rhetorically to indicate informality and other possible countercultural denotations and connotations.

Another potential function of unity is the way format might reflect content, or meaning. Asking students to include accompanying reflections or explanations with their multimodal products is one way to emphasize this kind of unity: the reflection should be similar enough to belong to the main product by repeating visual themes, layouts, colors, images, lines, etc. By requiring this, students have to shift from the idea that their product stands alone in space to the idea that their product and their reflection (in itself a rhetorical product) are in dialogue. Asking students to compose more than one product while stressing unity also asks them to explore more of the audience's expectations (such as working with variations to a theme) while maintaining some awareness regarding their overall purpose and goals. For students to value unity, they must also value the way all the various elements of a composition are in dialogue.

Layering

Layers are key to multimodal authoring because these texts are non-discursive. Whereas discursive texts rely on sequence, one utterance elaborating on the previous utterance, non-discursive texts rely on no specific ordering. In many cases, we read these kinds of texts at once, or in any order we choose. As such, non-discursive texts are complex, and this complexity comes from layering during the composing process. Layers provide depth, texture, complexity, nuance, even contradiction: all of which is important in creating multimedia products that move beyond simple representation/illustration. Many software programs designed for image, animation, and/or film must also allow for layers: sound on top of film, effects and filters on top of photos, loops and samples on top of backgrounds and scenes. Layers, in even small numbers, are dialogic.

Like the traditional canon of arrangement, layers produce tensions and resolutions between various elements of a composition. These tensions and resolutions can nourish the will-to-invent; as White has said, the will-to-invent comes from our "never-ending activity of discharging the desiring tension provoked in the organism in the course of its interaction with its environment" (85–86). One way to consider the changes in media over the centuries is in the number of compositional layers these media employ: in fact, when a text is said to *be* a multimedia text, what is often being pointed to are the various levels of layers and the different media that compose it. Layers *define* multimodality and multimedia throughout history, and this is especially true today in large part due to the way the interfaces built into computational software is modeled on the historical metaphors of painting and animation (the latter always previously reliant on layers). Layers can provide tension for the reader, just as juxtaposition can, and this tension is often the driving force of the composition.

Juxtaposition

When we juxtapose two types of text, the dialogue between them can result in the tensions and resolutions mentioned above, or the juxtaposition may simply add complexity and nuance (of tone, voice, design, and/or emotionality). Through the position of various elements, different conversations, or dialogues, are created, thereby providing the possibility of an argument through the spatiality of the elements involved: "Elements on a screen do not exist in isolation, but are interrelated in ways that are meaningful to users. If these interrelations are obscure, then the meanings of a page may also be obscure for many users" (Cranny-Francis 124). Juxtaposition is fundamental to argument, and, therefore, the rhetorical possibilities of multimedia text extend to persuasion. Collage, "the central technique of twentieth-century visual art," is reliant on juxtaposition and scale: two powerful meaning-making tools in multimodal text (Lanham 40).

> To replicate and juxtapose at will, as collage does, is to alter scale, and scaling change is one of the truly enzymatic powers of electronic text. When you click in the zoom box, you make a big decision: you are deciding on the central decorum of a human event, on the

boundary-conditions within which that event is to be staged, and hence on the nature of the event itself. (Lanham 41)

That is to say, juxtaposition forms the basis of many other possible functions and affects, and in the hands of a writer, juxtaposition of image can provide a powerful persuasive tool. Consider the image of the smoking aftermath at ground zero on 9/11 juxtaposed with the sound of a busy marketplace in which individual voices can be heard talking about food and clothing purchases. These two images together evoke powerful, affective, and persuasive meaning not possible if presented alone.

Perspective

Spatial considerations are very important, and in creating an architecture of space, multimodal composers must think about providing a vantage point or a point of view. Context is always important, but context can be manipulated with the right vantage point. In the case of visual texts, point of view might establish with whom we sympathize, or it might establish credibility (such as when a camera is focused on a subject from a downward angle, making the subject seem diminutive, trivial; or, conversely, when a camera focuses on a subject from an upward angle, making the subject seem exaggerated, or powerful). Similar to a review of the historical evolution of an idea, perspective in a multimedia composition provides the "outside-view" as well as privileging a particular interpretation.

The architecture of a composition is usually considered to be the manipulation of space, and the value of perspective works with space to help create an experience for the reader. In terms of web authoring and the use of potentially infinite digital space, the writer is often referred to as an architect:

> [Architecture] conveys an understanding of both the complexity of the task, and its combination of art and science. Just as architecture is more than building, so designing a web site is more than translating text into computer language. Architects create the space that is the living environment of a building by manipulating a range of materials ad meanings—building materials, shapes, light, colour, intertextual referents, contextual or locational factors. Web site designers do the same. For both architects and designers the major referent must be the social and cultural expectations of users. If users cannot find their way around a space—worse, if they cannot work out how to connect with that space, to include it in their everyday lives—they will simply avoid it. (Cranny-Francis 124)

Multimodal texts—whether a collage, web site, film, etc.—must construct a world in which the reader can reside. This world must be created for a particular audience (just as any rhetorical text is constructed for a particular audience), and the world must have one or more perspective built in. This is not to say that there is no room for multiple perspectives; on the contrary, non-discursive text is ideal for compositions that require multiple perspectives (exactly because they do not rely on sequence). But students must learn about perspective in multimodal composition because there may be a temptation to (1) always adopt their own particular perspective and, therefore, miss the influence of their audience; or (2) design without perspective in mind, sacrificing any sense that the space they build has purpose, or a goal. Writing any type of persuasive text requires imagining perspectives and, often, choosing at least one.[9]

Langer spends a great deal of time talking about space in *Feeling and Form*, becoming perhaps one of the first theorists to talk about virtual environments:

> Architecture creates the semblance of the World which is the counterpart of a Self. It is a total environment made visible. Where the Self is collective, as in a tribe, its Word is communal [...] And as the actual environment of a being is a system of functional relations, so a virtual "environment," the created space of architecture, is a symbol of functional existence [....] Similarly, the human environment, which is the counterpart of any human life, holds the imprint of a functional pattern; it is the complementary organic form. (98–99)

By characterizing the organic nature of function and form in this way, Langer defines the virtual environment as having the "imprint of a functional pattern" worked into the form itself. Form and function work together or not at all. The value of perspective might also be thought of as reflective of the kind of imprint function requires of form. Put in usability terms, perspective ensures usability by integrating the audience into the interface.

Other values of multimodal composition exist, but these I have found are the most important when asking students to employ non-discursive text. Perhaps what is also clear here is that these values, as well as the will-to-invent discussed already, depend heavily on the imagination. Eva Brann, in her ample work *The World of the Imagination: Sum and Substance*, makes clear that the imagination is not to be denied:

> What people brusquely deny as logicians and critics, they affirm as human beings in the intimate conversations in which [...] works of

prose, poetry, painting, plastic art, architecture, and music. Here, on common ground of the imagination, they point out to each other their discoveries: spots of delight and concealed signals and deft devices. Moreover they seem to regard all such communings as belonging within one universe of discourse and reference. (788)

As these values are practiced, as the full benefit of image is willed out of our imagination, we compose as we imagine.[10] It is a rarely perfect, never finished, and always exciting experience to image, and teaching students how to move into this world of composing the multimodal image we will no longer remain biased towards discursive text alone.

Cinematic Rhetoric

By imaging the future of multimodal composing, this section begins to sketch out where we are headed in rhetoric and composition if the current trends in composing are extended to their logical conclusion. Not only is rhetoric based not only on multiple modes, it is also the case that we are headed for an intellectual environment that will privilege multiple modes composed *in time*, as in cinema. This not-very-new cinematic rhetoric holds both exciting promise as well as a new set of challenges for teachers of writing, and as we move toward the increased ubiquity of computers and the simultaneous ubiquity of digital products, textual production will move more towards the cinematic and immersive, requiring writing teachers to be better equipped to analyze, instruct, and assess modes of text constructed within not only within space, but also constructed within time.

Lev Manovich, in *The Language of New Media*, makes the case that new media in general is moving us to a world that is becoming increasingly cinematic. This seems to be just an extension of the basic premise that as humans, we experience the world within time, and though we can theorize time as an abstraction, it is a very real abstraction for media:

> The printed word tradition that initially dominated the language of cultural interfaces is becoming less important, while the part played by cinematic elements is becoming progressively stronger. This is consistent with a general trend in modern society toward presenting more and more information in the form of time based audiovisual moving image sequences, rather than as [static] text. (78)

What this says about where we are heading in the newest forms of textual production is that texts, as they become more and more dynamic, are also more and more time-based, or experiential. This opens up non-discursive rhetoric beyond the static realm of textual production notable a century ago to textual production that demands being time-based. Web sites are more and more cinematic, with Flash and Shockwave animations, the success of YouTube, and the increasing broadband available to more and more internet users: "As computer culture gradually spatializes all representations and experiences, they are subjected to the camera's particular grammar of data access. Zoom, tilt, pan, and track—we now use these operations to interact with data spaces, models, objects, and bodies" (Manovich 80). Though film and film studies has been around for over a century, technology will do for cinematic text what digital photography has done for photographic text: it will become computable and, at the same time, more and more available to text producers. With the encroachment of cinema on the textual practices of people, corporations, civic groups, governments, and alliances comes the eventual insistence that our students write these texts (just like students are being asked to write web pages today). "Visual culture of a computer age," says Manovich, "is cinematographic in its appearance, digital on the level of its material, and computational (i.e., software driven) in its logic" (180). In short, writing teachers will need to teach the art of cinematic rhetoric, and we will do that the same way we always have: teaching students to understand the rhetorical situation, by helping them imagine and invent texts, and by giving them the tools and skills they need to produce text. The only way this will ever work, however, is if writing teachers understand and practice the way non-discursive text is rhetorical.

Richard Lanham suggests four changes for writing teachers due to the changes in textual production being offered by new technology and electronic literacy, the fourth of which is a similar prediction that writing will become more cinematic.[11] He states that "writing will be taught as a three-dimensional, not a two-dimensional art" (128). Other than the use of hypertext, Lanham points to animation and other 3-D advancements in particular:

> Ever since Greek rhetoric catalogued the basic figures of speech to recreate in a written culture some of the powers of oral speech and gesture, we have implied patterns—this is what one branch of rhetorical figuration is all about—but we have never let them complete themselves. Now they can explicate themselves in animations selected by the reader. The text will move, in three dimensions. Given the current state of digital animation programs, I think we'll come pretty soon to three-dimensional modeling of basic argumentative patterns. And we add the dimension of color [. . . .] And with better compression techniques and gigantic memory storage, we can add sound to our reading as well. Word, image, and sound will be inextricably intertwined in a dynamic and continually shifting mixture. (128).

Lanham's prescience here is remarkable, given this was written sometime before 1993. We are already witnessing many of these changes, and there are many new rhetorical products out there in need of analysis. To the extent that we can apply the "implied patterns" of ancient Greek rhetoric to today's cultural texts, the best result of this gradual movement is its reliance on our understanding of non-discursive text. To the degree a text can evoke emotional responses, inspire belief, or become articulate through image, that text is exhibiting non-discursive rhetoric.

One of the best ways to get students to experience many of the important facets of multimodal text is to ask them to create film—documentary film, especially. Not only is documentary film inherently rhetorical, it immediately asks students to consider the five multimedia values listed above: students must string together a collection of moving images; unify the various elements to convey a thesis, or point; layer transitions, sounds, music, cutaway shots, and still images to add to the complexity of the documentary; juxtapose a variety of images to underscore the main points and change the length of shots and distance of shots; and, finally, choose a perspective from which to film, interview, oppose, and, perhaps, change from time to time (students often need to figure out whether they should include themselves in the film as well). Such a project is challenging, but most computers today come preloaded with software that can help students create their own films, and their cell phones often have video capture capabilities.

Writing instructors not only need to consider non-discursive text as part of what they teach students; writing instructors must also be looking ahead to see what employers, governments, and the culture at large demand from their textual producers. If what we do for students has any value at all, we must be ready to adopt the various changes in textual production as they occur, and that includes the various theories and models we use to develop our curricula and assess our students' work.

Assessing Multimodality

Teachers who ask students to compose non-discursive texts based in image must learn to assess this kind of work. Assessment, especially in context of rhetoric and composition, is never an easy subject: consensus is difficult to find among members of the discipline, among departments, or even between instructors teaching the same course. This section deals with the very real possibility that some teachers would loathe to consider assigning multimodal projects to their students for the fear and intimidation of assessing them. By providing some simple techniques for assessment teachers will not have to hesitate assigning multimodal texts.

Obviously, assessing the traditional essay has always been a difficult matter (Baron, White, Lutz, Kamusikiri). Assessing multimodal texts has similar problems (Sorapure). On the other hand, there are at least three areas regarding the assessment of non-discursive text I would like to stress in this book as a way, I hope, to encourage writing teachers to assign multimodal texts in their classrooms: the myth of methodical multimodality and the use of reflective self-assessment.

The Myth of Methodical Multimodality

Just as Sharon Crowley and others have worked to dissuade scholars that the "methodical memory" reflected the "quality of authorial minds"—the more logical the writing, the more logical the mind that produced it—so too is there a myth of methodical multimodality. Multimodality (or monomodality, for that matter) does not reflect the "quality of authorial minds": there is no legitimacy to the notion that some of us are "more visual" or "more aural" than others when it comes time to create rhetorically appropriate texts for an audience—only, perhaps, that some of us are more practiced at it. By dispelling this myth, teachers and students cannot claim to "be less visual" or "be more visual" than others (and therefore more or less inclined toward composing multimodal texts). In fact, multimodality is a compositional form that comes from processes based in images which, coincidentally, happens to be closer to the way humans think than the chaining together of concepts as demanded by discursive text.

Part of the difficulty both students and teachers have who are unfamiliar with incorporating multimedia into their rhetorical texts stems from their inexperience in reading such texts. Just as any writing course stresses close reading as a way to improve writing, so must multimodal reading become a method of improving multimodal writing. As teachers of beginning film courses know, it takes some time to get students used to thinking about the intentionality of these texts. This requires practice in what Lanham calls "looking THROUGH" or looking AT" text:

> We are always looking first AT [the text] and then THROUGH it, and this oscillation creates a different implied ideal of decorum, both stylistic and behavioral. Look THROUGH a text and you are in the familiar world of the Newtonian interlude, where facts were facts, the world was really "out there," folks had sincere central selves, and the best writing style dropped from the writer as "simply and directly as a stone falls to the ground," precisely as Thoreau counseled. Look AT a text, however, and we have deconstructed the Newtonian world into Pirandello's and yearn to "act naturally." (5)

By looking AT a text we are basically revealing it as hypermediation, to use a term from Jay Bolter and Richard Grusin: "Where immediacy suggests a unified visual space, contemporary hypermediacy offers a heterogeneous space, in which representation is conceived of not as a window on the world, but rather as 'windowed' itself—with windows that open on to other representations or other media" (34). In other words, we see the puppeteer's strings, the wizard behind the curtain, and the mic above the head of the actors. The myth of the methodological multimedia student would have us believe that learning to see "AT" rather than "THROUGH" is a mental faculty closer to genetics than pedagogy, and that simply is not the case.

Once students learn how to read and analyze various multimodal texts, they will also begin to build their own will-to-invent. Writing teachers who do not attempt to foster and encourage a student's will-to-invent will wonder what went wrong as they assess the work they assigned. Successful completion of such writing assignments relies on a nonprocedural invention theory; moreover, it also relies on a writing teacher's willingness to challenge their students. Acknowledging non-discursive text, therefore, broadens what is available to writers during text generation. Invention can become a kind of "methodical memory"—a type of "mentalism" which mystifies text generation and, therefore, makes discovery a process of divination (Crowley 13).[12] By allowing students the ability to accept both discursive and non-discursive forms of symbol-making as legitimate in composition, by weighing discursive text and non-discursive text more equally, writers can combat the myth of methodical multimodality. After all, every assignment is a risk, and pedagogues must learn how to adjust their assignments over time to accommodate their particular student populations.

Reflective Self-assessment

Often touted as the panacea of assessment, self-assessment may not be as useful as some writing teachers might think, especially in terms of helping students to see the potential in the writing they do while, simultaneously, helping them to value the dynamic nature of most multimodal writing in new media today. Though reflection is for the most part a valuable exercise, it must be combined with a rigorous method of self-assessment that connects the process elements with the end product in such a way as to discourage any notions of rigidity or finality. As a changing, ever-evolving process, reflective self-assessment only works when practiced with plenty of outside input from the target audience. In the end, the most direct test for a textual product's success is whether or not that product is rhetorically successful, and in the context of the classroom, this audience may not be overtly obvious to some students (and thus unavailable to them through reflective self-assessment). Although I encourage reflection and self-assessment, it is only effective as long as the writing teacher realizes that the reflections they are getting are also rhetorical.

As I mentioned already at the beginning of this chapter, assigning a word-based, discursive reflection/narrative/exposition along with the more non-discursive, multimodal text not only asks that students put the two in dialogue (especially if the design of each is reflective of the other), but it also requires that students reveal the way they have willed the text into existence: that there is intent behind what they do. Trial and error or improvisation may work intuitively to get the text invented and made material in the medium in which the student is working, but the final product must be carefully considered and assessed against audience expectations. Like traditional, discursive text, the way the words first get put on the page can vary dramatically and there is no incorrect method; but also like traditional text, non-discursive text that remains and becomes part of the final product should be defensible, justified by what that student thinks the targeted audience requires. This is why reflective self-assessment can work, and this is also why reflective self-assessment is best paired with a rubric, or list of expectations with point values assigned to each element. Any disparity between what their reflection says and what their numeric self-assessment shows might be resolved with a conversation with the student. In the end, however, students who can be honest with themselves and create products with the audience in mind will benefit the most when there is not a writing teacher anywhere to be found.

Conclusions

I claim three important points about non-discursive rhetoric in this book: first, image, not word, is the basic unit of meaning-making, and image is primarily non-discursive; second, the affective domain need not rely on the false dualism of mind/body, and emotions are as much a part of our capacity to reason as they are part of our healthy mental lives; and, third, despite an obvious bias towards discursive text, we must assign and assess non-discursive text to students if they ever are to understand how image and the affective work together in rhetoric. As Louise Wetherbee Phelps stated in her essay, "Rhythm and Pattern in a Composing Life,"

> I discover [through reflection] how intimately tangled are my composing energies, my work, and my personal growth, daily life, and relationships [. . . .] There is a symbiotic relation between my composing life and the experience that it interprets, because

the power to connect not only feeds on the vitality of life but illuminates and changes its possibilities [. . . .] The use of language to compose meaning must, like any universal human act, have both great commonalities and incredible idiosyncrasy and individuality. (257, bold my emphasis)

Phelps describes here a non-sequential, nonlinear process full of emotion, intellectual curiosity, and a "generative urge to drive toward form"—an interesting way to put the will-to-symbolize. The integration of selves and the act of composing underscores the importance of non-discursive meaning-making. Like the claims for this book, Phelps brings into focus the composer as a connector, an illuminator, a generator, and a focuser: all images of "construing and constructing" to use Berthoff's terminology. Taken together, the three aforementioned claims stressed in this book make a case for the scholarship and pedagogy of non-discursive rhetoric, not to replace what we so often need to do with our symbolization (discursive textual production), but to not be ignored or brushed aside any longer by its dominance, either: as Langer puts it, "[the error] is in the very premise from which the doctrine proceeds, namely that all articulate symbolism is discursive" (88).

Multimodality, though nothing new, asks composers to understand and employ non-discursive rhetoric. Though the division between discursive and non-discursive text is—for the convenience of this analysis—somewhat contrived, setting forth any kind of procedural script for students to follow may be more teachable, but would nonetheless also be contrived. The *values* of non-discursive text—and the resulting composing model described in the last chapter—are intended, therefore, to help students generate connections as they compose multimodal texts. Like a playground stocked with equipment, composers are then free to build their texts (with their intended audience in mind, of course). These texts are wrought with the emotionality of our real, lived experiences; they are willed into existence, willed into composition, and willed into distribution. These multimodal texts are, therefore, images with both discursive and non-discursive elements rhetorically constructed for an audience. By accounting for both types of symbolization, this book provides a writing theory that, as Lynn Worsham put it, can bring forth a world.

Notes

Notes for Introduction

1. As printing became available as a new mass distribution system, centralization became easier due to the ability of the various governments to persuade via the new technology: "Printing fueled the strategic interests of nascent centralized state bureaucracies by providing the means by which standardized documents—from school textbooks, to public ordinances and fiscal regulations, to maps of the realm—could be mass reproduced and disseminated. In this way, printing provided the tools by which centralizing rulers could promote homogenous policies across territorially defined spaces and thus dissolve the cross-cutting and overlapping jurisdictions characteristic of the medieval world order" (Deibert 91–92).

2. "Philosophy," according to Wittgenstein, "is a fight against the fascination which forms of expression exert upon us" (27).

3. The terms "verbal" and "written" are traditional terms bound by genre and medium: they indicate a scholarly history of communication that generally means the conveyance of thought which is also called discourse. I do not rely on these terms because their connection to genre or medium is generally unhelpful, and because they are often used to describe discursive text exclusively.

4. Computerized Axial Tomography (CAT) uses x-rays and a computer to create images; Magnetic Resonance Imaging (MRI) uses magnesium and a computer to create images; and Positron Emission Tomography (PET) uses radioactive substances (positrons) to create images.

5. Consciousness is a difficult term to define, especially in context of interdisciplinary work. In later chapters, I define more precisely the way this term is being used, but for now it may be simpler to just refer to higher consciousness as what most of us think of when we think of the word "mind" and core consciousness as simply awake (though there are stages of sleep that are also conscious states).

6. "[T]he translation of visual images into verbal text—and vice versa—has always been a part of writing and speaking instruction" (Hobbs 28).

7. Kevin Porter's book, *Meaning, Language, and Time: Toward a Consequentialist Philosophy of Discourse*, calls for the explication of what is meant by the term "meaning" when used by theorists and scholars, and I have to agree with him. In fact, his book asks that theorists clarify their definition of the term meaning in a similar way that I have asked in the past that theorists define more closely their theory of language. I find no disagreement with Porter's assertion that meaning

is "constituted within" time (254), and that the "Meaning of an utterance or text (i.e., the totality of its consequences) must be treated as a propagating aggregate of meanings, not a seamless whole" (268). "Meaning," as used in this book, does not refer to a static, inconsequential notion of the word, nor do I intend the term "meaning" to be outside temporality—in fact, if anything, as I use the loose terminology of "discursive meaning" and "non-discursive meaning," I depend on the fact that it is the consequences of these two types of meaning through time that will define them—not any *particular* meaning at any *particular* time. This is also not to say that I am avoiding or otherwise assuming a definition of these two terms—they are defined in their own limited way within the text. Ultimately, though, my claims about my use of the term "meaning," and the meaning of this text in general, are, by Porter's account, not really a reflection of anything I might intend: "Once a writer exposes her text, even an autobiographical text, to readers, the Meanings of that text extends beyond her control; each consequence, however, unintended or even impossible from the perspective of the writer, is a member of the Meaning of that text" (314). Consequently, I sincerely agree that my intent as an author does not contribute to its meaning as much as its own evolution might: its own consequences or the lack thereof.

Notes for Chapter 1

1. James A. Herrick, in *The History and Theory of Rhetoric*, explains the Enlightenment project in rhetorical theory this way: "As a result of the expanding public domain and increasingly rhetorical public, a new understanding of rhetoric and oratorical skill gradually took hold as well. One ancient model that focused on winning a debate by any means available was losing ground [. . . .] [R]hetorical theorists of this period—George Campbell, Adam Smith, and others—[. . .] argued that rhetoric should teach how to forcefully communicate one's reasoned arguments" (180).

2. The term "information" has a very specific definition in communication theory. As chronicled in Stephen Johnson's book *Emergence: The Connected Lives of Ants, Brains, Cities, and Software*, Claude Shannon, after "interacting" with Alan Turing at Bell Labs, helped to begin the field of information theory in which he "explored the boundaries between noise and information" (44). Information, as the term is used here, is in opposition to "noise," or, perhaps, nondata. One of the problems with the Shannon-Weaver view of communication has everything to do with its ideal of perspicuity in the absence of noise. The word itself connotes a teleological signal, a purposeful, modernist sense of intended meanings. Mark Taylor, in his landmark book *The Moment of Complexity: Emerging Network Culture*, also makes the case that an "expanded notion of information makes it necessary to reconfigure the relation between nature and culture in such a way that neither is reduced to the other but that both emerge and coevolve in intricate interrelations"—that several "physical, chemical, and biological processes are also information processes" (4). Though it may indeed be changing, the term "information" is meant to be consistent with how it is often used in communication theory: data lacking interpretation.

3. I like Herrick's definition of rhetoric as "the systematic study and intentional practice of effective symbolic expression" because instead of using the term language (meaning discursive language), he uses the term "symbolic expression" which leaves the medium or the mode wide open for rhetorical use (7). In fact, Herrick emphasizes both the discursive (which he just calls "language") and non-discursive (which he calls art) aspects of rhetoric: "Language is the symbol system on which most of us rely for communicating with others on a daily basis. However, arts such as music, dance, theater, painting, and architecture also provide symbolic resources for communicating. In fact, human social life depends on our ability to use various symbol systems to communicate meanings to one another" (6).

4. This claim is one of the main tenets in cultural studies, and it has become a cornerstone of postmodern studies. It is perhaps the case that my view of text is much broader, however, than even this. "Text" is not just discursive; text is also non-discursive. Therefore, text cannot only be a worded description of a puppy; text can also be the images and emotions experienced from viewing an abstract expressionist painting of a puppy.

5. "In all senses of the word, writing thus *comprehends* language. Not that the word 'writing' has ceased to designate the signifier of the signifier, but it appears, strange as it may seem, that 'signifier of the signifier' no longer defines accidental doubling and fallen secondarity. 'Signifier of the signifier' describes on the contrary the movement of language: in its origin, to be sure, but one can already suspect that an origin whose structure can be expressed as 'signifier of the signifier' conceals and erases itself in its own production" (Derrida 7).

6. See Jacobson's *Style in Language* (1960) for his six constitutive factors in language: Addresser, Addressee, Context, Message, Contact, and Code (and the functions of these factors are Emotive, Cognitive, Referential, Poetic, Phatic, and Metalingual). The traditional sender-message-receiver paradigm, as I mean it here, is a view of language derived from communication theorists and made popular by scholars heavily indebted to twentieth-century linguistics tradition in composition studies. Specifically, in Kinneavy's *The Aims of Discourse*, he defines the traditional "communications triangle" in order to define each "aim" of discourse, allying the "aim" of narrative with the "sender" and the "aim" of expository with "receiver," et cetera.

7. Clearly, emotions are meaningful. But I find it is necessary to add to any description an explicit reference to meaning because (1) emotions are not always considered part of meaning when referring to texts due to the prevalence and bias towards discursive symbolization; and (2) emotion-as-meaning reiterates "meaning" as a term dependent on the receiver/audience as much, if not more so, than the sender/author.

8. It is rarely the case that the discursive and the non-discursive are ever separate products. In fact, even the most discursive of statements may carry with it an element of non-discursive tone, or implication, even connotation. In contrast, many primarily non-discursive products, such as mixed-media art pieces, include discursive elements as a way to compliment or complicate the non-discursive nature of the product. It may even be the case that the two do not exist in a dichotomy, but, instead, exist at the same time; what changes, then, is our *perception* of the

text and not the text itself (i.e., the non-discursive could be *read* as discursive, and vice versa).

9. Fleckenstein echoes this emphasis on the study of language in "Images, Words, and Narrative Epistemology" (1996) where she says "language ostensibly is the be-all and end-all of English studies: it is what we study, how we study, and why we study [. . . .] Understanding thought, self, and reality requires understanding language" (914).

10. *Speculative Instruments* by I. A. Richards (New York: Hartcort, 1955), pp. 115–16.

11. See Vivian Zamel (1988) for a summary of the influence these three language theorists has had on composition studies.

12. For a more complete explanation of the relationship between Kant and Cassirer, see the introduction in *Symbol, Myth, and Culture* (1979) by Donald Phillip Verene in which Cassirer is quoted as saying the following: "One ought to think of neo-Kantianism in functional terms and not as a substantial entity. What matters is not philosophy as a doctrinal system but as a certain way of asking philosophical questions" (4).

13. The importance of intuition and intuitive reasoning are a central theme in much of Langer's philosophy. In *Mind: An Essay on Human Feeling, Vol. II*, Langer states that the "catalyst which precipitated the new and unique power of speech was symbolic conception, the intuition of meaning" (310); and in volume III she states that "recognition of characteristics like form, relation, and every sort of meaning is the lowest denominator of intellect, the function of intuition" (49). Clearly, intuition plays a constitutive role in Langerian thought.

14. Langer enlarges this point by also criticizing positivism: "What is directly observable is only a sign of the 'physical fact'; it requires interpretation to yield scientific propositions. Not simply seeing is believing, but *seeing and calculating, seeing and translating.* . . . Yet if we did not attribute an elaborate, purely reasoned, and hypothetical history of causes to the little shivers and wiggles of our apparatus, we really could not record them as momentous results of experiment. The problem of observation is all but eclipsed by the problem of *meaning.* And the triumph of empiricism in science is jeopardized by the surprising truth that *our sense-data are primarily symbols* (*New Key* 20–21).

15. I am aware of the controversy surrounding the identities of V. N. Vološinov and M. M. Bakhtin and the respective authorship of some works: namely the claim by V. V. Ivanov that some works by Medvedev and Vološinov were actually written by M. M. Bakhtin. I support the decision made by the translators of one of those contested works, Matejka and Titunik, to treat these works as having separate authors. For more on this controversy and the translators' reasons, see the "Translator's Preface" in *Marxism and the Philosophy of Language.*

16. Vološinov summarizes Saussure this way: "[His] point of departure is a distinction among three aspects of language: *language-speech* (lagage), *language as a system of forms* (langue) and *the individual speech act—the utterance* (parole). Language (in the sense of *langue*: a system of forms) and utterance (parole) are constituents of language-speech, and the latter is understood to mean the sum total of all the phenomena—physical, physiological, and psychological—involved in the realization

of verbal activity" (59). What Vološinov seems to take issue with the most is the way the Saussurian school limits the study of language to the social (in opposition to the individual). Linguistics cannot study the utterance (parole) of any individual because it is too sporadic and unpredictable—in other words, too hard to objectify and observe scientifically.

17. Vygotsky, it may not be commonly known, also theorized about consciousness, emotions, imagination, and will. In other chapters, I will briefly address some of this lesser-known work.

18. I will explore this view of consciousness more fully in chapter 3.

19. Ernesto Grassi, in *Rhetoric as Philosophy: The Humanist Tradition*, values the way language is both social and within a physical time and place: "[S]o language can be effective only within a particular given historical time and a particular social situation [. . . .] In this way an understanding of language is formed that is distinguished from rationalistic logic because it stresses the primacy of language's historical character, dialectic, and topics. From this it necessarily follows that 'genuine' language is rhetorical, imagistic, and metaphorical, since this is the only kind that is formed with reference to the particularly confined state of the listener in time and space" (91).

20. The relationship between perception and cognition has a long history. See *Thought and Language*, edited by John Preston.

21. This is reminiscent of the Heisenberg Uncertainty Principle that, in general, states that any observed object is altered through the very act of its observation.

22. Langer is careful to make sure the reader does not assume that non-discursive forms are "inconceivable, mystical affairs" which are somehow made inarticulate simply because they are not discursive (89). The non-discursive, it must be stressed, works against dualist notions that the discursive defines reason and the non-discursive is pure, subjective, emotional, nonintellectual thought. By opposing and breaking down these dualisms, the non-discursive provides a place for image that is not simply "illustrative" or enigmatically aesthetic: the image is a language form capable of argument and reason just as it is capable of emotion and pure subjectivity. I will address the role of the affective domain on image in much more detail in the third chapter.

23. I mean to imply no particular proportionality with this figure between each element.

24. These are not experimental pedagogies at all. Instead, they are a result of increased distribution of images. Like the so-called "pictorial turn" of today, images enter the classroom not necessarily because there are more of them: images enter the classroom because the distribution methods for image got cheaper and, therefore, more prevalent. This is an important distinction that is covered more in the section "Image Production, Consumption, and Distribution" in chapter four.

25. "This means that imaging occurs in the specific modalities of visualizing, audializing, smelling in the mind's nose, feeling in the mind's muscles, tasting with the mind's tongue, and so on. There is, accordingly, no such thing as imagining in general—i.e., sensory-neutral imaging—since imaging always and only occurs in at least one of these particular sensory modalities. To image, then, is to imagine in a sensory-specific way" (Casey 41).

Notes for Chapter 2

1. "[I]mage—a message from the world that comes to consciousness through the senses. It may enter through the eye as shape and shade; it may enter the nose as odor; it may enter the ear as sound; it may tingle the tongue as taste; it may caress the skin as touch. Every strong memory exists as an image or a series or composite of images" (Bogarad and Schmidt 1189).

2. One consequence of a category of rhetoric termed "non-discursive rhetoric" is that it subsumes the various other categories of rhetoric that have been cropping up over the last few years: visual rhetoric becomes one kind of non-discursive rhetoric, as does each of the other rhetorics associated with its appropriate sense.

3. For obvious reasons, then, I prefer the term "image rhetorics" over "visual rhetorics" when talking about non-discursive rhetoric in general. If, on the other hand, I want to discuss visual elements of a text in particular, then perhaps the term "visual rhetoric" could be appropriate. Still, I prefer to discuss any kind of rhetorical analysis in terms of the non-discursive as opposed to discursive rhetorics, setting aside for as long as possible the issue of what sense gathered the data in the first place.

4. See, for example, "Twin Peaks and the Look of Television: Visual Literacy in the Writing Class" by Diane Shoos, Diana George, and Joseph Comprone.

5. In "Composition and the Circulation of Writing," Joseph Trimbur makes the case that "the circulation of writing should figure much more prominently in writing instruction" (190).

6. Stuart Selber expands the notion of literacy to include three types of literacy important to students working with technology: functional literacy, critical literacy, and rhetorical literacy. These "multiliteracies" are discussed more fully in chapter 4.

7. Though the results of this experiment were mixed, one interesting note by the authors was that students "became animated, eager to recite, and most cordial" during the use of the visual aid (326).

8. Surely, these authors only wanted to report their use of these "new" methods, but few of them investigated *why* such changes in pedagogy were cognitively important or exciting (or generative) to students.

9. See also Claude Gandelman's book, *Reading Pictures, Viewing Texts* (1991), in which he writes about "the relationship between the visual and the textual and sometimes about the equivalence of the visual and the verbal" (ix).

10. See the following for other appeals for visual literacy as justification for one media type, discipline, or method of interpretation: Shoos, George, and Comprone (1993) for television and ethics; Allen (1994) art and visual design; Glasgow (1994) reading skills; Miller (1994) for use of video; Jarvie (1995) for communication studies; and Flood and Lapp (1997, 1998) for pedagogical practices of using visuals in the classroom.

11. Though less about literacy and more about semiotics, see also "Reading Images: The Grammar of Visual Design" by Gunther Kress and Theo van Leeuwen, as well as "Social Semiotics" (1988) by Robert Hodge and Kress.

12. Kress and Theo Van Leeuwen, in *Multimodal Discourse: The Modes and Media of Contemporary Communication*, explicate a clearer theory of multimodality based in semiotics, one that I discuss more directly in chapter 4.

13. As mentioned before, this book asserts that all texts have both discursive and non-discursive elements. What makes a text primarily one or the other whether or not the text itself relies on a logical chain-of-reasoning which is sequentially organized to form an argument, or whether the text relies on a more intuitive logic free from such ordering (See Langer's explanation of these terms in chapter 1).

14. See Hesford (1981) and Kyle (1981) for more on the positive results such interactions between various literacies bring to writers.

15. For a more complete suggestion as to the history of how the visual entered the American classroom, see Lucille M. Schultz's *The Young Composers: Composition's Beginnings in Nineteenth-Century Schools*, particularly chapters 3 (No Ideas but in Things) and 4 (The Agency of Textbook Iconography).

16. I use the term "ought" purposely to highlight the implied morality these appeals of literacy often hold. Though I do not necessarily disagree with a moral obligation to make the illiterate literate, I do wish to point out that it is there and, consequently, it is bound by certain moral belief systems not necessarily inherent in the particular literacy itself.

17. See also Hampton (1990).

18. See Kaufer (1997).

19. One of the most prolific scholars in technical communication who has written about the use of visuals in the display of data is Edward R. Tufte. All three of his books on the subject—*The Visual Display of Quantitative Information* (1983), *Envisioning Information* (1990), and *Visual Explanations* (1997)—attempt to develop visual principles for the design and display of quantitative graphics.

20. Tebeaux rightly credits Stephen A. Bernhardt's CCC article, "Seeing the Text" (1986) as being the first in the field to dispute the essay's visual format as the norm, privileging instead "visually informative prose" found in the documents of typical workplace writing.

21. See Charles Kostelnick's "A Systematic Approach to Visual Language in Business Communication." *The Journal of Business Communication* 25.3 (1988): 29–48.

22. Michele S. Shauf's "The Problem of Electronic Argument: A Humanist's Perspective" (2001) warns against the proliferation of electronic vocabularies over humanist vocabularies, and she stresses how the technologist "reads chronologies as advancements" while the humanities "is the record of human attempts to address questions in which no advance whatever has been made" (36).

23. Richard Buchanan's essay, "Design and the New Rhetoric: Productive Arts in the Philosophy of Culture" claims that design (a word akin to "composition") has become a new form of rhetoric in a technological age, and, therefore, can benefit from "humanistic values and understanding" in order to improve our "cultural environments" (189–90).

24. See also the essay by Patricia Roberts and Virginia Pompei Jones. "Imagining Reasons: The Role of the Imagination in Argumentation" on how the visual can make an argument.

25. In fact, one important claim of this book is that visual, aural, haptic, gustatory, and olfactory rhetorics be grouped under the general label, non-discursive rhetoric. Each has its own modes of meaning-making, and each has its own relationship to discursive text, but such a label would avoid any type of privileging of one mode over the other as especially rhetorical (the visual, say, over the aural, or the aural over the olfactory) and better allow for hybrid rhetorics.

26. See Stafford (1999, 1997) for more about how the look of documents can (and needs to) change.

27. Craig Stroupe, in "Visualizing English: Recognizing the Hybrid Literacy of Visual and Verbal Authorship on the Web," calls for a new disciplinary process, one he terms "visualizing English," in which he proposes to keep the visual and the verbal in dialogue, forming "dialogically constitutive relations between words and images . . . which can function as a singly intended, if double-voiced, rhetoric" (609).

28. W. J. T. Mitchell, a scholar in image studies, actually refutes the claim that our culture is somehow more visual that it was before. At the 2001 Visual Rhetoric Conference, he stated that, on the contrary, images have always and consistently been a ubiquitous aspect of human life. Perhaps, if there is a contemporary focus on the visual, then what may have changed is our widespread ability to produce and disseminate the *same* images over and over again. Mitchell's books, *Picture Theory: Essays on Verbal & Visual Representation* (1994) and *The Language of Images* (1980), also help dispel some of the myths concerning the historical use of images.

29. Trimbur also acknowledges the importance of the "interpretive account" to the "meaning making" essay that often results from essay assignments centered on the analysis of cultural text (199). These essays therefore tend to allow the ideological influences of the circulation of these cultural texts to go largely unanalyzed.

30. For more on what I mean by cultural studies, see the following: "Cultural Studies: Reading Visual Texts" (1984) by Joel Foreman and David Shumway; "The Formations of Cultural Studies: An American in Birmingham" (1989) by Lawrence Grossberg; and Richard Johnson's "What is Cultural Studies Anyway?" (1986/1987).

31. For alternatives among types of visual analysis relevant to the classroom, see *Handbook of Visual Analysis* by Leeuwen and Jewitt (2001).

32. See also *Interpreting Visual Culture: Explorations in the Hermeneutics of the Visual* by Ian Heywood and Barry Sandywell: "From these different sources it appears that the place of perception and visuality in our understandings of human reality and the 'fate of the visual' in contemporary society and culture have merged to form the context for new alignments, critical projects, and interdisciplinary research in the arts, humanities and critical sciences" (ix).

33. Susan Sontag's book, *On Photography*, takes this point even further by claiming that "Photography has powers that no other image-system has ever enjoyed [. . . .] The primitive notion of the efficacy of images presumes that images possess the qualities of real things, but our inclination is to attribute to real things the qualities of an image" (158). Though I find Sontag's book a bit alarmist, this point about images giving credibility to reality resonates with me.

34. See also Jenny L. Nelson's essay, "Limits of Consumption: an Ironic Revision of Televisual Experience," for yet another example of such analysis.

35. In traditional discourse, the mind and the brain are held to be separate concepts: the mind indicating sentience and the brain indicating simply the organ itself. I will take up this issue as being part of the way *consciousness* becomes important later, but for now I will refer to both.

36. "When we recall the sensory aspects of past events, we image them. When we manipulate parts of existing images into new combinations and/or when we enrich images with affective associations, we imagine" (Sadoski 266).

37. Both Cassirer and Langer, like Vygotsky, also emphasize the social nature of language. They both stress the way meaning is made in communities through language, in the context of the social and not the singular.

38. It may be worth yet again to mention the important caveat that I use the word "primarily" here to emphasize that it is unlikely that an image or a printed text would ever be purely one form or another: the two forms mix, blur, even overlap. It is also the case that some images are primarily discursive—as in illustrations and diagrams, x-rays and CAT scans, et cetera—and that some printed texts are primarily non-discursive—as in the poetry of John Berryman and Wallace Stevens. In drawing this distinction, I intend to point out the way images and printed text are most often conceived, or used, in daily interactions; I do not intend to make a sweeping generalization regarding the propensity of one form or media over another. Indeed, I would be more inclined to argue the importance of the blend between the two forms in all texts, both discursive texts and non-discursive texts.

39. Laura Marks explains how haptics and the visual have and continue to be connected: "In my emphasis on haptic visuality and haptic criticism, I intend to restore a flow between the haptic and the optical that tour culture is currently lacking. That vision ceased to be understood as a form of contact and began to be understood as disembodied (and equated with knowledge) is a function of European post-Enlightenment rationality. Nevertheless, an ancient and intercultural undercurrent of haptic visuality continues to inform and understanding of vision as embodied and material. It is timely to explore how a haptic approach might rematerialize our objects of perception, especially now that optical visuality is being refitted as a virtual epistemology of the digital age" (xiii).

40. See Karen Burke LeFevre's *Invention as a Social Act* (1987) for one scholar's account as to how a purely discursive language theory affects thinking: "From many directions, then—linguistics, cognitive and developmental psychology, composition theory, technical writing pedagogy—comes evidence of assumptions that [discursive]language is not coextensive with thinking, that people are not dependent primarily on [discursive]language for what and how they think. The idea that some thinking may be nonverbal also receives support from introspective reports of certain artists and scientists. Albert Einstein is often cited as a representative of this view: 'The words or the language, as they are written or spoken, do not seem to play any role in my mechanism of thought,' Einstein said. 'The psychical entities which seem to serve as elements in thought are certain signs and more or less clear images. . . . [These elements] are, in my case, of visual and some of muscular

type. Conventional words or other signs have to be sought for laboriously only in a secondary stage' " (103).

41. I disagree. This is similar to the claim that silence is not meaningful because there is no sound (or text) there—that silence is by definition without meaning. Fleckenstein's point here also assumes that meaning comes from the object itself: from the symbol. But just as Langer has suggested, and as I have tried to emphasize here, meaning does not come to us from the symbol—it is our relationship to the symbol that creates the meaning: "No human impression is only a signal from the outer world; it always is *also* an image in which possible impressions are formulated, that is, a symbol for the conception of *such* experience" (*Feeling* 376).

42. Fleckenstein has an impressive history of research investigating image and its relationship to affectivity and cognition. Her dissertation explores the cognitive and affective links to expressive writing (1989); in 1989, she also published an article on the connections between imagery and emotion in "writing engagement" (*Teaching English in the Two-Year College*). Other relevant works include "An Appetite for Coherence: Arousing and Fulfilling Desires" (1992); "Mental Imagery, Text Engagement, and Underprepared Writers" (1994); and "Images, Words, and Narrative Epistemology" (1996). Her book *Embodied Literacies: Imageword and a Poetics of Teaching* (2003) emphasizes in part the difficulty of separating words from images.

Notes for Chapter 3

1. See specifically Kristie Fleckenstein's "Inner Sight: Imagery and Emotion in Writing Engagement" (1991) and "Images, Words, and Narrative Epistemology" (1996). In the former, Fleckenstein argues for a connection between "effortless" writing, mental imagery, and "previously felt emotions" (210); in the latter, she argues that "we need metaphors fusing image and language to undergird our conceptualization of being" (915).

2. W. Ross Winterowd's "Emerson and the Death of Pathos" warned against the notion that "creative writing is sacred while composition is profane," resulting in the death of *pathos*: "The death of pathos allows the writer to be radically transgressive, and in the process, the teacher's role is changed, for his or her only function is to respond sympathetically [. . . .] Invention, the very heart of rhetoric from the ancients onward, becomes introspection, and thus rhetoric tends to become expression" (37).

3. A term Antonio Damasio uses to describe consciousness. James Johnson ascribes a similar viewpoint to Langer: "Langer believes that 'the greatest advantage, however, to be gained from the conception of feeling as a phase of living process itself, instead of as a product or 'psychical correlate' of it, is that it contains implicitly the solution of the moot problems of 'consciousness' and 'the unconscious' " (66). Langer herself states that "Feeling, in the broad sense of whatever is felt in any way, as sensory stimulus or inward tension, pain, emotion, or intent, is the mark of mentality" (*Mind Vol. I* 4).

4. Berlin's book, *Writing Instruction in Nineteenth-Century American Colleges* states the influence this way: "In the [late eighteenth-century], the elective system

at the new American university—based, itself, on a faculty psychology—divided the entire academic community into discrete parts, leading to an assembly-line conception of education. As far as rhetoric is concerned, this meant that persuasive discourse—the appeal to the emotions and the will—was now considered to be possible only in oratory, and concern for it was thus relegated to the speech department. Discourse dealing with imagination was made the concern of the newly developed literature department. The writing course was left to attend to the understanding and reason, deprived of all but the barest emotional content. Encouraged by the business community, with the tacit approval of science departments, composition courses became positivistic in spirit and method" (9).

5. James T. Zebroski critiques Faigley and the entire categorization of expression through an informal textbook analysis: "In contrast to the increasingly shrill condemnations of a thing called expressivism [. . .], the data consistently show that expressivism *never* was a major, persuasive movement in college composition" (106). He also points out that the label "expressivism" came about through the socioeconomic demands of English departments: "The long repressed conflict in composition between English education and English, between the social sciences and the humanities, now rises to the surface but takes on distorted, reconfigured shapes. Critiques of "expressivism," "process," even "composition" are then a transference and projection of this basic, unresolved, repressed conflict, rather than solely philosophical differences" (109).

6. See W. Ross Winterowd's "Emerson and the Death of Pathos" (1996) for a critique on Emerson's focus on the individual and the basic argument as to why these authors are considered "Neo-Romantics" (38).

7. McLeod's work is reviewed by Kristi Fleckenstein in "Defining Affect in Relation to Cognition: A Response to Susan McLeod" in which she gently critiques McLeod's definitions of the affective domain in favor of one "based on the interweaving of affect and cognition" while simultaneously applauding McLeod's work (447). She sites Vygotsky and Frederic Bartlett as influences, and she reinforces the point that emotions are integral to thought and meaning-making.

8. This is similar, incidentally, to the way Damasio defines affect in his book *Looking for Spinoza: Joy, Sorrow, and the Feeling Brain* (2003).

9. Quintilian's *Institute's of Oratory* also theorizes at length the importance of emotions, and he sets out some specific rules that are intended to teach young rhetors how to deliver emotional appeals. See George Kennedy in *Quintilian* (1969) and Richard Katula in "Quintilian on the Art of Emotional Appeal" (2003) for a discussion of how emotions operate as a kind of non-discursive text in the courtroom.

10. It is actually remarkable how much Langer's concept of mind seems to be similar to how many neuroscientists theorize it today. She seems to anticipate exactly what scientists call the two main pathways the brain uses to process images: the "how" pathway (called "objective feeling" in Langer) and the "what" pathway (called "subjective feeling" in Langer).

11. Faigley considers Elbow's organic metaphor for the writing process "one of the standards of Romantic theory" and contends that such expressivism would result in writing that is "fragmentary and unfinished" because all of the errors and "false starts" would be evident in the final product (530). In order for writing to

be "coherent, it must also be mimetic and rhetorical" (530). But Faigley reduces Elbow's work to fit into his argument against expressivist writing: the organic metaphor is not the most central element of the book, nor does Faigley address its full implications for the Romantics (Gradin xvi).

12. Susan McLeod's book *Notes on the Heart: Affective Issues in the Writing Classroom* attempts to find answers to some of the research questions listed here. She attempts to weave a narrative that combines actual students in actual classrooms with dense, philosophical theory based in cognitive research: "We hope that by presenting a classroom context with illustrative vignettes, the research on affect will be more accessible for teachers like ourselves who want to understand our students better" (xiii). The result, though, is confusing because the two styles are irreconcilable: just when the narrative becomes convincing, it is interrupted with a very terse, conceptually challenging passage.

13. See Suzanne Clark's "Rhetoric, Social Construction, and Gender: Is It Bad to Be Sentimental?" (1994) and "Fight Club: Historicizing the Rhetoric of Masculinity, Violence, and Sentimentality (2001); also see Lynn Worsham's "Going Postal: Pedagogic Violence and the Schooling of Emotion" (1996) for an account of how the "rhetoric of pedagogic violence" affects emotions in teaching practice.

14. Also in Harre's collection, Claire Armon-Jones provides this succinct encapsulation of the social constructionist viewpoint on emotion: "The characterization of emotion as attitudinal and cognition-dependent is crucial to constructionism in the following respects. According to constructionism, a socioculturally constituted emotion is an acquired response [. . . .] Consequently, it is essential to constructionism that an account of emotion be given in which emotions are neither identifiable with, nor have the same ontological status as, phenomena such as sensation and perception" (43). This is remarkably similar to Demasio's definition of emotion as distinct from feeling.

15. For a good survey of the work being done to address the subjective in both philosophical and cognitive discourse, see *Philosophy in the Flesh* by George Lakoff and Mark Johnson (1999).

16. Of course, as already mentioned, it is possible that emotions can lead us astray, but it must also be acknowledged that emotions can work to focus our activities, enthrall us, motivate us in order to complete an arduous task.

17. Not all neuroscientists would acknowledge the importance of emotions in the same way as Damasio and Ramachandran, however. Joseph LeDoux, in his book *The Emotional Brain: The Mysterious Underpinnings of Emotional Life*, makes the point that most of our emotional processing is unconscious in the brain. The key question for him, then, is "the problem of how emotional information comes to be represented in working memory" (282). LeDoux agrees, though, that emotions shade every image we process in the brain.

18. Some patients with anosognosia, a complete unawareness of their own bodily condition or disease, do not know of their condition because the "cross-talk among regions involved in body-state mapping" have been damaged or diseased. Such cases, as well as phantom limb cases in which patients can still sense a limb that has been removed, highlight the importance of background feeling and body-mapping (*Descartes'* 153).

19. Damasio explains these processes this way: "(1) the view of a certain body state juxtaposed to the collection of triggering and evaluative images which caused the body state; and (2) a particular style and level of efficiency of cognitive process which accompanies the events described in (1), but is operated in parallel" (*Descartes'* 162–63).

20. See Lalicker's *The Interdisciplinary Imagination in the Teaching of Writing* and Crowley's *The Methodical Memory: Invention in Current-traditional Rhetoric.*

21. Martha Nussbaum, in *Upheavals of Thought* (2001) makes this point particularly well: "[U]nderstanding the relationship between emotions and various conceptions of the human good will inform our deliberations as we ask how politics might support human flourishing. If we think of emotions as essential elements of human intelligence, rather than just as supports or props for intelligence, this gives us especially strong reasons to promote the conditions of emotional well-being in a political culture: for this view entails that without emotional development, a part of our reasoning capacity as political creatures will be missing" (3).

22. There are, however, some neuroscientists trying to make the link between physical manifestation of emotions and brain pathology more vivid. See "Cortical Systems for the Recognition of Emotion in Facial Expressions" by Ralph Adolphs, et al. (1996).

23. Interestingly, Stocker also provides instances when any of these three emotional states can be counterproductive to rationality, therefore suggesting that even those characteristics regarded as nonaffective, or "cool," can actually become arational or irrational.

24. Ramachandran emphasizes this point through his observation of Capgras' delusion, as mentioned earlier in this chapter. He is especially determined to stress the importance of emotions to the way we make sense of images: "In each instance, when I look at the face, my temporal cortex recognizes the image—mother, boss, friend—and passes on the information to my amygdala (a gateway to the limbic system) to discern the emotional significance of the face. When this activation is then relayed to the rest of my limbic system, I start experiencing the nuances of emotion—love, anger, disappointment—appropriate to that particular face [. . . .] it occurred to me that [this] strange behavior might have resulted from a disconnection between these two areas (one concerned with recognition and the other with emotions)" (162). It would follow, then, that images carry with them an emotional component during the operation of a healthy brain.

25. Each of these categories, as Armstrong points out, is dialogical in that each is often in response to the one that comes before it.

26. For more on how Descartes viewed the mind and the body, and for an account of how a field such as mathematics has come to reject Descartes, see *Goodbye, Descartes: The End of Logic and the Search for new Cosmology of the Mind* by Keith Devlin (1997).

27. Behaviorist philosophers such J. B. Watson suggested that "all there is to mind are the physical actions of human beings" (Armstrong 4).

28. Armstrong cites two important works by each of these theorists: "Is Consciousness a Brain Process?" (1956) by U. T. Place; and "Sensations and Brain

Processes" (1959) by J. C. C. Smart. Though both articles theorize brain processes for mind, they stop short of attributing any particular process to any particular aspect of mind.

29. Causal theory, according to Armstrong (who was one of the proponents of this perspective), maintains that physical processes actually *cause* mental processes; Eliminativism (proposed by Paul Feyerabend and Richard Rorty) suggests that the term "mind" loses all meaning, and it takes the extreme position that "there are only physical processes in the brain"; and, thirdly, Functionalism (first proposed by Hilary Putnam and Jerry Fodor) "is the more or less prevailing orthodoxy about the mind-body problem" and it simply holds that mental processes can be named/categorized by the function they serve to the body (5–6).

30. James cites some of this important work, including Judith Butler's *Gender Trouble: Feminism and Subversion of Identity* (1990) and *Bodies that Matter: On the Discursive Limits of Sex* (1993). I would add Camille Paglia's *Sexual Personae* as well as *Feminine Principles and Women's Experience in American Composition and Rhetoric*, edited by Louise Wetherbee Phelps and Janet Emig.

31. Linda Brodkey and Michelle Fine, in "Presence of Mind in the Absence of Body" (1988), explain further the risk women take in presenting a mind without a body in scholarly discourse by recounting the experiences of two graduate students entering academia: "We see each women student as offering to pay an exorbitant, not to mention impossible, price for the coherent self represented in her narrative. In exchange for her 'mind,' she leaves her body to science" (88).

32. See also "Schooling the Postmodern Body: Critical Pedagogy and the Politics of Enfleshment" by Peter McLaren (1988); *Thinking Through the Body* by Jane Gallop (1988); and *Engendering Rationalities*, edited by Nancy Tuana and Sandra Morgan (2001).

33. Damasio published an article entitled "Individuals with Sociopathic Behavior Caused by Frontal Damage Fail to Respond Autonomically to Social Stimuli" in *Behavioral Brain Research* (Vol. 41, pages 81–94), and the content on that work shows up explicitly in chapter 3, "A Modern Phineas Gage."

34. On page 15: "Imagery is what we know of reality and serves as the core to our consciousness (Damasio, 1999)." Fleckenstein, interestingly, also cites Langer and Berthoff heavily in this essay.

35. A few of these scientists, such as A. C. Roberts and J. D. Wallis, contest these findings more on a methodological ground than a substantive one. In one study, "Inhibitory Control and Affective Processing in the Prefrontal Cortex: Neuropsychological Studies in the Common Marmoset," these authors contribute data that contradicts Damasio's, but they do so in such a way as to complicate or expand on this work. In this article, for example, Roberts and Wallis state that "While damage to the orbitofrontal cortex in humans and non-human primates can cause inflexibility, impulsiveness and emotional disturbance, the relationship between these effects are unclear" (252). Damasio was one of the first to claim the effects of damage to this area of the brain, and these scientists are simply complicating the findings by investigating relationships between each of the effects.

36. Because of a conference entitled *Unity of Knowledge: The Convergence of Natural and Human Science*, an edited collection of philosophers and scientists was

published with the same title (2001). In it, Damasio (one of the editors) states that "throughout the 20th century, the integrated brain and mind have often been discussed with hardly any acknowledgement that emotion does exist" in neuroscience (101). His point, therefore, becomes that because emotion did (and does) exist in philosophy and rhetoric, looking outside of his own field helps him integrate his work within a larger conversation.

37. In *Neurophilosophy: Toward a Unified Science of the Mind/Brain*, Patricia Smith Churchland defines the task of neurophilosophy this way: "[T]he framework for discussion of neuroscientifically relevant philosophy is the overarching question of the nature and possibility of devising a unified theory to explain how the mind-brain works" (8). She goes on to conclude that "[t]heories—of the large-scale, governing-paradigm, unifying-framework kind—are beginning to emerge, and they will evolve and come to structure both the research enterprise and, undoubtedly, our very way of thinking about ourselves." (481).

38. The myth of the homunculus is, simply, that there must be a "little person in the brain who 'sees' an inner television, 'hears' an inner voice, 'reads' the topographic maps, weighs reasons, decides actions" and so on (Churchland 406). It is, in effect, the personification of consciousness as consciousness.

39. This is similar to the conclusion in *The Mind and The Brain: Neuroplasticity and the Power of Mental Force* by Schwartz and Begley (2002).

40. One main factor in discussing the self in composition is to acknowledge the work of postmodernism, especially regarding self and identity. Though it may seem easy to debunk research on imagination, image, and the non-discursive on postmodern terms, the reverse is actually the case. My view of language, image, and the non-discursive is consistent with the postmodern view, and nowhere do I intend to substitute one grand narrative for another. In fact, this view of language, image, emotions, and consciousness works to disrupt the easy binaries suggested by some compositionists that anything that is not cold, reasoned, critical theory is automatically subject to charges of romanticism and/or atomistic thought. Derrida, Lyotard, and, more recently, James Berlin all espouse a view of language that rejects foundational and essentialist notions of subjects and objects of experience (See Derrida's *Of Grammatology* (1976), Lyotard's *The Postmodern Condition: A Report on Knowledge* (1984), and Berlin's *Rhetorics, Poetics, and Cultures: Refiguring College English Studies* (1996) for original texts). Another central element of postmodern thought is its insistence that we can no longer refer to a static, single self since language encompasses a dynamic, multilayered, historical relationship to worlds of symbolization. In fact, self becomes a term not necessarily describing the mind's core or essential quality, rather it describes one particular relationship with one particular reality created by language—as language shifts realities, so does the perception of self-change, resulting in a panoply of selves rather than a single, essentialized self.

41. Damasio and Ramachandran both investigated Phantom Limb Syndrome (PLS) in order to find some explanation of the body's continually evaluated sense of self and the brain's memory of self as it manifests bodily. Interestingly, Ramachandran in particular discovered a treatment for PLS through image: he built a mirrored box that allowed a patient to insert both the healthy limb and the amputated limb. By looking through the top of the box, the illusion was created that both limbs

existed. This treatment, given a few times a day, managed to ease some of the painful symptoms of PLS for some patients (Ramachandran 46–49).

42. See especially Adam Zeman's *Consciousness: A User's Guide* (2002).

43. According to Edelman and Tononi, EEG Patterns during epilepsy and sleep indicate how conscious experience "requires a differentiated neural process reflected in the diverse patterns of low amplitude, fast activity," and that the lack of differentiation—i.e., erratic waves—indicate unconsciousness (72).

44. Hertenstein et al., found that "humans can communicate numerous emotions with touch," such as "anger, fear, disgust, love, gratitude, and sympathy," at "much-better-than-chance levels" (528). Should the research expand beyond touching just one arm, researchers might find other emotions effectively communicated with touch alone.

45. Bacon and others saw human will as a faculty, as is consistent with the faculty psychology so prevalent at the time: "The justest divisions of human learning is that derived from the three different faculties of the soul, the seat of learning: history being relative to the memory, poetry to the imagination, and philosophy to the reason [. . .] Thus it is clearly manifest that history, poetry, and philosophy flow from the three distinct fountains of the mind, viz., the memory, the imagination, and the reason; without any possibility of increasing their number" (93). Lalicker among others refutes this faculty or associationist psychology as too limiting.

46. I use the term "linguistic" deliberately because when the reports say that Gage's language was normal, they mean his linguistic skills, his ability to form words and sentences, that remained intact. But what this study and others insist on is a broader notion of language that includes the way we use language in public as well as private. I argue that just because Gage could form sentences and words appropriate to questions (discursive language) does not mean he could *use language* the way he once could, nor does it mean that he did not lose other important language skills that are more non-discursive than reported in the historical documents.

47. Pre-writing, as described by D. Gordon Rohman and Albert Wlecke in their book *Pre-Writing: The Construction and Application of Models for Concept Formation in Writing* (1964), is organic and reliant on current self and a future, self-actualized self-important in discovery: "Based upon the twin concepts of 'plant-growth' and 'line-process,' we described the entire activity called 'writing' as a person's transformation of the events of his life into experienced conceptual structures revealed in language for the sake of his won self-actualization and for communication with other persons through commonly shared patterns of meaning [. . .] Once we had set up our problem in this conceptual frame, we defined 'pre-writing' as the stage of discovery in the writing process when a person transforms a 'subject' into his own categories" (13). This kind of categorization, Damasio reveals later in his book, is exactly part of what gets lost in patients with prefrontal brain damage.

48. See Peter Elbow's *Writing Without Teachers* (1973) and Donald Murray's *A Writer Teaches Writing* (1968) for full explanations of these techniques.

49. Present-future is a term derived from Damasio's concept taken to explain the cultural development of social conventions and ethical structures in humans: "[T]he strategies evolved in individuals to be able to realize that their survival

was threatened or that the quality of their postsurvival life could be bettered [. . .] could have evolved only in the few species whose brains were structured to permit the following: First, a large capacity to memorize categories of objects and events [. . .] Second, a large capacity for manipulating the components of those memorized representations and fashioning new creations by means of novel combinations [. . . .] Third, a large capacity to memorize the new creations described above, that is, the anticipated outcomes, the new plans, and the new goals. I call those memorized creations 'memories of the future' " (261–62).

Notes for Chapter 4

1. See Francois Lyotard's book *The Postmodern Condition* to get a description of the term "grand narrative."

2. George Pullman states that, in 1959, Daniel Fogarty replaced "current traditional rhetoric" with "new rhetoric" which was based on "the theories of language offered by I. A. Richards, Kenneth Burke, and S. I. Hayakawa: "All students in progressive classrooms were encouraged to revise their papers before they were graded, to seek peer council, and to get feedback from the professor before and during revisions [. . . .] Composition teachers were no longer editors and judges. Now they were coaches and fellow writers." (18–19). To see accounts of post-process theory, refer to Thomas Kent's anthology *Post-Process Theory: Beyond the Writing-Process Paradigm* in which composition as a field is revised: "[T]he work of Lyotard, Haraway, Harding, and many other theorists suggests that it is incumbent upon us all—especially, it would seem, those of us in rhetoric and composition—to challenge received notions of writing, of composition itself, to move away from a discourse of mastery and assertion toward a more dialogic, dynamic, openended, receptive, nonassertive stance" (14).

3. See Damasio in *Descartes' Error*, (102), for the way images are recalled in the brain.

4. Susan Wells, in her book *Sweet Reason: Rhetoric and the Discourses of Modernity*, discusses this connection between reason and desire: "The discourses of modernity [. . .] establish quite different relations between pleasure and reason, desire and discourse. They require a rhetoric that accepts partial and probable knowledge, not as an epistemic condition or an antistrophe to dialectic, but as a necessary reflex of the differentiation of discursive practices. A rhetoric for modernity imagines reason and desire not as two beasts of burden, however, yoked together, but as connected systems of signification, each essential to the power of the text" (140).

5. Sondra Perl defines "felt sense" as the stage in which "what is not yet in words but out of which images, words, and concepts emerge" (46–47).

6. Many theorists point to this process as the fundamental process underlying the learning process itself: the number of new dendritic connections between synapses in the brain is directly proportional to the amount of learning taking place: "If anything simple can be said about the awesome complexity of intelligence it may be that intelligence lies in *connecting*—not only connecting information to

information to weave the elemental fabric of knowledge, but connecting knowledge to action and to experience" (Perelman 151).

7. Scientists recently discovered that there is a particular region of the brain dedicated to the recognition of facial features (Halgren, et al. 69).

8. Classic among these debates is the commonly held assumptions between three dominant worldviews: positivist, phenomenological, and critical theory. Each integrates self and society at different levels, and each responds to the other based on those assumptions. One consequence of this book is to show that all three are important for many reasons, and that all three tend to simplify the role of consciousness and the will that is inherent in their perspectives.

9. The analogy I am thinking of here is the same as an alternating generator: through the alternation of current, electrons can propagate long distances. But there is resistance, and that resistance tends to limit the propagation according to certain physical properties. Composing in the same way will depend on certain "properties" of the writer—i.e., past experiences, sense of selves, primary and secondary feelings, state of consciousness, and future planning. It is the alternation between the two halves of this model which creates the energy and, of course, the possibility for new knowledge.

10. "Making Room, Writing Hypertext" by Collin Brooke claims that hypertext "calls our attention to discursive space in ways that the transparency of print no longer can," though I would add that hypertext also calls our attention to space-as-text—especially non-discursive text.

11. Many other texts make too much out of the notion that we are somehow *more* inundated with images now than in recent history, though the fact is that we are not: we may be better at distributing rhetorically composed images, but not more images in general. W. J. T. Mitchell, during his keynote speech at the Visual Rhetoric Conference (referenced in the next section of endnotes), called this sort of claim one of the "Ten Myths about Visual Culture": "We live in a predominantly visual era. Modernity entails the hegemony of vision and visual media," adding later that "We do not live in a uniquely visual era. The 'visual' or 'pictorial turn' is a recurrent trope that displaces moral and political panic onto images and so-called visual media. Images are convenient scapegoats, and the offensive eye is ritually plucked out by ruthless critique."

12. Berlin, in *Rhetorics, Poetics, and Cultures: Refiguring College English Studies*, also stresses the importance of consumption and production as integral to composition: "Producing and consuming are both interpretations (as all language is interpretive), requiring a knowledge of semiotic codes in which versions of economic, social, and political predispositions are inscribed. Since all language is interested, the task of the rhetor as well as the poet—and their readers—is a working out of semiotic codes. These codes are never simply in the writer, in the text, or in the reader. They always involve a dialectical relation of the three, a rhetorical exchange in which writer, reader, text, and material conditions simultaneously interact with each other through the medium of semiotic codes [. . . .] Thus, the signifying practices of a poetic or rhetoric are always historically conditioned, always responses to the material and social formations of a particular moment" (86–87). These semiotic codes, to use Berlin's terminology, include and are dependent on image.

13. "[W]e call the representation of one medium in another *remediation*, and we will argue that remediation is a defining characteristic of the new digital media" (45). Bolter and Grusin go on to explain that the goal for remediation is usually "to make [. . .] electronic interventions transparent," but the opposite is also true: "users of older media such as film and television can seek to appropriate and refashion digital graphics, just as digital graphics artists can refashion film and television" (48).

14. Collin Brooke's essay, "Forgetting to be (Post)Human: Media and Memory in a Kairotic Age," focuses on this trend to externalize memory: "We are separated from knowledge, and increasingly we come to rely on our environment rather than our own faculties [. . . .] [W]e do not perceive it as such. In many contexts, access to a text is accorded the same importance as knowledge itself [. . . .] [K]nowing where to look for knowledge is itself a sign of self-reliance and individuality. We are encouraged to think of ourselves as autonomous, only relying on others for help when absolutely necessary" (786).

15. See J. Murray's "White Space as Rhetorical Space: Usability and Image in Electronic Texts" for an account of the rhetorical use of white or blank space on websites.

16. This statement is similar to J. L. Lemke's claim in "Metamedia Literacy: Transforming Meanings and Media": "Signs must have some material reality in order to function as signs, but every material form potentially carries meanings according to more than one code. All semiotics is multimedia semiotics, and all literacy is multimedia literacy" (72).

Notes for Chapter 5

1. Rodowick, in *Reading the Figural, or, Philosophy after the New Media*, makes a similar point about broadening the term *writing* to include the figural: "What if we were to assume the figural and plastic arts, rather than standing outside of writing, were indeed themselves "written," that is, staged on the 'scene of writing,' as Derrida has considered it? First, as I have already pointed out, the symptomatic place that writing now occupies in film theory as a kind of epistemological limit would have to be overturned. Second, it would be necessary to interrogate how the problematic of "writing" might encounter and redefine, indeed, might be redefined by, the potential intelligibility of figural discourses, including the cinema" (79–80).

2. In *Imagination: A Study in the History of Ideas*, J. M. Cocking seems to imply that even as the Romantic Revolution began to redefine the value of image and imagination to aesthetics, the world of science continued to view epistemology as dependent on the "primary qualities" associated with rationalism. These qualities provided a functional way to categorize the *use* of the imagination and image primarily through the emphasis of one sense—sight—over all others: "The primary qualities were the scientific, quantitative concepts like shapes and mass; the secondary qualities were the *aesthetic* concepts of how things appear to the senses, how they *feel*. The new scientific rationalism was interested in primary qualities; the growing pre-Romantic sensibility in art was interested in secondary qualities; and these belonged, said Addison, to imagination, to the creative part of the mind" (273).

3. Part one of Carolyn Handa's book, *Visual Rhetoric in a Digital World: A Critical Sourcebook*, emphasizes repeatedly the need to bring multiliteracies—though the book talks mainly of visual literacies—to the pedagogy of the classroom. Craig Stroup, specifically, states that "the practice and teaching of this hybrid literacy will require that those of us in English studies reexamine our customary distinctions and judgments about literacy" (15); Gunther Kress claims that multimodality refashions traditional text into mixed genres, such that "[l]iteracy and communication curricula rethought in this fashion offer an education in which creativity in different domains and at different levels of representation is well understood," making it possible that "[t]he young who experienced that kind of curriculum might feel at ease in a world of incessant change" (54); J. L. Lemke insists that "[w]e certainly cannot afford to continue teaching our students only the literacies of the mid-twentieth century, or even to simply lay before them the most advanced and diverse literacies of today," finally recommending that "[w]e must help this generation learn to use these literacies wisely, and hope they will succeed better than we have" (91); and Charles Hill suggests that "we should recognize that this purity [of distinct forms of print or visual text] does not exist in the real world, and pedagogical efforts should be aimed toward helping students deal with combinations of picture, word, and symbol" (109).

4. The first Visual Rhetoric Conference was held in Bloomington, Indiana, in 2001 (information may still be found at http://www.uiowa.edu/~commstud/visual_rhetoric). The International Visual Literacy Association (IVLA) has an annual conference and information on their website about other publications relevant to image studies (http://www.ivla.org).

5. David Blakesley and Collin Brooke, as the editors of that special issue of *Enculturation*, state the following about the relationship between "text" and "image": "It is a world where theorists interrogate the no longer obvious or necessary distinction between texts and images, with profound ethical, political, and epistemological implications, as Mitchell and others have shown. We have served witness to the conflation of word and image in the astounding development of media technologies in the late twentieth century. By many measures, we have rediscovered the visual nature of rhetoric. As students and teachers adapt to these new technologies and venues for reading and writing, it will be important to understand the ways that words and images function rhetorically and together in the various forms of media and literature that grab our attention and so delicately direct the intention" (Introduction).

6. See Hocks' "Understanding Visual Rhetoric in Digital Writing Environments" for more on hybridity in digital texts.

7. The website "Encyclo: Olfactory Groups"—at OzMoz.com—is dedicated to fragrances and fragrance composition. Here is how they describe the way fragrances are developed: "A perfume creator composes a story around a central theme just as a writer would. That theme constitutes the main accord of the composition and will determine the family of the perfume, whereas, the secondary accords will indicate its subfamily. There are eight major families: Floral, Chypre, Oriental (Masculine and Feminine), Woody, Aromatic and Hesperide (Masculine and Feminine). Each one of those olfactive families being itself split into several subfamilies." Students,

in order to compose fragrances with these images of families, would have to first be able to identify them in a sample, invent, and then produce a fragrance of their own composition.

8. Rudolf Arnheim's book, *Visual Thinking*, also suggests that the role of image in the mind is elemental: "What we need to acknowledge is that perceptual and pictorial shapes are not only translations of thought products but the very flesh and blood of thinking itself and that an unbroken range of visual interpretation leads from the humble gestures of daily communication to the statements of great art" (134).

9. In the case of Renaissance painters, Michael Ann Holly's book, *Past Looking: Historical Imagination and the Rhetoric of the Image*, emphasizes the continuing and historical consequences of perspective: "the perspective system originated by Alberti can be construed not only as a painterly device that permits the artist to locate objects spatially in a certain manifest scheme of relationships, but also as a kind of cognitive map for the cultural historian whose directive is to relate events, attitudes, and personalities in a coherent temporal architectonic" (79). Analysis is also affected by perspective: "Analysis is not something that is superimposed on the structure of the work of art; it is instead a continuation of its importance, a playing out of its own expectations of what its ideal viewer should or should not be saying, of where he should come from, of where he should literally take his stand" (80).

10. "Imagining is a mental act that often appears to reveal itself more crucially in its performance than in any particular product it may bring forth" (Casey 40).

11. Lanham's other three changes for composition are (1) "the essay will no longer be the basic unit of writing instruction" (which is also a claim in this book); (2) "we can back off a turn or two on the thumbscrew of spelling instruction"; and (3) "the nature of punctuation surely will change." That Lanham would bother to predict about spelling and punctuation says more about his regard for composition as a discipline than about authentic future changes in the way we teach writing.

12. In Sharon Crowley's book *The Methodical Memory: Invention in Current-Traditional Rhetoric* (1990), invention becomes affected by the dominant faculty psychology of the eighteenth and nineteenth centuries, a movement in rhetoric she labels as "current-traditional" (xii). The result is that invention became a mechanized, institutionalized, repetitive exercise she calls a "form of intellectual poverty" which "shifts discursive authority away from students and onto the academy" (13). The result is a disempowered view of language: "If we grant that cultures are held together by the persuasive potential that exists within language (when they are not held together by the overt use of force, that is), we must grant the importance of rhetoric to such a culture. And we must further grant the importance of invention. When rhetoric is taught as a system of rules for arranging words, its students may overlook the fact that language, effectively used, can change the way people think and can move them to act [. . .] Skilled rhetoricians know how to invent culturally effective arguments. Thus they are able to exert noncoercive control over those who don't suspect the power that is in language" (168).

Works Cited

Adolphs, Ralph, Hanna Damasio, Daniel Tranel, and Antonio Damasio. "Cortical Systems for the Recognition of Emotion in Facial Expressions." *Journal of Neuroscience* 16.23 (1996): 7678–87.

Allen, D. "Teaching Visual Literacy—Some Reflections on the Term." *Journal of Art & Design Education* 13.2 (1994): 133.

Aristotle. "Rhetoric." *The Complete Works of Aristotle: The Revised Oxford Translation.* Ed. Jonathan Barnes. Vol. 2 of Bollingen Series 71. Princeton: Princeton UP, 1984.

———. "Nicomachean Ethics." *The Complete Works of Aristotle: The Revised Oxford Translation.* Ed. Jonathan Barnes. Vol. 2 of Bollingen Series 71. Princeton: Princeton UP, 1984.

———. "On Dreams." *The Complete Works of Aristotle: The Revised Oxford Translation.* Ed. Jonathan Barnes. Vol. 1 of Bollingen Series 71. Princeton: Princeton UP, 1984.

———. "Topics." *The Complete Works of Aristotle: The Revised Oxford Translation.* Ed. Jonathan Barnes. Vol. 1 of Bollingen Series 71. Princeton: Princeton UP, 1984.

Armon-Jones, Claire. "The Thesis of Constructionism." *The Social Construction of Emotions.* Ed. Rom Harre. New York: Blackwell, 1986.

Armstrong, D. M. *The Mind-Body Problem: An Opinionated Introduction.* Boulder: Westview P, 1999.

Arnheim, Rudolf. *Visual Thinking.* Berkeley: U of California P, 1969.

Bacon, Francis. *Advancement of Learning.* Ed. Joseph Devey. New York: Collier, 1902.

Bakhtin, M. M. *The Dialogic Imagination: Four Essays.* 1981. Ed. Michael Holquist. Trans. Caryl Emerson and Michael Holquist. Austin: U of Texas P, 1998.

Baron, Dennis. "The College Board's New Essay Reverses Decades Toward Literacy." *Chronicle of Higher Education* 51.35 (2005): B14–B15.

Barton, Ben F., and Marthalee S. Barton. "Ideology and the Map: Toward a Postmodern Visual Design Practice." *Professional Communication: The Social Perspective.* Ed. Nancy Blyler and Charlotte Thralls. Newbury Park: Sage Press, 1993. 49–78.

Berlin, James A. *Rhetorics, Poetics, and Cultures: Refiguring College English Studies.* Urbana: NCTE, 1996.

————. *Writing Instruction in Nineteenth-Century American Colleges.* Studies in Writing and Rhetoric 1. Carbondale: Southern Illinois UP, 1984.

Berthoff, Ann E. *Forming, Thinking, Writing.* 2nd ed. with James Stephens. Portsmouth: Boynton/Cook, 1982.

————. *Mysterious Barricades: Language and Its Limits.* Toronto: U of Toronto P, 2000.

Blakesley, David. *The Elements of Dramatism.* The Elements of Composition Studies Series 11. New York: Longman, 2002.

Blakesley, David, and Collin Brooke. "Introduction: Notes on Visual Rhetoric." *Enculturation* 3.2 (2001).

Bogarad, Carley Rees, and Jan Zlotnik Schmidt. "Reading and Writing about the Genres." *Legacies: Fiction, Poetry, Drama, Nonfiction.* Ed. Carley Rees Bogarad and Jan Zlotnik Schmidt. Fort Worth: Harcourt, 1995.

Bolter, Jay David, and Richard Grusin. *Remediation: Understanding New Media.* Cambridge: MIT P, 1999.

Brand, Alice. Introduction. "Part Five: Emotions." *Presence of Mind: Writing and the Domain Beyond the Cognitive.* Ed. Alice Brand, Emeritus Graves, and Richard Graves. Portsmouth: Boynton/Cook, 1994.

————. "Defining Our Emotional Life: The Valuative System—A Continuum Theory." *Presence of Mind: Writing and the Domain Beyond the Cognitive.* Ed. Alice Brand, Emeritus Graves, and Richard Graves. Portsmouth: Boynton/Cook, 1994.

————. "Defining Our Emotional Life: The Cool End (Plus Motivation)." *Presence of Mind: Writing and the Domain Beyond the Cognitive.* Ed. Alice Brand, Emeritus Graves, and Richard Graves. Portsmouth: Boynton/Cook, 1994.

————. "Hot Cognition: Emotions and Writing Behavior." *JAC* 6 (1985–86): 5–15.

————. "The Why of Cognition: Emotion and the Writing Process." *CCC* 38 (1987): 436–43.

————. "Social Cognition, Emotions, and the Psychology of Writing." *JAC* 11.2 (1991): 1–6.

Brann, Eva T. H. *The World of the Imagination: Sum and Substance.* Lanham: Rowman, 1991.

Britton, James. *Language and Learning: The Importance of Speech in Children's Development.* 1970. 2nd ed. Portsmouth: Boynton/Cook, 1993.

Brodkey, Linda, and Michelle Fine. "Presence of Mind in the Absence of Body." *Journal of Education* 170.3 (1988): 84–99.

Bronowski, Jacob. *The Origins of Knowledge and Imagination.* New Haven: Yale UP, 1978.

Brooke, Collin G. "Forgetting to be (Post)Human: Media and Memory in a Kairotic Age." *JAC* 20.4 (2000): 775–95.

————. "Making Room, Writing Hypertext." *JAC* 19.2 (1999): 253–68.

Buchanan, Richard. "Design and the New Rhetoric: Productive Arts in the Philosophy of Culture." *Philosophy and Rhetoric* 34.3 (2001): 183–206.

Burke, Kenneth. *A Rhetoric of Motives.* Berkeley: U of California P, 1969.

———. *Language as Symbolic Action: Essays on Life, Literature, and Method.* Berkeley: U of California P, 1966.

Burnett, Ron. *How Images Think.* Cambridge: MIT P, 2004.

Calvert, Clay. "Introduction." *Voyeur Nation: Media, Privacy, and Peering in Modern Culture.* Boulder: Westview P, 2000. 1–18.

Carter, Locke. "Argumentation in Hypertext: Writing Strategies and the Problem of Order in a Nonsequential World." *Computers and Composition* 20 (2003): 3–22.

Cassirer, Ernst. *Language and Myth.* Trans. Susanne K. Langer. New York: Dover, 1946.

———. *Essay on Man: An Introduction to a Philosophy of Human Culture.* 1944. New Haven: Yale UP, 1962/1969.

———. *Symbol, Myth, and Culture: Essays and Lectures, 1935–1945.* Ed. Donald Phillip Verene. New Haven: Yale UP, 1979.

Churchland, Patricia Smith. *Neurophilosophy: Toward a Unified Science of the Mind/ Brain.* Cambridge: MIT P, 1986.

Cocking, J. M. *Imagination: A Study in the History of Ideas.* New York: Routledge P, 1991.

Coles, William E. *The Plural I—and After.* Portsmouth: Boynton/Cook, 1988.

Crane, Tim, and Sarah Patterson. "Introduction." Ed. Tim Crane and Sarah Patterson. *History of the Mind-Body Problem.* London Studies in the History of Philosophy. London: Routledge, 2000.

Crane, Tim. *The Mechanical Mind: A Philosophical Introduction to Minds, Machines and Mental Representations.* New York: Penguin, 1995.

Cranny-Francis, Anne. *Multimedia: Texts and Contexts.* London: Sage, 2005.

Crowley, Sharon. *The Methodical Memory: Invention in Current-Traditional Rhetoric.* Carbondale: Southern Illinois UP, 1990.

Damasio, A. R., D. Tranel, and H. Damasio. "Individuals with Sociopathic Behavior Caused by Frontal Damage Fail to Respond Autonomically to Social Stimuli." *Behavioral Brain Research* 41 (1990): 81–94.

Damasio, Antonio. *The Feeling of What Happens: Body and Emotion in the Making of Consciousness.* New York: Harcourt, 1995.

———. *Descartes' Error: Emotion, Reason, and the Human Brain.* New York: Putnam's, 1994.

———. *Looking for Spinoza: Joy, Sorrow, and the Feeling Brain.* Orlando: Harcourt, 2003.

———. *Unity of Knowledge: The Convergence of Natural and Human Science.* Annals of the New York Academy of Sciences. Vol. 935. New York: New York Academy of Sciences, 2001.

Danto, Arthur C. "Mind as Feeling; Form as Presence; Langer as Philosopher." *Journal of Philosophy* 81.11 (1984): 641–47.

Deibert, Ronald J. *Parchment, Printing, and Hypermedia: Communication in World Order Transformation.* New York: Columbia UP, 1997.

Derrida, Jacques. *Of Grammatology.* 1967. Trans. Gayatri Chakravorty Spivak. Baltimore: Johns Hopkins UP, 1976.

Devlin, Keith. *Goodbye, Descartes: The End of Logic and the Search for a New Cosmology of the Mind*. New York: Wiley, 1997.

DeWitt, Scott Lloyd. *Writing Inventions: Identities, Technologies, Pedagogies*. New York: State U of New York P, 2001.

Dunn, Patricia A. *Talking, Sketching, Moving: Multiple Literacies in the Teaching of Writing*. Portsmouth: Boynton/Cook, 2001.

Edelman, Gerald M., and Giulio Tononi. *A Universe of Consciousness: How Matter Becomes Imagination*. New York: Basic Books, 2000.

Elbow, Peter. *Writing without Teachers*. New York: Oxford UP, 1973.

"Encyclo: Olfactory Groups." *Ozmoz: A New Look at Fragrance*. Ed. Levy, Julian. June 3, 2008. <http://www.ozmoz.com/Encyclopedia/Olfactory-groups>.

Faigley, Lester. "Competing Theories of Process: A Critique and Proposal." *College English* 48.6 (1986): 527–42.

Farnsworth, Rodney, and Avon Crismore. "On the Reefs: The Verbal and Visual Rhetoric of Darwin's Other Big Theory." *RSQ* 21.2 (1991): 11–25.

Fleckenstein, Kristie S. "Mental Imagery, Text Engagement, and Underprepared Writers." *Presence of Mind: Writing and the Domain beyond the Cognitive*. Portsmouth: Boynton/Cook, 1994. 125–32.

———. "Defining Affect in Relation to Cognition: A Response to Susan McLeod." *JAC* 11.2 (1991): 447.

———. "Inviting Imagery into Our Classrooms." *Language and Image in the Reading-Writing Classroom: Teaching Vision*. Mahwah: Erlbaum, 2002. 3–26.

———. "Writing Bodies: Somatic Mind in Composition Studies." *College English* 61.3 (1991): 281–306.

———. "Inner Sight: Imagery and Emotion in Writing Engagement." *TETYC* 18.3 (1991): 210–16.

———. *Embodied Literacies: Imageword and a Poetics of Teaching*. Studies in Writing and Rhetoric 24. Carbondale: Southern Illinois UP, 2003.

Fleckenstein, Kristie, Linda Calendrillo, and Demetrice Worley. *Language and Image in the Reading-Writing Classroom: Teaching Vision*. Mahwah: Erlbaum, 2002.

Flood, James, and Diane Lapp. "Visual Literacy: Broadening Conceptualizations of Literacy: The Visual and Communicative Arts." *Reading Teacher* 51.4 (1997): 342.

Flood, James, Diane Lapp, and Karen Wood. "Visual Literacy: Viewing: The Neglected Communication Process or 'When What You See Isn't What You Get.'" *Reading Teacher* 52.3 (1998): 300.

Flower, Linda, and John R. Hayes. "Problem Solving Strategies and the Writing Process." *College English* 39.4 (1977): 449–61.

———. "A Cognitive Process Theory of Writing." *CCC* 32 (1981): 365–87.

Foreman, Joel, and David R. Shumway. "Cultural Studies: Reading Visual Texts." *Cultural Studies in the English Classroom*. Ed. James Berlin and Michael J. Vivion. Portsmouth: Boynton/Cook, 1992. 244–61.

Fortenbaugh, W. W. *Aristotle on Emotion*. New York: Harper, 1975.

Fox, Roy F., ed. *Images in Language, Media, and Mind*. Carbondale: NCTE P, 1994.

Fulkerson, Richard. *Teaching the Argument in Writing*. Urbana: NCTE, 1996.

Gallop, Jane. *Thinking through the Body*. New York: Columbia UP, 1988.

Gandelman, Claude. *Reading Pictures, Viewing Texts*. Bloomington: Indiana UP, 1991.

Gilbert, Rita, and William McCarter. *Living with Art*. 2nd ed. New York: Knopf, 1988.

Gilyard, Keith. "Literacy, Identity, Imagination, Flight." *CCC* 52.2 (2000): 260–72.

Glasgow, Jacqueline N. "Teaching Visual Literacy for the 21st Century." *Journal of Reading* 37.6 (1994): 494.

Gradin, Sherrie L. *Romancing Rhetorics: Social Expressivist Perspectives on the Teaching of Writing*. Portsmouth: Boynton/Cook, 1995.

Grassi, Ernesto. *Rhetoric as Philosophy: The Humanist Tradition*. Trans. John Michael Krois and Azizeh Azodi. Carbondale: Southern Illinois UP, 1980.

Halgren, Eric, Tommi Raij, Ksenija Marinkovic, et al. "Cognitive Response Profile of the Human Fusiform Face Area as Determined by MEG." *Cerebral Cortex* 10.1 (2000): 69–81.

Hampton, Rosemary E. "The Rhetorical and Metaphorical Nature of Graphics and Visual Schemata." *RSQ* 20.4 (1990): 347–56.

Handa, Carolyn. "Letter from the Guest Editor: Digital Rhetoric, Digital Literacy, Computers, and Composition." *Computers and Composition* 18.1 (2001): 1–10.

Harre, Rom, ed. *The Social Construction of Emotions*. New York: Blackwell, 1986.

Harrington, Dana. "Hume's Concept of Taste in the Context of Epideictic Rhetoric and 18th-Century Ethics." *Scottish Rhetoric and Its Influences*. Ed. Lynee Lewis Gaillet. Mahwah: Hermagoras Press, 1998. 17–31.

Hassett, Michael, and Rachel W. Lott. "Seeing Student Texts." *Composition Studies* 28.1 (2000): 29–47.

Herrick, James A. *The History and Theory of Rhetoric: An Introduction*. 3rd ed. Boston: Allyn, 2005.

Hertenstein, Matthew J., Dacher Keltner, Besty App, et al. "Touch Communicates Distinct Emotions." *Emotion* 6.3 (2006): 528–33.

Hesford, Wendy S. "Visual Auto/biography, Hysteria, and the Pedagogical Performance of the 'Real.' " *JAC* 20.2 (2000): 349–89.

Heywood, Ian, and Barry Sandywell, eds. *Interpreting Visual Culture: Explorations in the Hermeneutics of the Visual*. New York: Rutledge, 1999.

Hill, Charles A., and Marguerite Helmers, eds. *Defining Visual Rhetorics*. Mahwah: Erlbaum, 2004.

Hobbs, Catherine. "Learning from the Past: Verbal and Visual Literacy in Early Modern Rhetoric and Writing Pedagogy." *Language and Image in the Reading-Writing Classroom: Teaching Vision*. Eds. Kristie S. Fleckenstein, Linda T. Calendrillo, and Demetrice A. Worley. Mahwah: Erlbaum, 2002. 27–44.

Hocks, Mary E. "Understanding Visual Rhetoric in Digital Writing Environments." *CCC* 54.4 (2003): 629–56.

Hocks, Mary E., and Michelle R. Kendrick. *Eloquent Images: Word and Image in the Age of New Media*. Cambridge: MIT P, 2003.

Hodge, Robert, and Gunther Kress. *Social Semiotics*. Ithaca: Cornell UP, 1988.

Holly, Michael Ann. *Past Looking: Historical Imagination and the Rhetoric of the Image.* Ithaca: Cornell UP, 1996.

Holsapple, Cortell K., and Warren Wood. "Experiments with Audio-Visual Aids in Teaching Freshman English." *College English* 13.6 (1952): 324–26.

International Visual Literacy Association. "What is Visual Literacy?" 1 May 2002. 13 Sep 2002. <http://www.ivla.org/organization/whatis.htm>.

Ione, Amy. *Innovation and Visualization: Trajectories, Strategies, and Myths.* Consiousness Literature and the Arts 1. New York: Rodopi, 2005.

James, Susan. "Feminism in Philosophy of Mind: The Question of Personal Identity." *The Cambridge Companion to Feminism in Philosophy.* Ed. Miranda Fricker and Jennifer Hornsby. New York: Cambridge UP, 2000. 29–48.

Jarvie, I. C. "Visual Literacy: Image, Mind, and Reality by Paul Messaris," *Communication Theory* 5.1 (1995): 89.

Johnson, James R. "The Unknown Langer: Philosophy from the New Key to the Trilogy of Mind." *Journal of Aesthetic Education* 27.1 (1993): 63–73.

Johnson, Mark. *The Body in the Mind: The Bodily Basis of Meaning, Imagination, and Reason.* Chicago: U of Chicago P, 1987.

Johnson, Stephen. *Emergence: The Connected Lives of Ants, Brains, Cities, and Software.* New York: Simon, 2001.

Katula, Richard A. "Quintilian on the Art of Emotional Appeal." *Rhetoric Review* 22.1 (2003): 5–15.

Kaufer, David S. "From *Tekhne* to Technique: Rhetoric as a Design Art." *Rhetorical Hermeneutics: Invention and Interpretation in the Age of Science.* Ed. Alan G. Gross and William M. Keith. Albany: State U of New York P, 1997. 247–78.

Kennedy, George A. *Quintilian.* New York: Twayne P, 1969.

Kenny, Anthony. *Will, Freedom and Power.* Oxford: Blackwell, 1975. Ed. Richard Kearney. *The Wake of Imagination: Toward a Postmodern Culture.* Minneapolis: U of Minnesota P, 1988.

Kent, Thomas, ed. *Post-Process Theory: Beyond the Writing Process Paradigm.* Carbondale: Southern Illinois UP, 1999.

Kinneavy, James L. *A Theory of Discourse: The Aims of Discourse.* New York: Norton, 1971.

Knoblauch, C. H. "Rhetorical Constructions: Dialogue and Commitment." *CE* 50.2 (1988): 125–40.

Kress, Gunther. *Literacy in the New Media Age.* Literacies 9. New York: Routledge, 2003.

Kress, Gunther, and Theo van Leeuwen. *Reading Images: The Grammar of Visual Design.* London: Routledge, 1996.

———. *Before Writing: Rethinking the Paths to Literacy.* London: Routledge, 1997.

Kyle, J. G. "Written Language in a Visual World." *Exploring Speaking-Writing Relationships: Connections and Contrasts.* Ed. Barry M. Kroll and Roberta J. Vann. Urbana: NCTE, 1981. 168–83.

Lakoff, George, and Mark Johnson. *Philosophy in the Flesh: The Embodied Mind and Its Challenge to Western Thought.* New York: Basic Books, 1999.

Lalicker, William B. "Social Constructionist Composition and the Hunger of Imagination." *Writing on the Edge* 3.1 (1991): 24–36.

———. *The Interdisciplinary Imagination in the Teaching of Writing.* Diss. University of Washington, 1987. Ann Arbor: UMI, 1987. 8713382.

Langer, Susan K. *Philosophy in a New Key: A Study in the Symbolism of Reason, Rite, and Art.* 1942, 1951. 3rd ed. Cambridge: Harvard UP, 1957.

———. *Feeling and Form: A Theory of Art.* New York: Scribner's, 1953.

———. *Problems of Art.* New York: Schribner's, 1957.

———. *Mind: An Essay on Human Feeling.* Vol. 1. Baltimore: Johns Hopkins, 1967.

———. *Mind: An Essay on Human Feeling.* Vol. 2. Baltimore: Johns Hopkins, 1972.

———. *Mind: An Essay on Human Feeling.* Vol. 3. Baltimore: Johns Hopkins, 1982.

Lanham, Richard. *The Electronic Word: Democracy, Technology, and the Arts.* Chicago: U of Chicago P, 1993.

LeDoux, Joseph. *The Emotional Brain: The Mysterious Underpinnings of Emotional Life.* New York: Simon, 1996.

Leeuwen, Theo van, and Carey Jewitt. *Handbook of Visual Analysis.* London: Sage, 2001.

LeFevre, Karen Burke. *Invention as a Social Act.* Carbondale: Southern Illinois UP, 1987.

Lemke, J. L. "Metamedia Literacy: Transforming Meanings and Media." *Visual Rhetoric in a Digital World.* Ed. Carolyn Handa. New York: Bedford/ St. Martins, 2004. 71–93.

Lucaites, John Louis, and Robert Hariman. "Visual Rhetoric, Photojournalism, and Democratic Public Culture." *Rhetoric Review* 20.1/20.2 (2001): 37–42.

Lyotard, Jean-Francois. *The Postmodern Condition: A Report on Knowledge.* 1979. Trans. Geoff Bennington and Brian Massumi. Theory and History of Literature Series. Vol. 10. Minneapolis: U of Minnesota P, 1999.

Manovich, Lev. *The Language of New Media.* Cambridge: MIT P, 2001.

Marks, Laura U. *Sensuous Theory and Multisensory Media.* Minneapolis: U of Minnesota P, 2002.

McLaren, Peter. "Schooling the Postmodern Body: Critical Pedagogy and the Politics of Enfleshment." *Journal of Education* 170.3 (1988): 53–83.

McLeod, Susan. "Some Thoughts about Feelings: The Affective Domain and the Writing Process." *CCC* 38.4 (1987): 426–34.

———. *Notes on the Heart: Affective Issues in the Writing Classroom.* Carbondale: Southern Illinois UP, 1997.

———. "The Affective Domain and the Writing Process: Working Definitions." *JAC* 11.1 (1990): 95–105.

Miller, Laverne. "Teaching Visual Literacy with Films and Video, 'the Moving Image,'" *Educational Media International* 31.1 (1994): 58.

Mitchell, W. J. T. *Iconology: Image, Text, Ideology.* Chicago: U of Chicago P, 1986.

———. *Picture Theory: Essays on Verbal and Visual Representation.* Chicago: U of Chicago P, 1994.

———. *The Language of Images.* Chicago: U of Chicago P, 1980.

Moffett, James. *Teaching the Universe of Discourse.* Portsmouth: Boynton/Cook, 1968, 1983.

Murray, Donald. *A Writer Teaches Writing.* Boston: Houghton Mifflin, 1968.

Murray, Joddy. "Michel de Certeau's Language Theory." *Journal of College Writing* 6.1 (2003): 19–33.

————. "White Space as Rhetorical Space: Usability and Image in Electronic Texts." *Rhetorical Agendas: Political, Ethical, Spiritual. Rhetorical Society of America Conference Proceedings.* Mahwah: Earlbaum, 2005. 145–50.

"National Council of Teachers of English (NCTE) Resolutions: On Viewing and Visually Representing as Forms of Literacy." NCTE Annual Business Meeting. Chicago, 1996. 4 June 2003. <http://www.ncte.org/resolutions/visually961996.shtml>.

Nelson, Jenny L. "Limits of Consumption: An Ironic Revision of Televisual Experience." *Rhetoric in the Human Sciences.* Ed. Herbert W. Simons. Newbury Park: Sage Press, 1989. 152–63.

Nussbaum, Martha C. *Upheavals of Thought: The Intelligence of Emotions.* New York: Cambridge UP, 2001.

Olson, Gary. "Toward a Post-Process Composition." *Post-Process Theory: Beyond the Writing Process Paradigm.* Ed. Thomas Kent. Carbondale: Southern Illinois UP, 1999: 7–15.

Ong, Walter J. *Orality and Literacy: The Technologizing of the Word.* New York: Routledge Press, 1982.

Paglia, Camille. *Sexual Personae: Art and Decadence from Nefertiti to Emily Dickinson.* New Haven: Yale UP, 1990.

Perelman, Lewis J. *School's Out: A Radical New Formula for the Revitalization of America's Educational System.* New York: Avon Books, 1992.

Perl, Sondra. "Understanding Composing." *The Writer's Mind: Writing as a Mode of Thinking.* Ed. Janice N. Hayes et al. Urbana: NCTE, 1983. 43–52.

Phelps, Louise Wetherbee. "Rhythm and Pattern in a Composing Life." *Writers on Writing.* Ed. Tom Waldrep. New York: Random, 1985. 241–57.

Phelps, Louise Wetherbee, and Janet Emig, eds. *Feminine Principles and Women's Experience in American Composition and Rhetoric.* Pitt Series in Composition, Literacy, and Culture. Ed. David Bartholomae and Jean Ferguson Carr. Pittsburg: U of Pittsburg P, 1995.

Pinker, Stephen. *How the Mind Works.* New York: Norton, 1997.

————. *The Language Instinct: How the Mind Creates Language.* New York: Harper, 1994.

Porter, Kevin J. *Meaning, Language, and Time: Toward a Consequentialist Philosophy of Discourse.* West Lafayette: Parlor Press, 2006.

Preston, John, ed. *Thought and Language.* Royal Institute of Philosophy Supplement. Vol. 42. Cambridge: Cambridge UP, 1997.

Pullman, George. "Stepping Yet Again into the Same Current." *Post-Process Theory: Beyond the Writing Process Paradigm.* Ed. Thomas Kent. Carbondale: Southern Illinois UP, 1999. 16–29.

Ramachandran, V. S., and Sandra Blakeslee. *Phantoms in the Brain: Probing the Mysteries in the Human Mind.* New York: Harper, 1998.

Richards, I. A. *Speculative Instruments.* Chicago: U of Chicago P, 1955.

Roberts, A. C., and J. D. Wallis. "Inhibitory Control and Affective Processing in the Prefrontal Cortex: Neuropsychological Studies in the Common Marmoset." *Cerebral Cortex* 10 (2000): 252–62.

Roberts, Patricia, and Virginia Pompei Jones. "Imagining Reasons: The Role of the Imagination in Argumentation." *JAC* 15.3 (1995): 527–41.

Rodowick, D. N. *Reading the Figural, or, Philosophy after the New Media.* Durham: Duke UP, 2001.

Rohman, D. Gordon, and Albert O. Wlecke. *Pre-Writing: The Construction and Application of Models for Concept Formation in Writing.* Cooperative Research Project. East Lansing: Michigan State UP, 1964.

Sadoski, Mark. "Imagination, Cognition, and Persona." *Rhetoric Review* 10.2 (1992): 266–78.

Sadoski, Mark, and Allan Paivio. *Imagery and Text: A Dual Coding Theory of Reading and Writing.* Mahwah: Erlbaum, 2001.

Saussure, Ferdinand. *Course in General Linguistics.* 1972. Ed. Charles Bally and Albert Sechehaye. Trans. Roy Harris. La Salle: Open Court Press, 1991.

Scharfstein, Ben-Ami. *Ineffability: The Failure of Words in Philosophy and Religion.* Albany: State U of New York P, 1993.

Schultz, Lucille M. *The Young Composers: Composition's Beginnings in Nineteenth-Century Schools.* Carbondale: Southern Illinois UP, 1999.

Schwartz, Jeffrey M., and Sharon Begley. *The Mind and the Brain: Neuroplasticity and the Power of Mental Force.* New York: Harper, 2002.

Searle, John. *Mind, Language and Society: Philosophy in the Real World.* London: Weidenfeld, 1999.

Selber, Stuart. *Multiliteracies for a Digital Age.* Studies in Writing and Rhetoric 26. Carbondale: Southern Illinois UP, 2004.

Selfe, Cynthia L. "Students Who Teach Us: A Case Study of a New Media Text Designer." *Writing New Media: Theory and Applications for Expanding the Teaching of Composition.* Ed. Anne Francis Wysocki, et al. Logan: Utah State UP, 2004. 43–99.

———. *Technology and Literacy in the Twenty-First Century: The Importance of Paying Attention.* Studies in Writing and Rhetoric 18. Carbondale: Southern Illinois UP, 1999.

Shauf, Michele S. "The Problem of Electronic Argument: A Humanist Perspective." *Computers and Composition* 18.1 (2001): 33–37.

Shoos, Diane, Diana George, and Joseph Comprone. "Twin Peaks and the Look of Television: Visual Literacy in the Writing Class." *JAC* 13.2 (1993): 459–76.

Sontag, Susan. *On Photography.* New York: Farrar, 1977.

Sorapure, Madeleine. "Between Modes: Assessing Students' New Media Compositions." Kairos 10.2 (Spring 2006). 10 Aug. 2006. <http://english.ttu.edu/kairos/10.2/>.

Spinuzzi, Clay. " 'Light Green Doesn't Mean Hydrology!': Toward a Visual-rhetorical Framework for Interface Design." *Computers and Composition* 18.1 (2001): 39–53.

Stafford, Barbara Maria. *Visual Analogy: Consciousness as the Art of Connecting.* Cambridge: MIT P, 1999.

———. *Good Looking: Essays on the Virtue of Images.* Cambridge: MIT P, 1997.

Stenberg, Shari J. "Embodied Classrooms, Embodied Knowledges: Re-thinking the Mind/Body Split." *Composition Studies* 30.2 (2002): 43–60.

Stocker, Michael, and Elizabeth Hegeman. *Valuing Emotions.* Cambridge: Cambridge UP, 1996.

Stroupe, Craig. "Visualizing English: Recognizing the Hybrid Literacy of Visual and Verbal Authorship on the Web." *College English* 62.5 (2000): 607–32.

Tayler, Mark C. *The Moment of Complexity: Emerging Network Culture.* Chicago: U of Chicago P, 2001.

Tebeaux, Elizabeth. "Ramus, Visual Rhetoric, and the Emergence of Page Design in the Medical Writing of the English Renaissance: Tracking the Evolution of Readable Documents." *Written Communication* 8.4 (1991): 411–45.

———. "Writing in Academe; Writing at Work: Using Visual Rhetoric to Bridge the Gap." *Journal of Teaching Writing* 7.2 (1988): 215–36.

Tremonte, Colleen. "Film, Classical Rhetoric, and Visual Literacy." *Journal of Teaching Writing* 14.1–2 (1995): 3–17.

Trimbur, John. "Composition and the Circulation of Writing." *CCC* 52.2 (2000): 188–219.

Tuana, Nancy, and Sandra Morgen, eds. *Engendering Rationalities.* Albany: State U of New York P, 2001.

Tufte, Edward R. *The Visual Display of Quantitative Information.* Cheshire: Graphics, 1983.

———. *Envisioning Information.* Cheshire: Graphics, 1990.

———. *Visual Explanations: Images and Quantities, Evidence and Narrative.* Cheshire: Graphics, 1997.

Vološinov, V. N. *Marxism and the Philosophy of Language.* Trans. Ladislav Matejka and I. R. Titunik. Cambridge: Harvard UP, 1973.

Vygotsky, L. S. *The Collected Works of L. S. Vygotsky.* 1932. Ed. Robert W. Rieber and Aaron S. Craton. Trans. Norris Minick. New York: Plenum, 1987.

———. *Thought and Language.* 1934. MIT P, 1986.

———. "Consciousness as a Problem of Psychology of Behavior." *Soviet Psychology* 17 (1979): 29–30.

Westbrook, Steve. "Visual Rhetoric in a Culture of Fear: Impediments to Multimedia Production." *College English* 68.5 (2006): 457–80.

White, Alex. *The Elements of Graphic Design: Space, Unity, Page Architecture, and Type.* New York: Allworth, 2002.

White, Edward M., William D. Lutz, and Sandra Kamusikiri, eds. *Assessment of Writing: Politics, Policies and Practices.* New York: MLA, 1996.

White, Eric Charles. *Kaironomia: On the Will-To-Invent.* Ithaca: Cornell UP, 1987.

Whitin, Phyllis E. "Exploring Visual Response to Literature." *Research in the Teaching of English* 30.1 (1996): 114–40.

Williams, Sean D. "Part 1: thinking out of the Pro-Verbal Box." *Computers and Composition* 18.1 (2001): 21–32.

Winterowd, W. Ross. "Emerson and the Death of *Pathos.*" *JAC* 16.1 (1996): 27–40.

Wittgenstein, Ludwig. *The Blue and Brown Books: Preliminary Studies for the "Philosophical Investigations."* New York: Harper, 1958.

Worsham, Lynn. "The Question Concerning Invention: Hermeneutics and the Genesis of Writing." *PRE/TEXT* 8.3–4 (1987): 197–244.

———. "Going Postal: Pedagogic Violence and the Schooling of Emotion." *JAC* 18.2 (1998): 213–46.

Wysocki, Anne Frances, Johndan Johnson-Eilola, Cynthia L. Selfe, and Geoffrey Sirc, eds. *Writing New Media: Theory and Applications for Expanding the Teaching of Composition*. Logan: Utah State UP, 2004.

Wysocki, Anne Frances. "Opening New Media To Writing: Opening and Justifications." *Writing New Media: Theory and Applications for Expanding the Teaching of Composition*. Ed. Anne Francis Wysocki, et al. Logan: Utah State UP, 2004. 1–41.

Yarnoff, Charles. "Contemporary Theories of Invention in the Rhetorical Tradition." *College English* 41.5 (1980): 552–60.

Zamel, Vivian. "Thinking beyond Imagination: Participating in the Process of Knowing." *Audits of Meaning: A Festschrift in Honor of Ann E. Berthoff*. Ed. Louise Z. Smith. Portsmouth: Boynton/Cook, 1988. 182–94.

Zebroski, James T. *Thinking through Theory: Vygotskian Perspectives on the Teaching of Writing*. Portsmouth: Boynton/Cook, 1994.

———. "The Expressivist Menace." *History, Reflection, and Narrative: The Professionalization of Composition, 1963–83*. Ed. Mary Resner and Debra Journet Boehm. Perspectives in Writing: Theory, Research, Practice. Vol. 3. Stamford: Ablex, 1999. 99–114.

Zeman, Adam. *Consciousness: A User's Guide*. New Haven: Yale UP, 2002.

Index